THE BEST OF
SALADS AND BUFFETS

THE BEST OF

SALADS
AND
BUFFETS

Christian Teubner and
Annette Wolter

Photography by
Christian Teubner

CHANCELLOR
PRESS

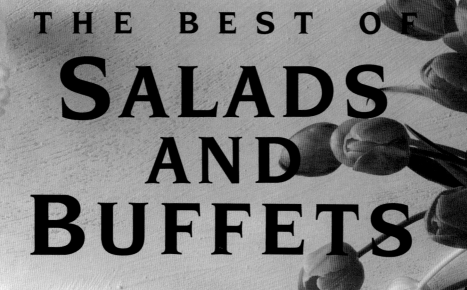

First published under the title
Kalte Köstlichkeiten wie noch nie
© Copyright by Gräfe und Unzer GmbH, München, 1980

English edition first published in 1982 by
The Hamlyn Publishing Group Limited
part of Reed International Books
under the title *The Best of Salads and Buffet Cookery*

© Copyright Reed International Books Limited 1982

This 1992 edition published by
Chancellor Press
Michelin House
81 Fulham Road
London SW3 6RB

ISBN 1 85152 133 X

Produced by Mandarin Offset
Printed and bound in Hong Kong

Useful Facts and Figures

Notes on metrication

In this book quantities are given in metric and Imperial
measures. Exact conversion from Imperial to metric measures
does not usually give very convenient working quantities and so
the metric measures have been rounded off into units of 25
grams. The table below shows the recommended equivalents.

Ounces	Approx g to nearest whole figure	Recommended conversion to nearest unit of 25
1	28	25
2	57	50
3	85	75
4	113	100
5	142	150
6	170	175
7	198	200
8	227	225
9	255	250
10	283	275
11	312	300
12	340	350
13	368	375
14	396	400
15	425	425
16 (1 lb)	454	450
17	482	475
18	510	500
19	539	550
20 (1¼ lb)	567	575

Note: When converting quantities over 20 oz first add the
appropriate figures in the centre column, then adjust to the
nearest unit of 25. As a general guide, 1 kg (1000 g) equals 2.2 lb
or about 2 lb 3 oz. This method of conversion gives good results
in nearly all cases, although in certain pastry and cake recipes a
more accurate conversion is necessary to produce a balanced
recipe.

Spoon measures All spoon measures given in this book are level
unless otherwise stated.

Can sizes At present, cans are marked with the exact (usually
to the nearest whole number) metric equivalent of the Imperial
weight of the contents, so we have followed this practice when
giving can sizes.

Liquid measures The millilitre has been used in this book and the following table gives a few examples.

Imperial	Approx ml to nearest whole figure	Recommended ml
$\frac{1}{4}$ pint	142	150 ml
$\frac{1}{2}$ pint	283	300 ml
$\frac{3}{4}$ pint	425	450 ml
1 pint	567	600 ml
$1\frac{1}{2}$ pints	851	900 ml
$1\frac{3}{4}$ pints	992	1000 ml (1 litre)

Oven temperatures

The table below gives recommended equivalents.

	°C	°F	Gas Mark
Very cool	110	225	$\frac{1}{4}$
	120	250	$\frac{1}{2}$
Cool	140	275	1
	150	300	2
Moderate	160	325	3
	180	350	4
Moderately hot	190	375	5
	200	400	6
Hot	220	425	7
	230	450	8
Very Hot	240	475	9

Notes for American and Australian users

In America the 8-oz measuring cup is used. In Australia metric measures are now used in conjunction with the standard 250-ml measuring cup. The Imperial pint, used in Britain and Australia, is 20 fl oz, while the American pint is 16 fl oz. It is important to remember that the Australian tablespoon differs from both the British and American tablespoons; the table below gives a comparison. The British standard tablespoon, which has been used throughout this book, holds 17.7 ml, the American 14.2 ml, and the Australian 20 ml. A teaspoon holds approximately 5 ml in all three countries.

British	American	Australian
1 teaspoon	1 teaspoon	1 teaspoon
1 tablespoon	1 tablespoon	1 tablespoon
2 tablespoons	3 tablespoons	2 tablespoons
$3\frac{1}{2}$ tablespoons	4 tablespoons	3 tablespoons
4 tablespoons	5 tablespoons	$3\frac{1}{2}$ tablespoons

An Imperial/American guide to solid and liquid measures

Imperial	American
Solid measures	
1 lb butter or margarine	2 cups
1 lb flour	4 cups
1 lb granulated or castor sugar	2 cups
1 lb icing sugar	3 cups
8 oz rice	1 cup
Liquid measures	
$\frac{1}{4}$ pint liquid	$\frac{2}{3}$ cup liquid
$\frac{1}{2}$ pint	$1\frac{1}{4}$ cups
$\frac{3}{4}$ pint	2 cups
1 pint	$2\frac{1}{2}$ cups
$1\frac{1}{2}$ pints	$3\frac{3}{4}$ cups
2 pints	5 cups ($2\frac{1}{2}$ pints)

NOTE: When making any of the recipes in this book, only follow one set of measures as they are not interchangeable.

Contents

Introduction

For two years we have selected, tested, cooked, garnished and photographed – now at last all is ready and we can present our comprehensive, fully illustrated guide to the best of salads and buffet cookery. For the first time, over 350 of the best and most original ideas for dishes and garnishes have been gathered together, each with its colour picture, and each explained in detail so as to ensure success for everyone, from the aspiring amateur cook to the accomplished professional.

The selection and organisation of our recipes has come about through careful consideration of all the different occasions on which a choice of cold dishes would be appropriate. We begin with open sandwiches and rolls which can be adapted to any purpose, from lunchtime snacks to party canapés; then there's a comprehensive selection of salads, first as crisp accompaniments, then as satisfying meals in themselves and as colourful party platters. Next, we feature a wealth of egg, vegetable, fish and meat dishes, with ideas for entertaining family and friends alike.

For really festive occasions we can offer the finest pâtés and terrines, rich recipes for all types of fish and seafood and simple to sophisticated suggestions for cold meat platters. For the gourmet, there are luscious concoctions of exotic fruits, or delicate aspic creations featuring fish, shellfish, chicken and vegetables.

And as well as heart warming savoury soups, we have also brought you some delicious traditional cold soups.

Finally, there's a section packed with ideas for many different occasions, ranging from a children's party to a classic cold buffet, taking in Danish, Swedish and Italian specialities on the way and culminating in a full-scale festive buffet for a special celebration.

The extra sections at the back of the book deal in detail with the basic recipes which appeal to those who really love every aspect of party catering: home-made breads and mayonnaises, pastries, stocks and aspics. Our detailed instructions and the clear line drawings put them well within the reach of any amateur cook. A chapter on drinks gives lots of ideas for what to serve with any kind of buffet food, whether it is for family and friends or for formal entertaining. Altogether, we feel sure that this is the most comprehensive handbook indispensable for anyone involved in successful salads and buffet cookery.

We hope you enjoy preparing or cooking, serving and eating these recipes. We know the results will win compliments from everyone around you.

Christian Teubner and Annette Wolter

Open Sandwiches

Ham and Egg

For each:
7 g/¼ oz soft butter
50 g/2 oz smoked ham, finely
    chopped
pinch curry powder
1 large slice brown bread
1 hard-boiled egg, shelled
1 teaspoon chopped fresh mixed
    herbs or a generous pinch
    dried mixed herbs
1 tablespoon mayonnaise
GARNISH
parsley sprig

Mix the butter with the ham
and curry powder and spread
the bread with the mixture.
Slice the egg and arrange on
top. Stir the herbs into the
mayonnaise and spoon over
the egg. Garnish with parsley.

Cheese Salad

For each:
2–3 leaves endive
1 large slice wholemeal bread
7 g/¼ oz soft butter
75 g/3 oz Edam cheese
½ hard-boiled egg
4 shelled walnuts
1 teaspoon chopped chives
1 tablespoon mayonnaise
1 teaspoon natural yogurt
salt and pepper
GARNISH
few grapes

Cut the endive into thin strips.
Spread the bread with the
butter and cover with the
endive. Dice the cheese and egg
and chop three of the shelled
walnuts. Mix these with the
chives, mayonnaise and yogurt
and season with salt and
pepper. Spread this mixture
over the endive and garnish
with grapes and the remaining
walnut.

Sausage and Peppers

For each:
1 large slice brown bread
7 g/¼ oz soft butter
½ green pepper, seeded
½ red pepper, seeded
1 small onion
75 g/3 oz ham sausage
1 tablespoon oil
1 teaspoon vinegar
1 teaspoon chopped parsley
salt and pepper

Spread the bread with the
butter. Slice the green pepper
into rings and arrange on the
bread. Finely dice the red
pepper. Peel the onion and
slice into rings, and cut the
sausage into small strips. Make
a dressing with the oil, vinegar,
parsley, salt and pepper. Stir
the dressing into the red
pepper, onion and sausage,
and arrange on the sandwich.

Salami and Egg Salad

For each:
1 large slice brown bread
7 g/¼ oz soft butter
6 thin slices salami
1 lettuce leaf
1 hard-boiled egg, shelled
3 mushrooms
½ tomato
1 teaspoon mayonnaise
1 tablespoon single cream
dash of lemon juice
salt and pepper
few capers (optional)

Spread the bread with the
butter and arrange the salami
slices on top. Add the lettuce.
Chop the egg and mushrooms,
dice the tomato, and mix these
ingredients with the
mayonnaise, cream and lemon
juice. Season and arrange on
the lettuce. Sprinkle with
capers, if used.

10

Open Sandwiches

Mussel and Cress

For each:
1 large slice brown or white bread
7 g/¼ oz soft butter
½ small onion, peeled
½ punnet mustard and cress
5 canned mussels

Spread the bread with the butter. Chop the onion very finely and sprinkle half over the bread. Snip the cress with scissors and sprinkle over the onion in a thick layer. Drain the mussels thoroughly and arrange them on the bed of cress. Garnish with the rest of the onion.

Smoked trout

For each:
1 large slice brown or white bread
7 g/¼ oz soft butter
1 (75-g/3-oz) smoked trout fillet
2 thin slices honeydew melon
1 teaspoon mayonnaise
1 teaspoon pickled pink peppercorns or a sprinkling of freshly ground white pepper

Lightly toast the bread and when cooled, spread with the butter. Cut the trout fillet in half and arrange on the bread. Remove the peel from the melon slices, scrape away the seeds and place the slices on the trout. Spoon over the mayonnaise and sprinkle with red peppercorns, if used, or white pepper.

Swiss Cheese Salad

For each:
2–3 lettuce leaves
1 large slice white bread
7 g/¼ oz soft butter
1 small tomato
½ small green pepper
75 g/3 oz Emmental cheese
1 teaspoon lemon juice
¼ teaspoon French mustard
salt and pepper
1 tablespoon oil
GARNISH
parsley sprig

Cut the lettuce into strips and arrange on the buttered bread. Neatly dice the tomato, pepper and cheese. Stir the lemon juice, mustard, salt and pepper into the oil and mix in the diced ingredients.
   Arrange on the lettuce and garnish with parsley.

Tomato and Fish

For each:
1 large slice brown bread
7 g/¼ oz soft butter
1 tomato
¼ teaspoon white pepper
2 canned sild or pilchards
¼ hard-boiled egg, cut lengthways
1 tablespoon mayonnaise
GARNISH
½ teaspoon canned lumpfish roe (optional)

Spread the bread with the butter. Slice the tomato and place on the bread. Sprinkle with pepper and top with the fish. Remove the yolk from the egg, mix with the mayonnaise and fill the egg white with the mixture. Garnish with lumpfish roe, if used, and place the egg in the centre of the sandwich.

Open Sandwiches

Vegetarian Special

For each:
75 g/3 oz frozen peas and carrots
1 tablespoon oil
1 teaspoon wine vinegar
salt and pepper
1 teaspoon chopped parsley
¼ teaspoon strong mustard
7 g/¼ oz soft butter
1 large slice wholemeal bread
2 leaves red endive or red cabbage
1 teaspoon whipped cream

Cook the frozen vegetables following the instructions on the packet and drain. Make a dressing with the oil, vinegar, salt, pepper and parsley and stir into the vegetables. Mix together the mustard and butter and spread over the bread. Arrange the red endive on the bread and top with the vegetables and whipped cream.

Mushroom with Egg

For each:
75 g/3 oz mushrooms
1 teaspoon lemon juice
1 teaspoon oil
salt and pepper
1 large slice white bread
½ clove garlic, crushed
15 g/½ oz soft butter
½ hard-boiled egg, chopped
1 teaspoon chopped fresh herbs

Slice the mushrooms very finely. Make a dressing with the lemon juice, oil, salt and pepper and pour over the mushrooms. Rub one side of the bread with the garlic. Melt half the butter in a pan and brown the garlic side of the bread in it. When cool, spread the other side with the rest of the butter and arrange the mushrooms on top. Sprinkle with chopped egg and herbs.

Pinwheels

1 white loaf
1 (225-g/8-oz) can tuna fish
1 small onion
2 tablespoons fresh grated horseradish, or bottled creamed horseradish
3 tablespoons whipped cream
¼ teaspoon salt
¼ teaspoon pepper
50 g/2 oz soft butter
GARNISH
6 small tomatoes
6 twists of lemon
mustard and cress

Remove the crust from the loaf and cut lengthways into six slices. Interleave the slices of bread with greaseproof paper and, with a rolling pin, roll out until thin. Then roll up each slice lengthways as for a sponge roll.

Drain the tuna fish and chop into small pieces. Peel and finely chop the onion. Blend the tuna fish, onion, horseradish, whipped cream, salt and pepper in the liquidiser, taste and adjust the seasoning as necessary. Unroll the bread slices, spread evenly with the butter, followed by the tuna fish mixture, and roll up again. Wrap each of the six rolls of bread in greaseproof paper, then in cooking foil and leave to stand in the refrigerator for 1 hour. Before serving, cut each roll into slices and arrange in a circle on individual plates. Garnish the centre of each plate with a small tomato, a twist of lemon, and a small bunch of cress.
Serves 6.

Sandwiches and Rolls

Danish Salami and Cucumber

For each:
1 slice granary bread
top half of 1 sesame roll
15 g/½ oz soft butter
¼ cucumber
salt and pepper
6–8 thin slices salami
chopped parsley

Spread the bread and half roll with the butter. Thinly slice the cucumber and season with salt and pepper. Arrange half the cucumber on the bread, cover with the salami, then follow with the rest of the cucumber. Sprinkle with parsley and top with the half roll.

Cook's Tip
This refreshing and satisfying roll makes an ideal snack for summer rambles. For an outing, wrap these rolls in cling-film or foil. An equally delicious variation would be sliced apple and cold roast pork, garnished with horseradish sauce.

Corned Beef and Egg

For each:
1 bread roll
15 g/½ oz soft butter
7 g/¼ oz cheese spread
2–3 lettuce leaves
2 slices canned corned beef
1 hard-boiled egg, shelled
½ gherkin

Cut the roll in half and spread each half with the butter, followed by the cheese spread. Place the lettuce and corned beef on the bottom half. Cut the egg into slices lengthways and the gherkin into fine strips. Arrange the egg and gherkin over the corned beef and top with the remaining half roll.

Cook's Tip
These rolls are also particularly suitable for picnics. As a variation, substitute cold pork or ham for the corned beef.

Brunch Slices

For each:
¼ teaspoon salt
pinch each black pepper and
  paprika pepper
100 g/4 oz pork fillet
25 g/1 oz dripping
2 large slices white bread
15 g/½ oz soft butter
2–3 lettuce leaves
1 hard-boiled egg
1 small onion, peeled
1 strip canned pimiento
2 tablespoons single cream
1 tablespoon whipped double
  cream
1 teaspoon curry powder
sprig dill (optional)

Rub the salt, black pepper and
paprika into the pork fillet.
Heat the dripping in a frying
pan and brown the fillet well
all over, turning frequently.
Reduce the heat and cook
gently for a further 10 minutes.
Remove the fillet from the pan

and when cool, cut into equal
slices.
   Spread the bread with the
butter. Arrange the lettuce on
one slice of bread followed by
the slices of pork. Shell and
finely chop the egg. Finely dice
the onion and pimiento, and
mix with the chopped egg,
single and double cream and
curry powder. Season to taste.
Spoon the mixture onto the
meat and top with the second
slice of bread. Garnish with a
dill sprig, if used.

Club Sandwich

For each:
2 small slices white bread
1 slice liver sausage
1 small slice wholemeal bread
1 tablespoon mayonnaise
1 slice ham
2–3 lettuce leaves
1 slice Cheddar or Edam cheese
small bunch radishes

Lightly toast the white bread.
Place the liver sausage on one
slice of toast and cover with
the wholemeal bread. Spread
the mayonnaise on top and
add, one after the other, the
ham, lettuce and cheese. Top
with the second slice of toast.
With a sharp knife cut the
sandwich diagonally in half
and secure each half with a
cocktail stick. Serve with the
radishes.

Cook's Tip

As a variation, you
could make this
sandwich using a slice of
cooked chicken instead
of the liver sausage, and
replacing the cheese with
a few tomato slices,
sprinkled with freshly
ground black pepper.

Sandwiches and Rolls

Baked Roquefort Slices

4 slices white bread
75 g/3 oz butter
8 slices smoked ham
100 g/4 oz Roquefort (or other blue cheese)
GARNISH
½ red pepper
½ green pepper

Preheat the oven to very hot (240 C, 475 F, Gas Mark 9). Cut the slices of bread in half. Melt the butter in a large pan and fry the bread in it until golden brown on both sides. Remove the bread from the frying pan and leave to cool. Cover each slice of bread with a slice of ham followed by a piece of Roquefort. Transfer to a baking sheet and bake for a few minutes in the oven until the cheese begins to melt but not brown. Remove the slices from the oven and allow to cool.

Wash the peppers, remove the seeds and cut into very fine strips. Garnish each slice of bread with a few strips of red and green pepper. *Makes 8.*

Cook's Tip

Unless you are baking large quantities of these slices at a time, using the oven will prove uneconomical. The same delicious result will be achieved if the slices are lightly grilled.

Tuscan 'Crostini'

1 (100-g/4-oz) packet Mozzarella cheese
8 slices white bread
2 cloves garlic
parsley sprigs
40 g/1½ oz canned anchovy fillets
2 tablespoons capers
6 tablespoons olive oil
¼ teaspoon freshly ground white pepper
100 g/4 oz black olives

Preheat the oven to very hot (240 C, 475 F, Gas Mark 9). Remove the Mozzarella from its packet of preserving liquid, wipe dry and slice. Remove the crusts from the bread and cut each slice in half. Peel and crush the garlic cloves. Wash, drain and finely chop the parsley. Blend together the anchovy fillets, capers and garlic in a liquidiser, or pass through a sieve to make a smooth paste. Stir 4 tablespoons of olive oil into the paste, followed by the chopped parsley. Season with pepper. Spread half the bread slices with the paste, top with the cheese and cover with another slice of bread. Sprinkle both sides of the crostini with the remaining oil, place on a baking sheet and bake for a few minutes in the preheated oven until golden brown. Turn once during baking. Remove the crostini from the oven, leave to cool slightly and serve with black olives. *Makes 8.*

15

Smörgåsbord Favourites

For each:

Egg and Tongue
1 hard-boiled egg
1 large slice brown bread
7 g/¼ oz soft butter
2–3 lettuce leaves
50 g/2 oz sliced smoked tongue
2 stuffed olives
¼ teaspoon capers

Shell and slice the egg. Spread the bread with the butter. Top with the lettuce, smoked tongue, egg, olives and capers.

Mariner's Breakfast
25 g/1 oz soft butter
1 large slice brown bread
2 smoked trout fillets
1 egg
1 teaspoon single cream
salt and pepper
a little chopped fresh parsley

Spread some butter on the bread and top with the trout fillets. Beat the egg with the cream, salt and pepper. Melt the remaining butter in a pan and scramble the egg mixture over a low heat. Spoon onto the trout and sprinkle with parsley.

Prawn and Mock Caviare
50 g/2 oz frozen or canned prawns
1 large slice white bread
7 g/¼ oz soft butter
2–3 lettuce leaves
twist of lime
1 teaspoon lumpfish roe

Allow frozen prawns to thaw or drain canned prawns. Spread the bread with the butter and top with the lettuce. Arrange the prawns on top and garnish with a twist of lime and the lumpfish roe.

Roast Beef and Egg
1 large slice brown bread
7 g/¼ oz soft butter
2–3 lettuce leaves
2 slices cold roast beef
1 wedge hard-boiled egg
¼ teaspoon grated horseradish (optional)
sprig parsley

Spread the bread with the butter. Top with the lettuce, roast beef slices, egg, horseradish and parsley.

Rollmop Herring
1 slice white bread
7 g/¼ oz soft butter
2–3 lettuce leaves
2 rollmop herrings
½ onion, cut widthways
4–5 capers

Spread the bread with the butter and top with the lettuce and rollmop herrings. Slice the onion into rings and place on the rollmops, together with the capers.

Blue Cheese and Walnut
1 slice crispbread
7 g/¼ oz soft butter
1 large tomato, sliced
salt and pepper
2 small slices Stilton cheese
1 shelled walnut

Spread the crispbread with the butter, top with the sliced tomato and season with salt and pepper. Arrange the Stilton on the tomato and garnish with the walnut.

Pâté and Bacon
1 round slice white bread
7 g/¼ oz soft butter
2–3 lettuce leaves
2 slices smooth liver pâté
1 bacon rasher

Spread the bread with the butter and top with the lettuce and liver pâté. Fry the bacon until crisp, cool slightly and place over the liver pâté.

From the Smörgåsbord

Smoked Mackerel

For each:
1 large slice rye bread
7 g/¼ oz soft butter
2–3 lettuce leaves
50 g/2 oz curd cheese
1 tablespoon single cream
pinch each salt, sugar and white pepper
¼ small pear
½ small banana
few drops lemon juice
100 g/4 oz smoked mackerel fillet
coarsely ground black pepper
GARNISH
dill sprig (optional)

Spread the bread with the butter and top with the lettuce. Mix together the curd cheese, cream, salt, sugar and white pepper. Wash and core the pear and coarsely grate into the mixture. Peel and dice the banana, add to the mixture and sprinkle with lemon juice. Stir well and spoon onto the lettuce. Cut the fish fillet into thick slices and arrange in a fan-shape on top. Sprinkle with coarsely ground black pepper, and garnish with dill, if used.

Cook's Tip
You can replace the mackerel fillet with cold roast pork, rolls of smoked tongue or diced smoked ham.

Spicy Chicken Livers

For each:
100 g/4 oz chicken livers
25 g/1 oz soft butter
¼ teaspoon salt
1 slice white bread
1 large lettuce leaf
1 tablespoon mayonnaise
2 teaspoons red wine
1 teaspoon cranberry sauce
½ red apple
few drops lemon juice
¼ teaspoon sugar
GARNISH
1 wedge lemon

Wash the chicken livers in cold water, trim and dry well. Melt half the butter in a pan and fry the livers for 8 minutes over a moderate heat, turning continuously. Season with salt and when cool, cut into equal slices.

Toast the bread, spread with the rest of the butter and top with the lettuce. Arrange the liver on the lettuce and spoon the mayonnaise on top. Mix the red wine with the cranberry sauce and spoon over the mayonnaise. Wash, core and coarsely grate the apple. Sprinkle with lemon juice and sugar and arrange around one corner of the bread. Garnish with a wedge of lemon.

Parma Ham and Fig

For each:
1 large slice crusty brown bread
7 g/¼ oz soft butter
4 slices Parma ham
freshly ground pepper
1 tablespoon mayonnaise
1 fresh fig, sliced

Spread the bread with the butter. Place the slices of ham individually on a board, sprinkle with pepper, roll up and arrange on the bread. Spoon the mayonnaise onto the ham, and top with the fig slices.

Asparagus Crispbread

For each:
2 tablespoons oil
1 tablespoon wine vinegar
pinch ground ginger
6–10 cooked asparagus shoots
1 slice crispbread
7 g/¼ oz soft butter
½ slice orange
¼ hard-boiled egg
1 tablespoon double cream
1 tablespoon Cointreau
grated rind of ¼ orange

Beat the oil with the vinegar and ground ginger, and marinate the asparagus in the mixture for 30 minutes, then drain. Spread the crispbread with the butter and top with the asparagus and orange slice. Chop the egg, beat with the cream, Cointreau and orange rind and spoon onto the asparagus.

Breakfast Special

For each:
2 thin bacon rashers
1 slice white bread
1 tablespoon mayonnaise
2–3 lettuce leaves
1 tomato
1 teaspoon finely chopped fresh chives (optional)

Remove the rind from the bacon, and grill or fry in a little fat until crisp. Leave on one side.

Lightly toast the bread and when cool, spread thickly with the mayonnaise. Wash the lettuce, dry well and place on the mayonnaise. Slice the tomato and arrange over the lettuce. Sprinkle with the chives, if used, and top with the bacon rashers.

Cook's Tip

You can stretch bacon rashers to make them thin. Lay them flat on a board and, holding them down at one end, pull the back of a knife blade right along their length.

From the Smörgåsbord

New Yorker

For each:
1 large slice rye bread
40 g/1½ oz full fat cream cheese
3 thin slices smoked salmon
½ small red onion, cut
*   widthways*

Spread the bread thickly with the cheese. Fold each slice of smoked salmon in half and arrange on the bread. Peel the onion, cut into rings and place over the smoked salmon.

Cook's Tip

If the onion topping does not appeal, you can season the cheese spread with freshly grated horseradish instead. Mix ½–1 teaspoon horseradish with the cream cheese and spread the bread with this mixture.

Beef Mayonnaise

For each:
1 large thin slice brown bread
1 tablespoon mayonnaise
3 slices cold roast beef
1 hard-boiled egg
GARNISH
¼ pickled cucumber, sliced

Thickly spread the bread with the mayonnaise. Fold the slices of roast beef in half lengthways and arrange in a fan-shape on the bread. Shell and slice the egg lengthways, and place on the beef. Garnish with the cucumber slices.

Cook's Tip

Roast beef sandwiches are just as delicious made with lightly toasted bread. In this case mix the mayonnaise with 1 teaspoon cranberry sauce and omit the pickled cucumber.

Smoked Eel and Salmon

For each:
1 egg
1 teaspoon chopped fresh mixed
herbs, or a generous pinch
dried mixed herbs
salt and white pepper
20 g/¾ oz soft butter
1 large slice brown bread
2–3 lettuce leaves
2 small smoked eel fillets
1 thin slice smoked salmon

Beat together the egg, herbs, salt and pepper. Melt 15 g (½ oz) butter in a pan, add the beaten egg and scramble over a low heat. Leave to cool slightly.
 Spread the bread with the rest of the butter. Wash and dry the lettuce thoroughly and place on the bread. Cut the bread in half with a sharp knife, and spread both halves

with the scrambled egg. Remove the skin from the smoked eel, and arrange on one half-slice of bread. Roll up the smoked salmon slice and place on the other half.

Cook's Tip
Most kinds of smoked fish can be used in this recipe.

Bavarian Cornets

For each:
1 large slice brown bread
7 g/¼ oz soft butter
2–3 lettuce leaves
1 small onion
50 g/2 oz pickled red cabbage
few drops lemon juice
pinch sugar
salt and pepper
2 small slices cold roast pork
1 teaspoon strong mustard
1 tablespoon whipped double
cream
¼ teaspoon coarsely ground
black or green pepper

Spread the bread with the butter. Wash the lettuce, dry thoroughly and place on the bread. Peel and finely dice the onion. Mix the red cabbage with the lemon juice and half the diced onion, add the sugar and season to taste. Place the red cabbage on the lettuce.

Form the roast pork into cones and arrange on top.
 Stir the mustard into the whipped cream, transfer to a piping bag fitted with a star-shaped nozzle and pipe into the meat cones. Sprinkle with the remaining diced onion and coarsely ground pepper.

From the Smörgåsbord

Gourmet's Delight

For each:
2–3 lettuce leaves
1 large slice brown bread
7 g/¼ oz soft butter
100 g/4 oz cooked chicken breast
1 canned peach half
1 tablespoon mayonnaise
chopped parsley

Wash the lettuce and dry thoroughly. Spread the bread with the butter and place the lettuce on top. Skin the chicken breast, slice thinly and arrange in layers on the lettuce. Drain the peach half, cut into equal slices, and place in a fan-shape on the chicken. Spoon the mayonnaise into a piping bag fitted with a star-shaped nozzle and pipe two swirls onto the peaches. Sprinkle with chopped parsley.

Cook's Tip

When ripe peaches are in season, use one of these in preference to a canned one. Scald the fresh peach by placing it in an ovenproof bowl and pouring on boiling water. Leave for a few seconds, then take out the peach and remove the skin. Cut the peach in half, remove the stone and slice one half as above.

Danish Sandwiches

For each:
25 g/1 oz soft butter
1 slice white bread
1 lettuce leaf
1 slice Tilsit or Cheddar cheese
2 canned sardines
2 large slices tomato
½ onion
salt and coarsely ground black pepper
1 teaspoon grated Emmental or Edam cheese

Melt the butter in a small frying pan and brown the bread in it on both sides. Leave to cool.
    Wash the lettuce, dry well and place on the bread. Top with the Tilsit or Cheddar. Drain the sardines, lay them diagonally across the cheese and arrange the sliced tomato on top. Peel and finely dice the onion. Sprinkle on the tomato, followed by the salt, pepper and grated Emmental or Edam cheese.

Cook's Tip

Danish Sandwiches can be topped with canned anchovy fillets cut into strips instead of sardines. Soak the anchovies first in a little milk, as they tend to be very salty.

21

Super Spreads

Stilton Spread

175 g/6 oz Stilton cheese (or
    other blue cheese)
100 g/4 oz sliced salami
3 small gherkins
10 pickled cocktail onions
4 shelled walnuts
1 teaspoon grated horseradish
1 tablespoon natural yogurt
3 tablespoons mayonnaise
pinch salt
5 drops Tabasco sauce

Place the cheese in a large bowl
and break up with a fork. Cut
the salami into thin strips.
Finely dice the gherkins. Drain
and chop the cocktail onions.
Chop the walnuts. Stir salami,
gherkins, onions and walnuts
into the cheese, together with
the horseradish, yogurt,
mayonnaise, salt and Tabasco
sauce. Adjust the seasoning.

Egg and Pepper Spread

5 hard-boiled eggs
200 g/7 oz soft butter
½ red pepper
1 small onion, peeled
¼ teaspoon salt
pinch each celery salt, white
    pepper, curry powder and
    cayenne pepper

Cut the eggs in half and
remove the yolks. Place the egg
yolks and butter in a bowl and
mix together until smooth.
Finely dice the egg whites.
Wash the pepper, remove the
seeds and dice the flesh finely,
together with the onion. Stir
the diced egg white, pepper
and onion into the butter and
egg yolk mixture. Season with
salt, celery salt, pepper, curry
powder and cayenne.

Emmental Spread

225 g/8 oz Emmental cheese
4 canned baby sweet corn cobs,
    drained
10 stuffed olives
½ clove garlic
small bunch fresh mixed herbs
    (dill, chives, parsley and
    rosemary) or a generous
    pinch of each herb in its dried
    form
175 g/6 oz soft butter
1 teaspoon pickled green
    peppercorns (optional)
salt and pepper

Finely dice the cheese. Finely
chop the sweet corn cobs and
olives. Peel and crush the
garlic, and wash, dry and chop
the fresh herbs, if used.
    Beat the butter until light
and fluffy. Work in the cheese,
sweet corn, olives, garlic and
herbs. Drain and add the

peppercorns, if used. Season to
taste, cover and leave to stand
in the refrigerator for
1–2 hours.

Cook's Tip

These spreads are only
mildly seasoned. If you
prefer hotter, saltier or
sharper spreads, season
accordingly.

Cottage Cheese with Ginger and Honey

225 g/8 oz cottage cheese
3 tablespoons double cream
1 piece preserved stem ginger
3 tablespoons honey
25 g/1 oz cut mixed peel

Sieve the cottage cheese into a bowl. Lightly whip the cream and fold into the cheese. Finely dice the ginger and stir into the mixture, then stir in the honey. Chill the cottage cheese in the refrigerator. Serve garnished with cut mixed peel.

Cottage Cheese with Apple

225 g/8 oz cottage cheese
1 crisp dessert apple
½ large onion
salt

Sieve the cottage cheese into a bowl. Peel and quarter the apple. Remove the core and grate the apple coarsely. Peel and finely chop the onion. Stir the apple and onion into the cottage cheese and season with salt. Chill before serving.

Cook's Tip
You can serve these spreads as sauces with hard-boiled eggs (page 98) or as fillings for tomatoes (page 176).

Cottage Cheese with Herbs

225 g/8 oz cottage cheese
small bunch fresh mixed herbs
* (chives, dill and parsley), or*
* ½ teaspoon each dried chives,*
* dill and parsley*
1 small onion
1 clove garlic
¼ teaspoon salt
generous pinch freshly ground
* white pepper*

Sieve the cottage cheese into a bowl. Wash and finely chop the fresh herbs, if used. Peel the onion and garlic clove and grate both very finely. Stir the herbs, onion, garlic, salt and pepper into the cottage cheese, taste and adjust the seasoning as necessary. Chill before serving.

Cottage Cheese Salad

225 g/8 oz cottage cheese
small bunch radishes
1 small red pepper
1 small onion
1 medium pickled cucumber
¼ teaspoon Tabasco sauce
¼ teaspoon salt

Sieve the cottage cheese into a bowl. Wash, trim and finely chop the radishes. Wash the red pepper, cut it in half, remove the seeds and dice finely. Peel and grate the onion. Finely dice the pickled cucumber. Stir the radishes, pepper, onion and cucumber into the cheese. Season with Tabasco sauce and salt, and chill before serving.

Luxury Party Loaf

4 eggs
1 long French loaf
5 tablespoons mayonnaise
1 small lettuce
225 g/8 oz sliced ham sausage
1 carrot
1 stick celery
bunch radishes
1 onion
2 tablespoons wine vinegar
4 tablespoons oil
1 tablespoon chopped parsley
salt and pepper
175 g/6 oz frozen peas
225 g/8 oz sliced salami
100 g/4 oz Edam or Cheddar
  cheese
2 tablespoons natural yogurt
¼ teaspoon paprika pepper
GARNISH
few dill and parsley sprigs

Hard-boil the eggs, plunge into cold water, shell and leave to cool. Slice the outer crust off the top of the loaf lengthways, to within 5 cm/2 inches of each end. Scoop out some of the bread, and coat the inside of the loaf with 4 tablespoons mayonnaise. Separate the lettuce into leaves; wash, drain thoroughly and use to line the inside of the loaf.

Cut the ham sausage into fine strips. Wash and scrape the carrot and slice into small fingers. Wash the celery and radishes, chop the celery and slice the radishes very finely. Peel the onion and cut into rings. Place the sausage, carrot, celery, radishes and onion rings together in a bowl. Whisk the vinegar with the oil and chopped parsley, season with salt and pepper and stir into the salad.

Blanch the frozen peas in boiling water for 5 minutes, drain and leave to cool. Cut the salami into fine strips, dice the cheese, and place the peas, salami and cheese together in a bowl. Make a dressing with the remaining mayonnaise, the yogurt and paprika, season with salt and pepper and stir into the salami mixture. Fill the inside of the loaf with alternate spoonfuls of the ham sausage and salami salads. Slice each egg into eight wedges and arrange in the salad. Garnish with sprigs of parsley and dill. *Serves 8*

Cook's Tip

For an evening party you can prepare the fillings in advance and fill the loaf shortly before you need it. The lettuce leaves should prevent the bread from becoming soggy. Once filled, keep the loaf loosely wrapped in cling-film in a cool place until you are ready to serve it.

Mosaic Loaf

1 small light rye loaf
175 g/6 oz soft butter
2 hard-boiled eggs
½ cooked carrot
50 g/2 oz canned mushrooms
100 g/4 oz ham
1 spring onion
1 tablespoon capers
pinch celery salt
½ teaspoon salt
½ teaspoon pepper
10 stuffed olives, sliced

Cut off one end of the loaf.
With a long, sharp knife, cut
all round the inside of the loaf
1 cm/½ inch from the crust and,
using your hand, scoop out the
bread from inside.

Place the butter in a bowl
and beat until light and creamy.
Shell the hard-boiled eggs, cut
them in half and remove the
yolks. Sieve the yolks into the
butter and mix well. Finely
dice the egg whites and the

carrot. Drain the mushrooms
and chop finely, together with
the ham, spring onion and
capers. Stir all the chopped
ingredients into the butter
mixture, followed by the sliced
olives. Season with celery salt,
salt and pepper. Spoon the
mixture into the loaf, filling it
completely, and pressing down
so that no spaces are left.
Replace the piece originally
sliced off, wrap the loaf in
kitchen foil and leave to stand
for a few hours in the
refrigerator.

Stuffed Party Rolls

6 Vienna rolls
450 g/1 lb curd cheese
4 drops Tabasco sauce
20 ml/1 fl oz white wine
¼ teaspoon salt
¼ teaspoon white pepper
2 tablespoons chopped fresh
  mixed herbs, or 2 teaspoons
  dried mixed herbs
1 green pepper
2 gherkins
225 g/8 oz ham
100 g/4 oz cooked chicken
6 button mushrooms
50 g/2 oz pistachio nuts
  (optional)
2 teaspoons grated root ginger
1–2 teaspoons chopped mixed
  peel
20 ml/1 fl oz sherry

Slice off one third of each roll
and scoop out all the bread
from inside. Place half the curd

cheese in a bowl and stir in the
Tabasco, white wine, salt,
pepper and herbs. Wash the
green pepper, remove the seeds
and dice the flesh finely, with
the gherkins and half the ham.
Mix the ham, pepper and
gherkins into the curd cheese.

Finely chop the remaining
ham, the chicken, mushrooms
and pistachios, if used, and mix
in a separate bowl with the
remaining curd chese. Add the
grated root ginger, chopped
mixed peel and sherry. Fill
three of the rolls with the wine
and herb mixture, and the
remaining three rolls with the
chicken and ginger mixture.
Set the two sections of each
roll back together again, wrap
in cooking foil and leave to
stand for a few hours in the
refrigerator. *Serves 6*

Cheese Bonnets

100 g/4 oz Cheddar or
  Emmental cheese
bunch parsley
2 tablespoons curd cheese
4 tablespoons mayonnaise
1 tablespoon wine vinegar
12 thin slices salami
12 slices French bread
40 g/1½ oz butter

Dice the cheese very finely.
Wash and dry the parsley, keep
a few sprigs to one side and
finely chop the rest. In a bowl
mix the curd cheese with the
mayonnaise, vinegar and
chopped parsley. Add the
diced cheese.

  Cut a straight line to the
centre of each slice of salami
and fold the cut edges over
each other to make a bonnet.
Toast the bread and leave to
cool slightly, then spread with
butter. Place spoonfuls of
cheese salad on each slice of

bread and cover each spoonful
with a salami bonnet. Garnish
with parsley sprigs. *Makes 12*

Cook's Tip
You can make this
recipe into a sandwich
snack by cutting rounds
from large white slices of
bread using a pastry
cutter. For this larger
size you will need to
double the quantities for
the cheese salad, and to
make the bonnets from
slices of Mortadella or
garlic sausage.

Savoury Butter Slices

150 g/5 oz soft butter
pinch salt
¼ teaspoon lemon juice
bunch chives
2 tablespoons grated Cheddar
  or Emmental cheese
1 teaspoon paprika pepper
50 g/2 oz smoked ham
2 hard-boiled eggs, shelled
1 tablespoon single cream
50 g/2 oz lobster or crab paste
8 small slices white bread
GARNISH
2 radishes
4 stuffed olives
4 chillies
4 small gherkins

Cream the butter with the salt
and lemon juice and divide
into three equal portions.
Wash, dry and finely slice the
chives, and mix into one
portion of butter. Stir the

grated cheese and paprika into
the second portion. Finely dice
the ham and eggs and stir into
the third portion of butter
followed by the cream. The
lobster or crab paste makes the
fourth topping. Spread two
slices of bread with half of
each, then cut the slices in half
and trim off the crusts.

  Slice the radishes and olives.
Cut the gherkins into a fan-
shape by slicing almost to the
bottom of each and spreading
out the sections. Garnish the
chive butter fingers with radish
slices, the cheese and paprika
butter with chillies, the ham
and egg butter with gherkins
and the lobster or crab paste
with olives. *Makes 16*

Party Nests

225 g/8 oz butter
¼ teaspoon salt
pinch white pepper
1 teaspoon lemon juice
1 punnet mustard and cress
75 g/3 oz shelled walnuts
10 small rounds wholemeal
bread
pinch each celery salt, garlic
salt and ground ginger
2 drops Tabasco sauce
3 strips canned pimiento
10 small rounds pumper-
nickel bread
GARNISH
parsley sprigs

Cream half the butter with the
salt, pepper and lemon juice.
Snip the cress with scissors,
rinse in cold water and leave to
drain. Chop the walnuts.
Spread the wholemeal bread
with the butter and sprinkle
cress round the edges. Place
the chopped walnuts in the

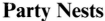

centre of each round.
   Stir the celery salt, garlic
salt, ginger and Tabasco into
the remaining butter. Drain the
pimiento and dice finely. Place
the butter mixture in a piping
bag fitted with a small star-
shaped nozzle and pipe round
the edges of the pumpernickel
bread. Fill the centres with the
diced pimiento. Wash and dry
the parsley, break into sprigs
and use to garnish each round.
(Use a pastry cutter to make
the bread rounds.) *Makes 20*

Smoked Fish Canapés

bunch chives
100 g/4 oz soft butter
1 tablespoon grated fresh
horseradish, or bottled
creamed horseradish
generous pinch each salt and
garlic salt
4 slices wholemeal bread
400 g/14 oz smoked halibut or
haddock
2 firm tomatoes
GARNISH
dill or parsley sprigs
2 lettuce leaves
coarsely ground black pepper

Wash the chives, dry well and
slice very finely. Cream the
butter with the horseradish,
salt, garlic salt and chives, and
spread on the bread. Cut each
slice diagonally to form two
triangles. Skin the fish, remove
any bones and cut into pieces

to fit the bread triangles. Place
one piece of fish on each
triangle.
   Wash, dry and slice the
tomatoes. Wash the dill or
parsley and the lettuce and
allow to drain. Place a slice of
tomato on half the pieces of
fish and tuck half a lettuce leaf
under the rest. Garnish with a
dill or parsley sprig. Sprinkle
with pepper before serving.
Makes 8

Cheese Sticks

450 g/1 lb Edam or Emmental
    cheese, in slices 1 cm/½ inch
    thick
50 g/2 oz thinly sliced salami
24 stuffed olives
2 small firm tomatoes
GARNISH
parsley sprigs

Cut the cheese into 1-cm/
½-inch cubes. Roll up the
salami slices. Thread each
salami roll onto a cocktail stick
with an olive, a small parsley
sprig and a cheese cube.
    Wash, dry and cut the
tomatoes into eight wedges.
Thread the tomato wedges
onto cocktail sticks, each with
an olive and a cheese cube.
Thread the remaining cheese
cubes onto sticks, interspersed
with olives, and garnish with
parsley sprigs.

Stuffed Tomatoes

25 g/1 oz long-grain rice
4 tomatoes
1 tablespoon mayonnaise
1 tablespoon single cream
1 tablespoon chopped fresh
    mixed herbs or 1 teaspoon
    dried mixed herbs
1 tablespoon grated Cheddar
    cheese
salt and white pepper
6 stuffed olives

Cook the rice following the
instructions on the packet,
drain and leave to cool. Wash
and dry the tomatoes. Slice off
the tops to make lids, scoop
out the seeds from inside and
discard. Mix the rice with the
mayonnaise, cream, herbs and
grated cheese. Season with salt
and pepper. Slice the olives
and stir into the rice mixture.
Stuff the tomatoes with the
mixture and replace the lids.
Makes 4

Curried
Croquettes

2 onions
parsley sprigs
450 g/1 lb minced beef, lamb or
    pork
2 eggs
2 tablespoons breadcrumbs
2 teaspoons mild curry powder
¼ teaspoon salt
¼ teaspoon black pepper
oil for deep-frying
GARNISH
mandarin segments, pineapple
    segments, maraschino
    cherries, grapes, blue and
    Camembert cheese, a
    sprinkling of chopped nuts,
    stuffed olives, chillies, canned
    baby sweet corn cobs, lettuce
    leaves and parsley

Peel the onions and chop
finely. Wash, dry and chop the
parsley. Place the mince in a
bowl and mix thoroughly with
the chopped onion, parsley,
eggs, breadcrumbs, curry
powder, salt and pepper. Wet
your hands and form the meat
into small balls. Heat the oil
for deep-frying to 180 C/350 F.
Place a few balls at a time in
the hot oil and deep-fry for 5–8
minutes. Remove from the oil
with a draining spoon and
drain on kitchen paper. Thread
the curry balls onto cocktail
sticks and garnish as liked with
pieces of fruit, cheese and
vegetables. Wash and drain the
lettuce, use to line a dish and
arrange the curried croquettes
on top.

Savoury Titbits

Gherkins and Smoked Ham
10 thin slices smoked ham
½ teaspoon coarsely ground
black pepper
10 small gherkins

Dates and Cream Cheese
10 dates
1 hard-boiled egg, shelled
2 tablespoons single cream
1 (75-g/3-oz) packet full fat
cream cheese
¼ teaspoon finely chopped dill
(optional)
¼ teaspoon chopped borage
(optional)

Olives and Bacon
10 thin slices streaky bacon
10 stuffed olives

Sprinkle the ham with the
pepper. Wrap each gherkin in
a slice of ham and secure with
a cocktail stick.

Slice the dates open

lengthways and remove the
stones. Cut the egg in half.
Sieve the yolk into a bowl, add
the cream and cream cheese
and stir until smooth. Mix in
the herbs, if used. Transfer the
mixture to a piping bag fitted
with a small star-shaped nozzle
and pipe into the dates. Keep
the stuffed dates in a cool place
until you are ready to serve
them.

Fry the bacon until cooked
on both sides. Drain for a few
minutes on absorbent kitchen
paper. Wrap a stuffed olive in
each slice of bacon, securing
with a wooden cocktail stick.
Return the bacon rolls to the
frying pan and fry in hot fat
until crisp, turning
occasionally.

Game and Mushroom Croquettes

450 g/1 lb mushrooms
100 g/4 oz ham
bunch parsley
50 g/2 oz butter
100 g/4 oz plain flour
150 ml/¼ pint milk
4 egg yolks
2 egg whites
575 g/1¼ lb game
50 ml/2 fl oz Madeira wine
pinch salt
¼ teaspoon black pepper
1 teaspoon ground allspice
100 g/4 oz dried breadcrumbs
oil for deep-frying

Clean the mushrooms and cut
off the tips of the stalks. Finely
chop the ham and parsley.
Melt half the butter in a
saucepan, sprinkle on 25 g/1 oz
flour and stir over the heat
until golden. Gradually add

the milk and simmer the sauce
for 10 minutes, stirring
continuously. Leave the sauce
to cool slightly, then stir in two
egg yolks.

Beat the two remaining egg
yolks with the egg whites. Skin
and trim the game, and mince
twice through the finest blade
of the mincer. Mix the mince
with the sauce, ham, parsley,
25 g/1 oz flour, the remaining
butter, the Madeira, salt,
pepper and allspice, and knead
to form a smooth dough. Wet
your hands and surround each
mushroom with a ball of the
mixture, lightly pressing the
meat together. Coat the balls
with the remaining flour, then
the beaten egg and finally the
breadcrumbs. Heat the oil for
deep-frying to 180 C/350 F. Fry
the croquettes for 6–8 minutes
until brown and crispy. Drain
on absorbent kitchen paper
and leave to cool. Serve with
Cumberland sauce or
cranberry jelly.

Canapés and Snacks

Prawn Croquettes

225 g/8 oz frozen prawns
25 g/1 oz butter
50 g/2 oz plain flour
150 ml/¼ pint milk
2–3 teaspoons lemon juice
¼ teaspoon salt
¼ teaspoon white pepper
1 tablespoon chopped fresh
  parsley, or 1 teaspoon dried
  parsley
1 egg, beaten
100 g/4 oz dried breadcrumbs
oil for deep frying

Place the prawns in a dish, cover and leave to thaw. Drain and chop finely. Melt the butter in a saucepan. Sprinkle on half the flour and stir over the heat until it becomes golden in colour. Gradually add the milk and, stirring continuously, bring slowly to the boil, when the sauce will thicken. Add the chopped prawns, lemon juice, salt, pepper and parsley. Continue cooking for about 2 minutes until the mixture becomes firm, again stirring continuously. Chill the prawn mixture.

Wet your hands and, on a lightly floured surface, form the mixture into a long roll. Cut into small pieces and shape into croquettes. Dip the croquettes in the remaining flour, then in beaten egg and finally in breadcrumbs. Heat the oil for deep-frying to 180 C/ 350 F and fry the croquettes for about 6–8 minutes until golden brown. Drain on absorbent kitchen paper and leave to cool. *Makes 18*

Cheese Fritters

350 g/12 oz matured Gouda or
  Cheddar cheese, in slices
  2 cm/1 inch thick
150 g/5 oz thinly sliced smoked
  streaky bacon
2 eggs
25 g/1 oz plain flour
100 g/4 oz dried breadcrumbs
oil for deep-frying
FOR THE SAUCE
1 (500-g/15·9-oz) carton
  natural yogurt
¼ teaspoon salt
pinch celery salt
¼ teaspoon ground white pepper
generous pinch ground ginger
3 tablespoons chopped fresh
  mixed herbs (parsley, chives,
  dill, a little rosemary and
  sage) or 2 teaspoons dried
  mixed herbs

Cut the cheese into 2-cm/ 1-inch cubes. Wrap each cube in a slice of bacon and secure with a wooden cocktail stick.

Beat the eggs. Dip the cheese and bacon cubes in the flour, then in the beaten egg and finally in breadcrumbs. Heat the oil for deep-frying to 180 C/ 350 F and fry the cubes for 4–6 minutes until golden brown. Drain on absorbent kitchen paper and leave to cool.

In a small bowl mix the yogurt with the salt, celery salt, pepper, ginger and mixed herbs. Serve the sauce with the cubes as a dip.

Melon and Ham Canapés

3 slices white bread
20 g/¾ oz soft butter
12 thin small slices smoked ham
¼ honeydew melon
12 mandarin segments (fresh or canned)

Remove the crusts from the bread and cut the slices into quarters to give 12 small squares. Spread each with butter. Fold the slices of smoked ham in half and place one on each piece of bread. Remove the seeds from the melon, scoop out the flesh with a melon scoop or small spoon, and arrange the melon balls on the ham. Top each canapé with a mandarin segment. *Makes 12*

Salmon Canapés Tartare

6 (6-cm/2½-inch) rounds white bread
25 g/1 oz soft butter
2 leeks
275 g/10 oz smoked salmon
GARNISH
1 lime or lemon, sliced
dill or parsley sprigs

Butter the bread rounds. Wash and trim the leeks, and slice into 6-cm/2½-inch lengths. Remove the outer leaves and blanch the centres in a little boiling water for 2 minutes. Drain the leeks and allow to cool. Roll out the leaves and trim exactly to cover each bread round. Coarsely mince the smoked salmon, divide onto the rounds and garnish each canapé with a slice of lime and a dill or parsley sprig.

Ham Rolls with Horseradish Cream

8 slices roast ham
200 ml/7 fl oz double cream
¼ teaspoon salt
1 tablespoon fresh grated horseradish
1 tablespoon orange juice
GARNISH
½ orange
8 stuffed olives

Place the slices of ham individually on a kitchen board. Whip the cream with the salt until very stiff and stir in the horseradish and orange juice. Spread half of each slice of ham with all but two tablespoons of the mixture, and roll up the slices. With a teaspoon, fill the larger opening of each roll with the remaining horseradish cream, and arrange the rolls on a flat dish.

Wash and dry the orange, and without peeling it, cut into thin slices. Cut the orange slices in half and use to garnish the dish, together with the stuffed olives. *Makes 8*

Cook's Tip

If you have no fresh horseradish you can use ready-grated, bottled horseradish. In this case you should add more seasoning to the cream, since bottled horseradish has less taste than the fresh variety.

Party Canapés

400 g / 14 oz full fat cream
    cheese
100 ml / 4 fl oz soured cream
¼ teaspoon salt
¼ teaspoon curry powder
pinch sugar
1 teaspoon tomato ketchup
½ teaspoon paprika pepper
1 teaspoon mild French mustard
100 g / 4 oz soft butter
50-60 cheese biscuits
50 g / 2 oz blue cheese
50 g / 2 oz Cheddar cheese
50 g / 2 oz sliced smoked tongue
GARNISH
prawns, caviare, smoked
    salmon, sliced salami, hard-
    boiled eggs, tomatoes,
    cucumber, chillies, gherkins,
    stuffed olives, truffles,
    radishes, walnuts, canned
    baby sweet corn cobs, capers,
    mushrooms, avocado pear
    cubes, mustard and cress, dill,
    parsley, strips of lettuce and
    fruit of your choice

Beat the cream cheese with the
soured cream and salt until
light and fluffy, then divide
into three portions. Leave one
portion on one side. Mix the
second portion with the curry
powder and sugar, and the
third portion with the tomato
ketchup and paprika.
    Work the mustard into the
butter and use to butter the
biscuits. Cut the blue cheese
and Cheddar into small cubes
and the smoked tongue into
small pieces. Top each biscuit
with a piece of cheese or
smoked tongue. Place the three
portions of cream cheese into
separate piping bags fitted with
star-shaped nozzles and pipe
an equal quantity of biscuits
with each flavour. Top the
biscuits with any of the
garnishes suggested, as shown
in the photograph.
Makes 50-60

Dominoes

1 hard-boiled egg
175 g/6 oz full fat cream cheese
3 tablespoons single cream
½ teaspoon salt
pinch white pepper
1 teaspoon strong mustard
generous pinch saffron
(optional)
½ teaspoon tomato purée
¼ teaspoon paprika pepper
few drops lemon juice
pinch sugar
1 tablespoon chopped fresh
mixed herbs or 1 teaspoon
dried mixed herbs
1 (227-g/8-oz) packet
pumpernickel bread

Shell the hard-boiled egg, remove the yolk from the white and discard the white. Beat together the cheese, cream and salt until creamy. Divide into four portions. Stir the white pepper and mustard into the first portion. Pass the egg yolk

through a sieve and stir into the second portion, followed by the saffron, if used. Mix the third portion with the tomato purée and paprika and the fourth with the lemon juice, sugar and mixed herbs. Spread the pumpernickel slices alternately with the four flavours of cheese. Stack the slices neatly one above the other and top with a fifth slice of pumpernickel. Place a flat plate on top of the bread to prevent the edges curling up, and leave to stand in the refrigerator for 1 hour. Before serving cut the bread into squares or rectangles with a sharp knife.

Cheese and Herb Crackers

225 g/8 oz curd cheese
3 tablespoons single cream
1 teaspoon lemon juice
½ teaspoon salt
generous pinch cayenne pepper
generous pinch sugar
½ small onion
2 tablespoons chopped fresh
mixed herbs (chervil, chives,
parsley, dill) or 1 teaspoon
dried mixed herbs
24 cheese biscuits
GARNISH
1 large carrot
24 mild chillies
parsley sprigs

Wash and scrape the carrot and blanch in a little boiling water for 2 minutes, then drain and leave to cool.
    Beat the curd cheese with the cream, lemon juice, salt, cayenne and sugar until

smooth. Peel and grate the onion. Fold it into the cheese mixture together with the mixed herbs. Transfer the mixture to a piping bag fitted with a star-shaped nozzle and pipe onto the biscuits.
    Cut the carrot into 24 slices. Using a patterned pastry cutter or a knife, shape the carrot slices into flower shapes. Garnish each biscuit with a slice of carrot, a chilli and a parsley sprig. *Makes 24*

Pork Fillet en Croûte

PASTRY
350 g/12 oz flour
½ teaspoon salt
175 g/6 oz butter or margarine
1 egg yolk
100 ml/4 fl oz water
FILLING
450 g/1 lb roast fillet of pork
25 g/1 oz butter
25 g/1 oz flour
100 ml/4 fl oz stock
1 egg
salt and pepper
pinch ground nutmeg
beaten egg to glaze

Sift the flour and salt into a bowl. Rub the butter or margarine into the flour until the mixture resembles fine breadcrumbs. Form a well in the centre of the mixture and pour in the egg yolk and water. Quickly knead all the ingredients together to form a dough. Wrap in cooking foil or greaseproof paper and leave to stand in the refrigerator for 30 minutes.

To make the filling, chop the pork fillet and pass it twice through the finest blade of the mincer. Melt the butter in a large pan, sprinkle in the flour and stir until it begins to brown. Gradually add the stock and simmer for 5–7 minutes, stirring continuously. Remove the pan from the heat. Separate the egg, beat the yolk and stir into the sauce. Season with salt, pepper and ground nutmeg, and add the minced pork. Whisk the egg white until stiff and fold into the mixture.

Preheat the oven to hot (220 C, 425 F, Gas Mark 7). Take the pastry out of the refrigerator and divide into three. Return two portions to the refrigerator until needed, and roll out the third to a round on a lightly floured surface. Grease the base and side of a 25-cm/10-inch pie tin. Place the pastry round in the tin, trimming round the edges to fit. Keep the pastry trimmings. Prick the base several times with a fork.

Roll out the second piece of dough into a long, even strip and use to line the side of the tin. Press the join between the base and side firmly together. Spoon the filling into the tin and smooth the surface. Roll out the remaining dough to a round the size of the tin and place over the filling, trimming off any excess pastry from the edges. Press the top firmly to the pastry side, and prick several times with a fork. Use half the beaten egg to brush over the top of the pie.

Roll out any left-over pastry until quite thin, and cut out leaves and half-moon shapes. Make a thin roll to decorate the centre of the pie. Paint these trimmings with more egg, arrange on the pie and paint the top of the pie once more with the rest of the beaten egg. Bake in the oven for 30 minutes. After baking, leave the pie to cool in the tin for 15 minutes, then turn out onto a cooling tray.

Meat Pasty

PASTRY
225 g/8 oz flour
pinch salt
100 g/4 oz butter or margarine
1 egg yolk
1 tablespoon cold water
FILLING
1 onion
50 g/2 oz mushrooms
25 g/1 oz butter
225 g/8 oz minced beef
2 tablespoons chopped parsley,
*   or 2 teaspoons dried parsley*
100 g/4 oz ham
2 tablespoons fresh white
*   breadcrumbs*
20 ml/1 fl oz brandy
salt and pepper
pinch each ground nutmeg and
*   dried marjoram*
¼ teaspoon grated lemon rind
beaten egg to glaze

Make the pastry following the
method for Pork Fillet en
Croûte (opposite), cover and

chill for 30 minutes.
   To make the filling, peel the
onion and chop finely, together
with the mushrooms. Melt the
butter in a large pan and fry
the onion until soft. Add the
minced beef and cook until
browned all over. Stir in the
mushroom and parsley. Finely
dice the ham. Mix the
breadcrumbs into the meat,
followed by the diced ham,
brandy, salt, pepper, nutmeg,
marjoram and lemon rind.
   Preheat the oven to
moderately hot (200 c, 400 f,
Gas Mark 6). Roll out the
pastry into two oval shapes.
Spread one with the filling and
place the other on top. Trim
any excess pastry off the edges
to fit, and press the edges
firmly together. Prick the top
several times.Roll out the
pastry trimmings and cut out
shapes for decoration. Brush
the top with beaten egg, add
the trimmings and bake for
60–75 minutes.

Liver Pasties

PASTRY
450 g/1 lb brioche dough (see
*   page 231)*
FILLING
100 g/4 oz chicken livers
75 g/3 oz pig's liver
175 g/6 oz pork fillet
175 g/6 oz bacon
grated rind of ½ orange
2 teaspoons paprika pepper
pinch each ground ginger,
*   allspice and basil*
¼ teaspoon rosemary
1 bay leaf
20 ml/1 fl oz brandy
50 g/2 oz shallots
1 clove garlic, peeled
4 tablespoons single cream
1 egg white
40 g/1½ oz fresh white
*   breadcrumbs*

Make a brioche dough. Line
12 brioche moulds or deep
patty tins with two thirds of
the dough.

   For the filling, roughly chop
the livers, pork and bacon. Add
the orange rind, spices, herbs
and brandy. Peel and dice the
shallots, crush the garlic and
add to the liver mixture. Cover
with cooking foil or cling film
and leave to marinate for
1 hour. Then add the cream,
egg white and breadcrumbs
and blend the mixture in the
liquidiser. Spoon the mixture
into the lined moulds or patty
tins. Roll out lids from the
remaining dough, dampen the
edges and use to cover the
pasties, pressing the edges well
together. Make decorations, if
liked, out of any left-over
pastry trimmings and place on
top of the pasties. Bake in a
moderately hot oven (200 c,
400 f, Gas Mark 6) for 20–25
minutes. Turn out on a wire
rack and leave to cool.
Makes 12

Pâtés en Croûte

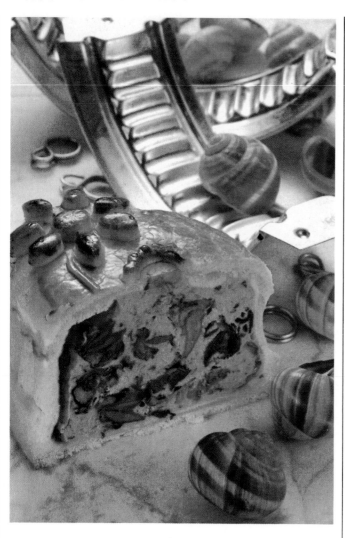

Pâté d'Escargots

100 g/4 oz shallots
40 g/1½ oz butter
1 small egg white
50 g/2 oz fresh white
  breadcrumbs
1 tablespoon single cream
100 g/4 oz lean veal
pinch salt and pepper
6 tablespoons double cream
1 (198-g/7-oz) can snails
2 cloves garlic
1 tablespoon Pernod
1 tablespoon brandy
100 ml/4 fl oz light stock
1 teaspoon chopped fresh
  thyme, or pinch dried thyme
225 g/8 oz shortcrust pastry (as
  for Meat Pasty, page 53)

Peel and dice the shallots. Fry
half of them in 25 g/1 oz of the
butter, then leave to cool. Beat
the egg white and mix with the
breadcrumbs and single cream.
Cut the veal into strips. Blend
together the veal, bread

mixture, fried shallots, salt and
pepper in the liquidiser. Fold
in the whipped double cream.
   Drain the snails, but keep
the liquid on one side. Cut the
snails in half. Peel and crush
the garlic cloves. Melt the
remaining butter in a pan, fry
the rest of the shallots until
soft and add the Pernod and
brandy. Add the stock, the
juice from the canned snails,
the garlic and thyme and
season to taste. Bring to the
boil and simmer until the
liquid evaporates, and add the
snails. Leave the mixture to
cool, then stir it into the veal
purée. Line a 600-ml/1-pint
mould or a 450-g/1-lb loaf tin
with the shortcrust pastry (see
page 200) and spoon in the
filling. Cover with a pastry lid.
Bake in a moderately hot oven
(200 C, 400 F, Gas Mark 6), for
15 minutes, then turn the oven
down to moderate (180 C,
350 F, Gas Mark 4) for a
further 30–40 minutes. *Serves 4*

Haddock and Salmon Pasty

1½ (370-g/13-oz) packets
  frozen puff pastry
150 g/5 oz frozen prawns
450 g/1 lb haddock fillet
450 g/1 lb plaice fillets
1 teaspoon salt
generous pinch ground nutmeg
½ teaspoon white pepper
1 egg
1 teaspoon chopped fresh
  parsley, or pinch dried
1 teaspoon chopped fresh dill, or
  pinch dried dill
225 g/8 oz fresh salmon
beaten egg yolk to glaze

Thaw the puff pastry as
directed on the packet. Place
the frozen prawns in a bowl,
cover and leave to thaw. Skin
and trim the haddock fillet and
cut into two pieces. Mince the
plaice fillets twice and season
with salt, nutmeg and pepper.

Whisk the egg and stir into the
minced plaice. Drain and chop
the prawns and add to the
mixture with the herbs.
   On a lightly floured surface
roll out the pastry to form two
long oval shapes. Place one
haddock fillet on one piece of
pastry. Cover with half the
plaice and prawn stuffing. Lay
the salmon on top. Spread the
remaining fish stuffing over the
salmon and top with the
second haddock fillet. Cover
the fish with the second piece
of pastry. Press the edges
firmly together, trimming off
any excess pastry. Make
decorations from the
trimmings. Glaze the pastry
with the egg yolk and arrange
the decorations on top. Bake in
a moderately hot oven (200 C,
400 F, Gas Mark 6) for 20
minutes, then turn the oven
down to moderate (180 C,
350 F, Gas Mark 4) and bake
for a further 40 minutes.
Serves 4

Country Terrine

2 rabbit (or hare) legs
450 g/1 lb lean pork
200 g/7 oz bacon
salt and freshly ground black
  pepper
generous pinch grated nutmeg
12 juniper berries
4 bay leaves
1 tablespoon dried mixed herbs
  (marjoram, thyme, sage,
  savory)
20 ml/1 fl oz brandy
2 eggs
225 g/8 oz smoked belly pork
300 g/12 oz thinly sliced bacon
  fat or streaky bacon
100 g/4 oz pork dripping

Trim and bone the rabbit or
hare legs and remove any skin.
Finely dice the rabbit, pork
and bacon. Mix the diced meat
together in a bowl and add the
salt, pepper, nutmeg, half the
juniper berries, one bay leaf,
the herbs and brandy. Cover
the mixture with cooking foil
or cling-film and leave to
marinate in the refrigerator for
at least 12 hours.

Blend the marinated meat, a
little at a time, in the liquidiser,
then chill for a further 2–3
hours. Whisk the eggs and add
to the meat purée, beating
vigorously for at least
10 minutes. Remove the rind
from the belly pork. Finely
dice the pork and stir into the
meat purée. Season to taste.
Line a 1.15-litre/2-pint
ovenproof earthenware dish
with a lid with overlapping
slices of bacon fat or streaky
bacon (see page 201) and fill
with the meat mixture. Smooth
the top and decorate with the
remaining bay leaves and
juniper berries. Cover with a
sheet of buttered greaseproof
paper.

Heat the oven to moderate
(180 C, 350 F, Gas Mark 4).
Place the lid on the dish, stand
the dish in a bain-marie
containing enough boiling
water to come up to within
2 cm/1 inch of the edge of the
terrine, and bake in the oven
for 2 hours. The water should
not be allowed to boil, and
should reach a maximum of
80 C (175 F). During cooking
the meat will shrink away from
the sides slightly. After
cooking, take the dish out of
the bain-marie and leave to
cool. Melt the pork dripping
and pour round the edge of the
pâté. Leave the dripping to set.
This terrine can be kept in the
refrigerator for up to two
weeks.

Cook's Tip

Before starting to make
a pâté, terrine or
galantine, please refer to
pages 199 – 201, where
methods of preparation
are explained in more
detail.

Mushroom Terrine

225 g/8 oz veal or pork fillet
50 g/2 oz white breadcrumbs
100 g/4 oz shallots, chopped
50 g/2 oz butter
1 egg white
150 ml/¼ pint single cream
generous pinch each salt,
    pepper, ginger and allspice
900 g/2 lb mushrooms, or 800 g/
    1¾ lb mushrooms and 100 g/
    4 oz diced truffles
3 tablespoons oil
1 small clove garlic
225 ml/8 fl oz chicken stock
½ teaspoon each dried basil,
    thyme, sage and caraway
150 ml/¼ pint white wine aspic
    (see page 202)

Dice the meat and place in a
bowl with the breadcrumbs.
Melt half the butter in a pan,
fry half the shallots until soft
and add to the meat. Whisk
the egg white with half the
cream, the salt, pepper and
spices. Pour over the meat,
cover with cooking foil and
leave to marinate for 1 hour.
Slice the mushrooms. Fry
them in the oil; strain and keep
the liquid on one side. Place
the mushrooms in a bowl. Peel
and chop the garlic. Melt the
remaining butter and fry the
rest of the shallots with the
garlic. Add the mushroom
juice, the chicken stock, herbs
and caraway seeds, bring to the
boil and simmer until reduced
by half. Strain over the
mushrooms. Cover and leave
to marinate for 1 hour. Blend
the meat mixture until smooth;
add the remaining cream. Fold
in the mushroom mixture and
diced truffle, if used, and
transfer to a greased terrine.
Cover, place in a bain-marie
and cook in a moderate oven
(180 C, 350 F, Gas Mark 4) for
1–1¼ hours. Pour over wine
aspic when cooled. Allow to set.

Rabbit Terrine

1.5 kg/3 lb boned rabbit
225 g/8 oz gammon
1 onion
2 shallots
1 clove garlic
2 sticks celery
2 carrots
rabbit, beef or chicken bones
few peppercorns
1.5 litres/2¾ pints water
25 g/1 oz butter
100 g/4 oz diced chicken livers
20 ml/1 fl oz brandy
225 g/8 oz ham
100 g/4 oz button mushrooms
2 eggs
1 teaspoon thyme
1 teaspoon dried sage
½ teaspoon allspice
pinch ground cardamom
350 g/12 oz thinly sliced bacon
    fat or streaky bacon
few sprigs fresh sage, bay leaf

Finely mince half the rabbit
together with the gammon.

Chop the rest into large pieces.
    Peel and dice the onion,
shallots and garlic clove. Wash
and chop the celery and
carrots. Place all the vegetables
in a pan together with the
bones, peppercorns and water,
bring to the boil and simmer
for 2 hours, skimming from
time to time, until reduced to
250 ml/8 fl oz. Strain, return to
the heat and simmer again
until reduced by half. Strain.
    Melt the butter, fry the
chicken liver and pour the
brandy over the top. Dice the
ham and mushrooms. Beat the
eggs. Mix the liver, ham,
mushrooms, eggs, minced
rabbit and gammon, rabbit
chunks, herbs and spices into
the stock and stir well. Line a
large terrine with overlapping
slices of bacon fat or streaky
bacon (see page 201) and fill
with the mixture. Decorate
with sage sprigs and a bay leaf.
Cover and bake in a bain-
marie for 2 hours.

Terrines and Galantines

Veal Terrine

350 g/12 oz veal fillet
225 g/8 oz lean pork
225 g/8 oz bacon
salt and pepper
¼ teaspoon each dried basil,
   sage and thyme
50 g/2 oz fresh white
   breadcrumbs
1 egg white
150 ml/¼ pint double cream
2 shallots
1 clove garlic
225 g/8 oz calf's liver
25 g/1 oz butter
20 ml/1 fl oz brandy
20 ml/1 fl oz Cointreau
225 g/8 oz mushrooms
100 g/4 oz ham
2 tablespoons chopped parsley
generous pinch each ground
   ginger and cardamom
350 g/12 oz thinly sliced bacon
   fat or streaky bacon

Dice the veal, pork and bacon
and place in a bowl. Season
with salt, pepper and dried
herbs and sprinkle with the
breadcrumbs. Whip the egg
white with the cream and pour
over the top. Cover with
cooking foil and leave to
marinate in the refrigerator for
at least 12 hours. Then take
out of the refrigerator, blend in
the liquidiser and chill again.

Peel and chop the shallots
and garlic clove. Dice the calf's
liver. Melt the butter in a pan
and fry the shallots, garlic and
liver. Pour over the brandy and
Cointreau. Slice the
mushrooms and ham. Mix
together the liver, shallots,
mushroom, ham, parsley and
spices, add salt and stir into
the meat purée. Line a
1.15-litre/2-pint earthenware
dish with overlapping slices of
bacon fat or streaky bacon (see
page 201) and fill with the
meat. Cover and stand the dish
in a bain-marie. Bake in a
moderate oven (180 C, 350 F,
Gas Mark 6) for 2 hours.

Italian Veal Galantine

1 kg/2¼ lb boned breast of veal
salt and pepper
350 g/12 oz veal fillet
350 g/12 oz loin of pork
225 g/8 oz bacon
1 bay leaf
1 teaspoon each chopped fresh
   thyme and basil, or pinch
   each dried thyme and basil
1 onion
25 g/1 oz butter
1 clove garlic, crushed
20 ml/1 fl oz Grappa or brandy
50 g/2 oz fresh white
   breadcrumbs
3 tablespoons single cream
1 egg
100 g/4 oz ham
25 g/1 oz chopped pistachio nuts
1.75 litres/3 pints veal or
   chicken
175 g/6 oz crystallised fruits

Rub the breast of veal with salt
and pepper. Cut the veal fillet,
pork and bacon into strips and
place together in a bowl.
Sprinkle with seasoning and
herbs. Cut the onion into rings.
Melt the butter in a pan and
fry the onion and garlic. Add
to the strips of meat, together
with the Grappa or brandy,
and breadcrumbs. Beat the
cream with the egg and pour
over the top. Cover the meat
mixture with cooking foil and
chill in the refrigerator for
1 hour, then blend in the
liquidiser. Dice the ham and
mix into the meat purée,
together with the pistachios, if
used. Spread the purée over the
breast of veal, roll it up and tie
with thin string at 2-cm/1-inch
intervals.

Pour the stock into a large
pan and bring to the boil. Add
the breast of veal and simmer
gently for 60–70 minutes.
Leave the veal to cool in the
stock. Then strain and serve
with the crystallised fruits.

Crudités

Crudités

1 small root celeriac
½ cauliflower
100 g/4 oz corn salad or
    watercress
2 small heads red endive
4 small tomatoes
½ cucumber
4 small carrots
1 red pepper
2 medium onions
12 stuffed olives
freshly ground black pepper
juice of 1 lemon
2 tablespoons chopped fresh
    mixed herbs (chives, parsley,
    tarragon, dill)
6 tablespoons oil
3 tablespoons wine vinegar
½ teaspoon salt
1 (150-g/5.3-oz) carton natural
    yogurt
GARNISH
1 hard-boiled egg (optional)
parsley sprig

Wash and scrape the celeriac,
peel if necessary, and boil in
salted water in a covered pan
for 20 minutes. Wash the
cauliflower, break into florets
and blanch in a little boiling
salted water for 5 minutes,
then drain. Trim and wash the
corn salad or watercress and
allow to dry. Separate the red
endive leaves, wash and leave
to drain. Cut the tomatoes into
quarters. Finely slice the
cucumber. Wash and scrape
the carrots and grate into fine
strips. Cut the stalk off the red
pepper, remove the seeds and
pith and slice the flesh into
strips. Peel the onions, cut into
rings and divide into two
portions. Carefully mix one
portion with the tomato and
the other with the red pepper.
Halve the olives widthways.
Drain the celeriac and allow to
cool, then slice. Arrange all the
salad ingredients, except for
the olives, in portions on a
large serving dish. Sprinkle
with black pepper, lemon juice
and 1 tablespoon chopped
herbs, and scatter the olives
over the top. Beat the oil with
the vinegar, salt, the remaining
herbs and the yogurt, and
either spoon the dressing over
the salad or serve separately.
Shell the egg, if used, cut into
eight wedges and place in the
centre of the salad as a garnish.
Top with the parsley sprig.
Serves 4

Corn Salad with Peach Dressing

450 g/1 lb corn salad
½ clove garlic
¼ teaspoon salt
2 tablespoons peach chutney
4 tablespoons red wine vinegar
2 tablespoons oil
1 teaspoon sugar
juice of ½ lemon
2 tablespoons chopped fresh
  mixed herbs (lemon balm,
  mint, chives) (optional)
1 tablespoon chopped almonds

Trim the corn salad, wash
thoroughly under cold running
water and shake dry. Then
arrange in a bowl.

Peel and finely chop the
garlic and crush with the salt.
Beat the peach chutney with
the crushed garlic, wine
vinegar, oil, sugar, lemon juice
and chopped herbs, if used,
and pour over the corn salad.

Sprinkle with chopped
almonds before serving.
Serves 4

Cook's Tip

Apple chutney can be
substituted for peach
chutney.

Carrot and Apple Salad

4 medium carrots
2 dessert apples
50 g/2 oz shelled walnut halves
2 teaspoons lime juice
2 teaspoons sugar
1 (150-g/5.3-oz) carton natural
  yogurt

Wash, scrape and coarsely
grate the carrots. Peel the
apples, remove the cores with
an apple corer and grate
coarsely. Gently mix the grated
apple and carrot together in a
bowl.

Keep one of the walnut
halves on one side and chop
the rest. Beat the lime juice,
chopped walnuts and sugar
into the yogurt, and pour half
the yogurt dressing over the
carrot and apple salad. Leave
the salad to stand for 15
minutes. Spoon the rest of the

dressing over the salad just
before serving and top with the
remaining walnut. *Serves 4*

Cook's Tip

You can make this salad
richer by substituting
soured or single cream
for the yogurt, or using
half yogurt, half cream
in the dressing.

Crudités

Celery and Avocado Salad

1 stick celery
1 green pepper
2 medium onions
3 medium carrots
2 ripe avocados
1 teaspoon orange juice
1 teaspoon lemon juice
4 tablespoons oil
1 tablespoon wine vinegar
salt and pepper
¼ teaspoon strong mustard
GARNISH
1 firm tomato
parsley sprig

Wash, trim and thinly slice the celery. Cut the green pepper in half, remove the seeds and pith and slice into strips. Peel the onions and cut into rings. Wash, scrape and coarsely grate the carrots. Mix the celery, pepper, onion and carrot together and arrange on a salad platter.

Peel, halve and stone the avocados. Slice the flesh lengthways and place on a dish. Mix the orange and lemon juice together and pour over the avocado. Beat the oil with the vinegar, salt, pepper and mustard, and sprinkle over the salad platter, then top the salad with the avocado slices. Wash the tomato, cut into eight wedges and use to garnish the salad, together with the parsley. *Serves 4*

Chinese Cabbage Salad

450 g/1 lb Chinese cabbage
1 large head red endive
50 g/2 oz fresh young spinach
bunch chives
4 tablespoons oil
2 tablespoons wine vinegar
salt and white pepper
¼ teaspoon soya sauce

Halve the Chinese cabbage lengthways, wash thoroughly under cold running water and drain. Cut off the stalk and slice the leaves into 1-cm/½-inch wide strips. Trim off any damaged parts of the red endive, cut away the stalk, and separate the endive into leaves. Tear the larger leaves in half, then wash them with the spinach and shake dry. Gently mix the Chinese cabbage, red endive and spinach together in a large bowl.

Wash and finely slice the chives. Beat the oil with the vinegar, salt, pepper and soya sauce, and pour the dressing over the salad. Sprinkle the chives over the top. *Serves 4*

Fennel Salad

2 heads fennel
½ cucumber
2 firm tomatoes
bunch radishes
small bunch chives
1 onion
4 tablespoons olive oil
2 tablespoons wine vinegar
½ teaspoon salt
pinch sugar
coarsely ground black pepper

Wash and trim the fennel and cut into thin strips. Wash and dry the cucumber, cut into thick slices and cut the slices into strips. Slice the tomatoes into eight wedges. Clean, trim and slice the radishes. Mix the fennel, cucumber, tomato and radish together in a bowl.

Wash the chives and chop finely. Peel and finely dice the onion. Beat the oil with the vinegar, salt, sugar and diced onion and pour over the salad.

Before serving, sprinkle the fennel salad with chopped chives and freshly ground black pepper. *Serves 4*

Corn Salad with Wheat Grains

4 tablespoons wholewheat
  grains
100 g/4 oz corn salad
1 crisp dessert apple
1 small orange
100 g/4 oz cottage cheese
3 tablespoons oil
1 tablespoon wine vinegar
salt and pepper
25 g/1 oz chopped hazelnuts

Wash the wheat grains in cold water, place in a bowl and cover with more cold water. Leave to stand for 24 hours, then drain, rinse through with fresh water and return the damp wheat to the bowl. Cover the bowl and leave to stand for a further 24 hours, then rinse again and leave the wheat to drain. By now the wheat should have begun to germinate and will be ready to eat, although it will remain edible for 2 more days as long as it is kept moist.

Trim, wash and thoroughly drain the corn salad. Wash, dry and quarter the apple, remove the core and slice. Peel the orange, separate into segments and remove the skin from each segment. Cut the flesh into pieces, discarding the pips. Mix the corn salad, apple and orange together and sprinkle with the germinated wheat grains. Top with the cottage cheese. Beat the oil with the vinegar, salt, pepper and chopped hazelnuts and pour over the salad. *Serves 4*

Cook's Tip
You can buy wholewheat grains in most healthfood shops.

Light Salads

Mixed Pepper Salad

*4 medium peppers, green and
  yellow for preference
1 onion
1 clove garlic
½ teaspoon salt
3 tablespoons wine vinegar
8 tablespoons oil
2 teaspoons chopped fresh
  mixed herbs (parsley, basil,
  marjoram, burnet) or
  1 teaspoon dried mixed herbs
½ teaspoon coarsely ground
  white pepper*

Wash the peppers and cut off
the stalks with a sharp knife.
Slice the peppers into very thin
rings and trim away the seeds
and core. Peel the onion and
cut into equally thin rings. Cut
the garlic clove in half and,
with the cut side, wipe round
the inside of a salad bowl.
Arrange the pepper and onion

rings in the bowl.
  Beat together the salt,
vinegar and oil, and pour this
dressing over the salad. Cover
and leave to stand at room
temperature for 30 minutes.
Just before serving, sprinkle
the salad with the herbs and
freshly ground white pepper.
Serves 4

Celery and Carrot Salad

*4 medium carrots
2 sticks celery
½ lemon
pinch sugar
3 tablespoons double cream
½ teaspoon pickled green
  peppercorns, crushed, or
  ¼ teaspoon freshly ground
  black pepper
½ teaspoon salt*

Wash and trim the carrots,
peel or scrape if necessary,
then grate them coarsely into
long strips. Wash the celery,
remove the leaves and slice the
celery stalks very finely. Place
the carrot and celery in a salad
bowl. Squeeze the lemon and
sprinkle the juice over the
vegetables. Add the sugar, and
lightly toss the salad. Beat the
cream with the crushed green
peppercorns, or black pepper,

and the salt, pour over the
salad and mix in at the table.
Serves 4

Cook's Tip

Many recipes do not use
celery leaves, but these
need not be wasted.
They can go into the
stock pot, or be chopped
and used to sprinkle on
soup just before serving.

Red Endive Salad with Piquant Dressing

¼ *lettuce*
3 small heads red endive
1 yellow pepper
1 red onion
4 fresh basil leaves, or a pinch dried basil
3 tablespoons natural yogurt
3 tablespoons single cream
¼ *teaspoon each salt and celery salt*
1 tablespoon pickled green peppercorns, or 1 teaspoon freshly ground white pepper

Wash the lettuce and red endive, separate the leaves and allow to drain. Use the lettuce to line a salad bowl. Cut the stalk off the pepper and slice the pepper into rings, trimming away the seeds and core. Peel the onion and also slice it into rings. Mix together the pepper, onion and red endive. Finely chop the fresh basil, if used. Beat the yogurt with the cream, salt, celery salt, basil and green peppercorns, or white pepper, and pour it over the endive salad. Leave to stand for a few minutes, then transfer the salad to the lettuce-lined bowl. *Serves 4*

Cook's Tip

For extra piquancy, grate the ends of one or two red endive stems and add to the salad dressing.

Balkan Tomato Salad

675 g / 1½ lb firm tomatoes
100 g / 4 oz mozzarella or fetta cheese
1 small onion
2 leaves each fresh lemon balm and mint (optional)
1 clove garlic
20 black olives
1 tablespoon lemon juice
2 tablespoons wine vinegar
salt and freshly ground black pepper
8 tablespoons olive oil
1 hard-boiled egg

Wash, dry and slice the tomatoes. Break up the cheese with a fork. Peel and finely dice the onion. Wash the fresh herbs, if used, and chop coarsely. Cut the garlic clove in half and rub the cut side round the inside of a large salad bowl. Place the tomato, cheese, onion and olives in the bowl and sprinkle with the herbs, if used. Beat together the lemon juice, vinegar, and salt until the salt has dissolved, then add the pepper and oil. Sprinkle the dressing over the salad, cover and leave to stand at room temperature for 30 minutes.

Shell the egg and cut into eight wedges. Before serving, toss the salad and garnish with the egg. *Serves 4*

Light Salads

Chicory and Fruit Salad

4 small heads chicory
2 grapefruit
2 fresh mandarins or ½ (312-g/ 11-oz) can mandarin segments
3 tablespoons oil
1–2 tablespoons fresh lime juice
1 teaspoon sugar
generous pinch ground ginger
½ teaspoon coarsely ground black pepper
½ teaspoon strong mustard
1 lime

Wash, trim and dry the chicory, separate the leaves and use to line four individual bowls. Peel the grapefruit, removing all the pith. Separate the segments, carefully remove the skin and cut each segment into quarters, discarding any pips. Peel the fresh mandarins, if used. Cut the segments in half and remove any pips. Drain and halve the canned mandarins. Beat the oil with the lime juice, sugar, ginger, pepper and mustard, and pour over the grapefruit and mandarin segments. Mix thoroughly, cover, and leave to stand for a few minutes.

Wash and dry the lime and cut into very thin slices. Transfer the fruit to the individual bowls lined with chicory, and garnish with the lime slices. *Serves 4*

Mussel and Bean Sprout Salad

225 g/8 oz fresh bean sprouts
1 large cooked carrot
1 (250-g/8¾-oz) can mussels
8–10 strips canned pimiento
2 tablespoons canned baby sweet corn cobs (optional)
2 pickled cucumbers
2 tablespoons pickled cocktail onions
2 tablespoons oil
1 tablespoon soy sauce
1 tablespoon lemon juice
¼ teaspoon each pepper and sugar

Wash the bean sprouts and allow to drain. Slice the carrot. Drain the mussels, pimiento, the baby sweet corn cobs, if used, and the pickled cucumbers. Cut the pimiento and sweet corn cobs into pieces, and the pickled cucumbers into very thin slices.

Mix all the above ingredients in a bowl, together with the pickled cocktail onions. Beat the oil with the soy sauce, lemon juice, pepper and sugar, and pour over the salad. *Serves 4*

Cook's Tip

As a variation, make this salad with prawns instead of mussels. Omit the carrot, baby sweet corn cobs and cocktail onions, and use one or two freshly grated crisp apples instead.

Bamboo Shoot Salad

1 (540-g/1 lb 3-oz) can bamboo
    shoots
1 clove garlic
1 teaspoon salt
2 tablespoons oil
2 teaspoons fresh lime or lemon
    juice
generous pinch cayenne pepper

Drain the bamboo shoots, cut
into thin slices and place in a
bowl. Peel and finely slice the
garlic. Sprinkle the garlic with
the salt and crush with the
blade of a knife. Beat the oil
with the lime or lemon juice,
crushed garlic and cayenne
pepper, and pour over the
bamboo shoots. Cover and
leave to stand for a few
minutes. *Serves 4*

Cook's Tip
Although traditionally
part of a Chinese meal,
Bamboo Shoot Salad
makes a delicious
accompaniment to any
meat or poultry dish. It
goes particularly well
with cold chicken for a
summer buffet.

Mixed Salad Platter

¼ head endive
3 firm tomatoes
1 red onion
1 stick celery
100 g/4 oz French beans
10 stuffed olives
1 hard-boiled egg
½ clove garlic
6 tablespoons olive oil
3 tablespoons wine vinegar
salt and pepper
2 tablespoons chopped fresh
    mixed herbs, or 2 teaspoons
    dried mixed herbs

Wash the endive, separate the
leaves and drain thoroughly.
Line a large dish with the
endive leaves.
   Wash and slice the
tomatoes. Peel the onion and
cut into fine rings. Wash the
celery and cut into strips. Trim
the French beans, blanch in a

little boiling salted water for
8 minutes, then drain. Slice the
olives. Shell the egg and cut
into eight wedges. Arrange all
the salad ingredients on the
bed of endive.
   Peel and crush the garlic
clove. Beat the oil with the
vinegar, garlic, salt, pepper and
herbs. Sprinkle the dressing
over the salad, cover and leave
to stand in the refrigerator for
10 minutes. *Serves 4*

Light Salads

Iceberg Salad with Port Dressing

*1 small Iceberg or Webb's
    Wonder lettuce
½ cucumber
100 g/4 oz mushrooms
4 firm tomatoes
2 hard-boiled eggs
6 tablespoons oil
3 tablespoons wine vinegar
100 ml/4 fl oz port
salt and white pepper
small bunch fresh tarragon, or
    1 teaspoon dried tarragon
1 punnet mustard and cress*

Wash and trim the lettuce, allow to drain and break into large pieces. Wash and slice the cucumber. Clean and trim the mushrooms and cut small ones into quarters, or larger ones into eight. Wash, dry and quarter the tomatoes. Shell the eggs and cut each into eight wedges. Place all the salad ingredients together in a bowl.

Beat the oil with the vinegar, port, salt and pepper. Pour the dressing over the salad and toss carefully. Wash, drain and chop the fresh tarragon, if used. Snip the cress with kitchen scissors, rinse in cold water and allow to drain. Sprinkle the tarragon and cress over the salad. *Serves 4*

Corn Salad with Orange

*350 g/12 oz corn salad
2 oranges
4 tablespoons oil
2 tablespoons wine vinegar
½ teaspoon salt
1 teaspoon pickled green
    peppercorns or ½ teaspoon
    freshly ground white pepper
3 tablespoons double cream
1 teaspoon fresh lime or lemon
    juice
2 tablespoons brandy*

Trim the corn salad, wash thoroughly in cold water and allow to drain. Peel the oranges, removing all the pith and skin attached to the segments, and cut into very fine slices. Place the corn salad in a bowl. Beat the oil with the vinegar and salt and pour over the salad. Cover and leave to stand for a few minutes.

Arrange the salad in a serving bowl and garnish with the orange slices. Leave a few green peppercorns, if used, on one side, and crush the rest. Whip the cream with the lime or lemon juice, the brandy and crushed peppercorns or white pepper, and spoon into the centre of the salad. Sprinkle with the reserved green peppercorns, if used. *Serves 4*

Red Endive and Spinach Salad

1 medium head red endive
225 g/8 oz young spinach
½ (396-g/14-oz) can artichoke
  hearts
2 onions
1 clove garlic
1 hard-boiled egg
5 tablespoons olive oil
3 tablespoons wine vinegar
salt and white pepper

Wash the red endive, remove the outer leaves and discard them. Slice off the stem and grate it. Separate the remaining leaves and allow to drain. Wash and trim the spinach, removing any long stalks. Drain the artichoke hearts and cut each in half. Peel the onions and slice into fine rings. Cut the garlic clove in half, and use the flat side to rub round the inside of a salad bowl. Place the red endive, spinach and artichoke hearts in the bowl and scatter the onion rings over the top. Shell and chop the egg.

  Beat the oil with the vinegar, salt, pepper and grated endive stem, and pour this dressing over the salad. Sprinkle with the chopped egg before serving. *Serves 4*

Spring Salad

1 lettuce
100 g/4 oz young spinach
3–4 radishes
small bunch each fresh
  tarragon, dill and parsley, or
  1 teaspoon each dried
  tarragon, dill and parsley
1 crisp dessert apple
1 onion
2 hard-boiled eggs
3 tablespoons dry sherry
2 tablespoons oil
2 teaspoons wine vinegar
1 teaspoon lemon juice
½ teaspoon sugar
salt and white pepper

Wash and trim the lettuce, separate the leaves and tear into pieces. Allow to drain, then place in a large dish. Wash, trim and drain the spinach, radishes and fresh herbs, if used. Cut the radishes into very fine slices, and chop the herbs. Wash and quarter the apple, remove the core and slice. Peel the onion and slice into fine rings. Shell the eggs and cut each into eight wedges. Beat the sherry with the oil, vinegar, lemon juice, sugar, salt and pepper. Add the spinach, radish, apple and onion to the lettuce, pour over the dressing and toss lightly. Sprinkle the herbs over the salad and garnish with the egg wedges. *Serves 4*

Light Salads

Mushroom Salad

350 g/12 oz mushrooms
½ (150-g/5-oz) can prawns
3 tablespoons oil
2 teaspoons wine vinegar
2 teaspoons lemon juice
salt and pepper
pinch sugar
2 tablespoons sherry
small bunch parsley and chives

Clean and trim the mushrooms and cut into very thin slices. Drain the prawns, rinse in cold water and allow to dry. Mix the prawns and mushrooms together in a salad bowl. Beat the oil with the vinegar, lemon juice, salt, pepper, sugar and sherry, and pour over the salad. Cover and leave to stand in the refrigerator for 30 minutes.

Wash, drain and chop the parsley and chives, and mix into the salad just before serving. *Serves 4*

Cook's Tip

If you prefer a milder dressing, use apple juice instead of the vinegar.

For a variation, you can replace the prawns with boiled or smoked ham, cut into thin strips.

Asparagus Salad

340 g/12 oz fresh or canned
    asparagus
½ teaspoon each salt and sugar
3 tomatoes
4 hard-boiled eggs
5 tablespoons oil
3 tablespoons wine vinegar
salt and pepper
small bunch parsley

Wash the fresh asparagus, if used, and lightly scrape the bases of the stems. Bring a little water to the boil in a wide, shallow pan with the salt and sugar. Add the fresh asparagus, cover, and simmer over a low heat for about 20 minutes, or until the shoots are tender.

Cut a cross into the base of each tomato, stand each briefly in boiling water, then drain and peel off the skins. Cut the tomatoes into quarters, scoop away the seeds and finely dice

the flesh. Drain the fresh asparagus, rinse in cold water and allow to cool. Drain the canned asparagus, if used. Cut the asparagus shoots into 2.5-cm/1-inch lengths. Shell the eggs and cut each into eight wedges. Arrange the asparagus, tomato and egg on a flat dish.

Beat the oil with the vinegar, season the dressing to taste, and pour over the salad. Cover and leave to stand in the refrigerator for 20 minutes. Wash, drain and finely chop the parsley, and sprinkle over the salad just before serving. *Serves 4*

Cucumber and Dill Salad

1 cucumber
1 clove garlic
4 tablespoons natural yogurt
2 teaspoons lemon juice
1 small onion
small bunch fresh dill, or
*   1 teaspoon dried dill*
salt and freshly ground black
*   pepper*

Wash and dry the cucumber. Cut it into thick slices, then cut each slice into thin strips and place in a bowl.

Peel and crush the garlic clove. Beat the yogurt with the lemon juice and garlic. Peel the onion and grate into the yogurt dressing. Wash and drain the fresh dill, if used. Keep one small sprig on one side and chop the rest. Stir the salt, pepper and dill into the yogurt dressing, pour over the cucumber and garnish with the remaining sprig of fresh dill, if used. *Serves 4*

Cook's Tip

If fresh or dried dill is hard to find, you can still make a delicious and refreshing cucumber salad using fresh mint in the yogurt dressing instead.

Celeriac Salad

450 g/1 lb celeriac root
juice of 1 lemon
3 tablespoons olive oil
1 tablespoon wine vinegar
¼ teaspoon each salt and sugar
½ punnet mustard and cress

Peel the celeriac, wash in cold water and allow to drain. Cut the celeriac into large pieces, then grate into long, thin strips. Sprinkle the lemon juice over the celeriac to prevent it discolouring.

Beat the oil with the vinegar, salt and sugar. Stir the dressing into the salad, cover and leave to stand at room temperature for 20 minutes. Snip the mustard and cress with kitchen scissors, wash and leave to drain. Before serving, sprinkle the cress over the celeriac salad. *Serves 4*

Cook's Tip

If you find raw celeriac indigestible, you can make this salad with cooked celeriac instead. Place the whole celeriac root in a pan containing boiling salted water, cover, and simmer over a low heat for 20–30 minutes. Allow to cool before cutting into thick strips.

Seasonal Sausage Salad

2 eggs
½ round lettuce
½ cos lettuce
bunch radishes
bunch spring onions
100 g/4 oz ham sausage or meat
　loaf, thinly sliced
100 g/4 oz Mortadella sausage
bunch fresh mixed herbs
　(parsley, chives, dill, lovage,
　tarragon)
3 tablespoons wine vinegar
6 tablespoons oil
salt and white pepper
generous pinch sugar
4 tablespoons mayonnaise

Hard-boil the eggs for 10
minutes, plunge into cold
water, shell and leave to cool.
Then cut each into eight
wedges.
　Wash the lettuces, separate
the leaves and drain

thoroughly. Trim, clean and
thinly slice the radishes. Wash
the spring onions, cut off the
roots and chop the rest. Cut
the ham sausage or meat loaf
slices in half, and the
Mortadella into strips. Line a
flat serving dish with the
lettuce leaves, and arrange all
the salad ingredients on top.
　Wash and drain the fresh
herbs, keep a few sprigs on one
side and finely chop the
remainder. Beat the vinegar
with the oil, salt, pepper and
sugar. Mix the herbs into the
dressing and pour over the
salad. Spoon the mayonnaise
into the centre of the salad
platter, and garnish with the
remaining sprigs of herbs.
Serves 4

Cook's Tip

If spring onions are not
obtainable, replace them
with 1 large Spanish
onion, peeled and cut
into fine rings. As a
variation you could add
2 tomatoes, peeled and
quartered, and 100 g/
4 oz young French
beans, blanched in a
little boiling salted water
for 10 minutes.
　In autumn when cos
lettuce is out of season,
replace it with a handful
of watercress, or
mustard and cress.

Salads as Main Meals

Iceberg Lettuce with Garnished Eggs

4 eggs
1 Iceberg or Webb's Wonder
  lettuce
½ red pepper
8 stuffed olives
1 (150-g/5.3-oz) carton natural
  yogurt
2 tablespoons mayonnaise
1 teaspoon mild French mustard
½ teaspoon lemon juice
salt and white pepper
1 (58-g/2-oz) jar lumpfish roe

Hard boil the eggs for 10-12 minutes, plunge into cold water, shell and leave to cool.

Wash and trim the lettuce, and cut off the stem. Slice the lettuce into quarters, drain well and arrange on four individual plates. Wash the red pepper, remove the seeds and dice. Cut the olives in half. Beat the yogurt with the mayonnaise, mustard, lemon juice, salt and pepper, pour over the lettuce quarters and sprinkle with the diced red pepper. Cut the eggs in half lengthways, garnish with the lumpfish roe and olives, and place two halves on each plate. *Serves 4*

Cook's Tip

Instead of garnished eggs, you could serve stuffed eggs with the salad (see pages 140 – 143).

Tuna Fish Salad

2 (198-g/7-oz) cans tuna
18 stuffed olives
175 g/6 oz pickled cocktail
  onions
175 g/6 oz cooked beetroot
4 tablespoons mayonnaise
1 (150-g/5.3-oz) carton natural
  yogurt, or 1 (142-ml/5-fl oz)
  carton soured cream
¼ teaspoon salt
½ teaspoon paprika pepper
1 tablespoon tomato purée
GARNISH
1 hard-boiled egg
4 sprigs dill (optional)

Drain the tuna thoroughly, break up with a fork and place in a bowl. Slice 10 olives very finely, cut the remainder in half, and keep these on one side. Rinse the cocktail onions in cold water and drain. Cut the beetroot into strips. Add the sliced olives, cocktail onions and beetroot to the tuna and mix well.

Beat the mayonnaise with the yogurt or soured cream, the salt, paprika and tomato purée. Pour the dressing over the tuna salad and mix in gently, then arrange the salad on four individual plates. Shell the egg, cut into eight wedges and garnish each portion with two wedges of egg, four olive halves and a sprig of dill, if used. *Serves 4*

Cook's Tip

If you prefer a milder salad, substitute diced banana and strips of chicory for the cocktail onions and olives.

Salads as Main Meals

Cucumber and Prawn Salad

225 g/8 oz frozen or canned
prawns
1 cucumber
1 tablespoon wine vinegar
salt and white pepper
¼ teaspoon grated lemon rind
¼ teaspoon sugar
3 tablespoons oil
½ punnet mustard and cress

Place the frozen prawns in a bowl, cover and leave to thaw at room temperature, then drain. Drain canned prawns, rinse in cold water and allow to dry. Wash and dry the cucumber and cut in half lengthways. Scrape away the seeds with a grapefruit spoon or teaspoon, and slice the cucumber halves very finely. Mix the prawns and cucumber together in a bowl.

Beat the vinegar with the

salt, pepper, lemon rind and sugar. Add the oil. Stir the dressing into the prawns and cucumber, cover and leave to stand at room temperature for 1 hour. Snip the cress with kitchen scissors, rinse in cold water and drain well. Sprinkle the cress over the salad before serving. *Serves 4*

Exotic Chicken Salad

175 g/6 oz frozen peas
575 g/1¼ lb cooked chicken
100 g/4 oz canned asparagus
tips
100 g/4 oz mushrooms
100 g/4 oz canned or fresh
pineapple
4 tablespoons mayonnaise
6 tablespoons natural yogurt
2 tablespoons brandy
1 teaspoon lemon juice
salt and pepper
pinch each sugar and curry
powder
GARNISH
1 lime
4 sprigs dill (optional)

Cook the frozen peas following the instructions on the packet, drain and leave to cool. Remove any skin or bones from the chicken and cut into 2-cm/1-inch pieces. Drain and

halve the asparagus tips. Clean, trim and finely slice the mushrooms. Drain the canned pineapple, if used, and cut the fresh or canned pineapple into small pieces. Place all the ingredients together in a bowl.

Beat the mayonnaise with the yogurt, brandy, lemon juice, salt, pepper, sugar and curry powder. Pour the salad dressing over the chicken and vegetable mixture and stir in gently. Cover and leave to stand at room temperature for 1 hour. Wash the lime, rub dry and cut four very thin slices from the centre. Arrange the salad on four individual plates and garnish each portion with a slice of lime and a dill sprig, if liked. *Serves 4*

Potato and Sausage Salad

450 g/1 lb potatoes
225 g/8 oz frozen French beans
225 g/8 oz ham sausage,
  unsliced
bunch radishes
2 small onions
bunch each parsley and chives
100 g/4 oz mayonnaise
1 tablespoon mild French
  mustard
2–3 teaspoons lemon juice
salt and pepper

Wash and peel the potatoes, and boil them in salted water for 20–25 minutes. Drain and leave to cool.

Cook the beans following the instructions on the packet, and drain. Slice the ham sausage thickly, then cut the slices into strips. Wash, trim and slice the radishes. Peel the onions and cut into rings.

Wash and finely chop the parsley and chives. Slice the potatoes, and mix all the salad ingredients together in a bowl.

Beat the mayonnaise with the mustard, and add lemon juice and seasoning to taste. Serve the mustard dressing separately with the salad.
Serves 4

Sweet Corn and Cheese Salad

225 g/8 oz ham sausage,
  unsliced
225 g/8 oz Edam or Gouda
  cheese
2 small onions
1 red pepper
1 green pepper
4 firm tomatoes
1 pickled cucumber
1 (283-g/10-oz) can sweet corn
1 tablespoon wine vinegar
3 tablespoons oil
½ teaspoon mild French mustard
salt and black pepper
pinch each sugar, paprika
  pepper and cayenne pepper

Cut the ham sausage and cheese into equal strips. Peel the onions and cut into rings. Wash, trim and quarter the red and green peppers, remove the seeds and cut into strips. Wash the tomatoes and slice,

together with the pickled cucumber. Drain the sweet corn. Mix all the above ingredients together in a bowl.

Beat the vinegar with the oil, mustard, salt, pepper, sugar, paprika and cayenne. Stir the dressing into the salad, cover and leave to stand at room temperature for 30 minutes. Taste and adjust seasoning before arranging on four individual plates. *Serves 4*

Salads as Main Meals

Swiss Salad

225 g/8 oz Emmental cheese
225 g/8 oz ham
2 sticks celery
225 g/8 oz cooked macaroni
1 tablespoon wine vinegar
1 egg yolk
pinch each salt, pepper, paprika
    pepper, sugar and garlic salt
3 tablespoons oil
50 g/2 oz shelled walnuts
225 g/8 oz canned morello
    cherries, drained

Dice the cheese, ham and
celery, and mix in a bowl with
the macaroni. Beat the vinegar
with the egg yolk and
seasoning and gradually add
the oil. Pour the dressing over
the salad and sprinkle with the
walnuts and cherries. *Serves 4*

Huntsman's Salad

1 lettuce
½ cucumber
small bunch radishes
4 firm tomatoes
2 hard-boiled eggs, shelled
8 game and mushroom
    croquettes (see page 29)
French dressing (see page 57)

Wash and slice all the salad
ingredients, place in a bowl
with the croquettes and add
the dressing. *Serves 4*

Rice Salad

450 g/1 lb frozen mixed
    vegetables
225 g/8 oz rice
225 g/8 oz salami, unsliced
1 apple
¼ root celeriac, peeled
150 g/5 oz natural yogurt
1 tablespoon lemon juice
3 tablespoons oil
salt and pepper
2 tablespoons chopped parsley

Cook the frozen vegetables
and the rice separately,
following the instructions on
the packets, drain and leave to
cool. Dice the salami, apple
and celeriac. Mix all the
ingredients together. Beat the
yogurt with the lemon juice,
oil, salt, pepper and parsley,
and pour over the rice salad.
Serves 4

Balkan Salad

1 green pepper
1 red pepper
1 yellow pepper
1 large red onion
225 g/8 oz fetta or mozzarella
*   cheese*
FRENCH DRESSING
2 tablespoons wine vinegar
4 tablespoons olive oil
salt and white pepper
pinch sugar
generous pinch dried oregano

Wash the peppers, cut the stalk off each and slice the peppers into thin rings. Remove the seeds and pith. Peel the onion and cut into rings, as thinly as possible. Break the cheese up with a fork. Mix the salad ingredients lightly together in a bowl.

Beat the vinegar with the oil, salt, pepper and sugar. Stir in the oregano. Sprinkle the French dressing over the salad, cover and leave to stand at room temperature for a few minutes. *Serves 4*

Cook's Tip
If you find raw peppers indigestible, blanch the rings in a little boiling water for 3 minutes. Then plunge into cold water and leave to drain.

Chicken Salad with Ham and Cheese

1 small lettuce
2 firm tomatoes
2 cooked chicken breasts
100 g/4 oz ham, unsliced
100 g/4 oz Gruyère or
*   Emmental cheese*
1 clove garlic
1 egg yolk
150 ml/¼ pint oil
salt and freshly ground white
*   pepper*
generous pinch sugar
1 tablespoon lemon juice
generous pinch strong mustard
*   powder*
GARNISH
parsley sprig

Wash the lettuce, break into leaves and allow to drain. Wash, dry and slice the tomatoes. Remove any skin from the chicken and cut the chicken, ham and cheese into equal strips. Cut the garlic in half and rub all round the inside of a salad bowl with the flat edge. Then line the bowl with lettuce. Arrange the tomato, ham, chicken and cheese on the bed of lettuce and garnish with parsley.

Make sure the egg yolk and oil are at room temperature. Whisk the egg yolk, salt, pepper and sugar, using a hand whisk or an electric whisk, until it begins to thicken. Add the oil gradually, a few drops at a time. As soon as the mayonnaise begins to thicken, stir in the lemon juice and mustard. Taste and adjust seasoning, and serve the mayonnaise separately with the salad. *Serves 4*

Rice and Tuna Salad

225 g/8 oz rice
1 red pepper
1 (198-g/7-oz) can tuna
100 g/4 oz pickled cocktail
   onions
2 tablespoons capers
1 tablespoon lemon juice
salt and white pepper
grated rind of ½ lemon
6 tablespoons mayonnaise
GARNISH
parsley sprig

Cook the rice following the instructions on the packet, drain, and rinse through with cold water. Then drain again and leave to cool. Wash the red pepper and cut it in half. Remove the stalk and seeds, then dice the pepper. Drain the tuna and break up with a fork. Drain the cocktail onions, and place the rice, red pepper, tuna and onions together in a bowl.

Beat the capers, lemon juice, salt, pepper and grated lemon rind into the mayonnaise. Mix the mayonnaise into the salad ingredients, cover and leave to stand for a few minutes. Garnish with a parsley sprig just before serving. *Serves 4*

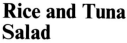

Cook's Tip
You can cook the rice for your salad while preparing another rice dish. If covered it will keep in the refrigerator for 3–4 days.

Piquant Beef Salad

450 g/1 lb cooked lean beef
2 small onions
2 pickled cucumbers
2 cooked medium carrots
1 red pepper
100 g/4 oz mushrooms
1 large dessert apple
small bunch parsley
3 tablespoons vinegar
6 tablespoons oil
1 teaspoon Worcestershire
   sauce
pinch garlic salt
½ teaspoon black pepper

Cut the meat into 2-cm/1-inch cubes. Peel the onions and cut into rings. Thinly peel the pickled cucumbers and slice, together with the carrots. Wash and quarter the red pepper, remove the stalk and seeds and cut into strips. Clean, trim and quarter the mushrooms, cutting any larger mushrooms into eight. Peel, halve, and core the apple, and cut into small slices. Wash, drain and finely chop the parsley. Beat the vinegar with the oil, Worcestershire sauce, garlic salt, pepper and parsley. Mix all the salad ingredients together in a bowl, pour over the dressing, cover and leave to stand at room temperature for 1 hour. *Serves 4*

Haricot Bean Salad

225 g/8 oz haricot beans
½ teaspoon dried thyme
1 stick celery
¼ small root celeriac
1 medium carrot
2 small onions
20 stuffed olives
6 tablespoons oil
3 tablespoons wine vinegar
salt and pepper
GARNISH
2 strips canned pimiento
parsley sprig

Soak the haricot beans in twice their volume of cold water for at least 12 hours. Then drain and place in a pan with fresh water, together with the thyme. Do not add salt at this stage, as it tends to toughen the skin of the beans. Cover the pan, bring to the boil and simmer over a low heat for 1 hour.

Wash the celery and cut into thick slices. Wash, peel and dice the celeriac and carrot. Peel the onions and cut into rings. Mix all the vegetables together, place in a pan containing a little boiling salted water, cover and simmer for 15–20 minutes until cooked. Drain the haricot beans and vegetables separately and leave to cool.

Cut the stuffed olives in half. Beat the oil with the vinegar, salt and pepper. Mix the beans and vegetables in a bowl, pour over the dressing and sprinkle the salad with the olives. Cover and leave to stand for 30 minutes. Before serving, thinly slice the pimiento and use to garnish the salad, together with the parsley sprig. *Serves 4*

Potato Salad with Cream Dressing

1 kg/2¼ lb new potatoes
100 g/4 oz ham, unsliced
2 pickled cucumbers
1 dessert apple
2 shallots
1 egg yolk
salt and pepper
1 tablespoon wine vinegar
6 tablespoons oil
150 ml/¼ pint single cream
small bunch parsley

Wash the potatoes, and without peeling them, place in boiling salted water. Simmer over a high heat for 20–25 minutes, drain and leave to cool.

Cut the ham into strips and slice the pickled cucumbers. Peel the apple, cut it in half and remove the core, then slice also into strips. Peel and finely chop the shallots. Peel and slice the potatoes.

Beat the egg yolk with the salt, pepper and vinegar, and gradually add the oil, a little at a time. Stir in the shallots and cream. Mix all the salad ingredients lightly together in a bowl and pour over the cream dressing. Cover and leave to stand at room temperature for 30 minutes. Wash, drain and finely chop the parsley, and sprinkle over the salad before serving. *Serves 4*

Salads as Main Meals

Sauerkraut Salads

Sauerkraut and Smoked Fish
*450 g/1 lb canned or bottled
    sauerkraut*
3 sticks celery
1 small red pepper
1 large dessert apple
1 (198-g/7-oz) can tuna
10 stuffed olives
225 g/8 oz smoked fish
3 tablespoons oil
juice of 1 lemon
salt and pepper
generous pinch sugar

Place the sauerkraut in a large
bowl and toss with two forks.
Wash and chop the celery. Cut
the red pepper in half, remove
the seeds and stalk and slice
the flesh into strips. Wash, core
and dice the apple. Drain and
flake the tuna, keeping the oil
on one side. Add the celery,
red pepper, apple and tuna to

the sauerkraut. Cut the olives
in half, and the smoked fish
into slicés. Mix both into the
sauerkraut.
    Beat together the tuna oil,
fresh oil, lemon juice, salt,
pepper and sugar. Stir the
dressing into the salad, cover
and leave to stand at room
temperature for 30 minutes.
Serves 4

Sauerkraut and Ham
*450 g/1 lb canned or bottled
    sauerkraut*
350 g/12 oz ham
4 slices canned pineapple
*5 tablespoons canned pineapple
    juice*
1 tablespoon honey
2 tablespoons oil
2 tablespoons lemon juice
pinch salt

Place the sauerkraut in a large
bowl and toss lightly. Finely
dice the ham. Drain and chop
the pineapple slices, and mix

the pineapple and ham into the
sauerkraut. Gently heat the
pineapple juice in a pan and
dissolve the honey in it. Stir the
oil, lemon juice and salt into
the pineapple juice. Pour the
dressing over the salad, cover
and leave to stand at room
temperature for 30 minutes.
Serves 4

Sauerkraut and Fruit
*450 g/1 lb canned or bottled
    sauerkraut*
175 g/6 oz grapes
2 small dessert apples
1 large ripe pear
1 small onion
juice of 1 lemon
¼ teaspoon each salt and sugar
2 tablespoons cranberry sauce

Place the sauerkraut in a bowl
and toss lightly. Wash all the
fruit and allow to drain. Cut
the grapes in half and remove
the pips. Quarter the apples
and the pear, remove the cores

and slice thinly. Peel and dice
the onion, and stir the onion
and fruit into the sauerkraut.
Beat the lemon juice with the
salt and sugar, pour over the
salad, cover and leave to stand
for 30 minutes. Stir in the
cranberry sauce just before
serving. *Serves 4*

Cook's Tip

Any of these salad
combinations will go
well with a blanched red
cabbage. Add 2 table-
spoons vinegar to the
water when blanching
red cabbage to preserve
the colour.

Cervelat Salad

*350 g/12 oz Cervelat sausage,
    unsliced*
1 red pepper
1 green pepper
3 medium tomatoes
2 crisp dessert apples
2 gherkins
1 tablespoon lemon juice
1 teaspoon paprika pepper
¼ teaspoon white pepper
generous pinch mustard powder
4 tablespoons mayonnaise

Remove the skin from the
Cervelat and cut the sausage
into thick slices. Cut each slice
into narrow strips. Wash the
peppers, cut them in half and
remove the seeds, then cut also
into thin strips. Dip the
tomatoes briefly into boiling
water, plunge into cold water,
peel and cut into quarters.
Remove the seeds. Peel, core
and dice the apples. Mix all
these ingredients together and
arrange on four individual
plates.
 Peel the gherkins and dice
finely. Stir the lemon juice,
paprika, white pepper,
mustard and diced gherkin
into the mayonnaise, and
spoon the dressing over the
salad portions. *Serves 4*

Seville Meat Salad

100 g/4 oz cold roast pork
100 g/4 oz cold roast beef
100 g/4 oz ham
2 green peppers
4 medium tomatoes
10 black olives, stoned,
10 stuffed olives
1 onion
*100 g/4 oz pickled cocktail
    onions*
4 tablespoons oil
2 tablespoons wine vinegar
salt and white pepper
small bunch parsley

Cut the pork, beef and ham
into equal strips. Wash and
halve the peppers, remove the
seeds and cut into thin strips.
Dip the tomatoes into boiling
water, then plunge into cold
water and peel. Cut into
quarters and scoop away the
seeds. Halve the olives if liked.
Peel the onion and cut into
rings. Drain the cocktail
onions, and mix all the salad
ingredients together in a bowl.
 Beat the oil with the vinegar,
salt and pepper and pour the
dressing over the salad.
Arrange on four individual
plates. Wash the parsley, allow
to drain and chop finely.
Sprinkle over the salad before
serving. *Serves 4*

Pea Salad

4 eggs
350 g/12 oz frozen young peas
4 firm tomatoes
225 g/8 oz mushrooms
225 g/8 oz green grapes
225 g/8 oz ham
3 tablespoons wine vinegar
4 tablespoons oil
salt and pepper
1 tablespoon chopped fresh
parsley
4 tablespoons mayonnaise
4 tablespoons tomato purée
4 tablespoons double cream
dash Worcestershire sauce

Hard-boil the eggs for 10 minutes, plunge into cold water, shell and leave to cool. Cook the frozen peas following the instructions on the packet, rinse through with cold water and leave to drain. Peel the tomatoes, cut each into eight and remove the seeds. Clean, trim and finely slice the

mushrooms. Wash and peel the grapes, cut them in half and remove the pips. Cut the ham into strips. Mix the peas, tomato, mushroom, grapes and ham together in a bowl.

Beat 2 tablespoons vinegar with the oil, salt and pepper and pour over the salad. Cover and leave to stand for 15 minutes. Cut the eggs into eight wedges, arrange on the salad, and sprinkle with the parsley.

Beat the mayonnaise with the remaining vinegar, the tomato purée, cream and Worcestershire sauce, season to taste and serve separately with the salad. *Serves 4*

Broccoli Salad

575 g/1¼ lb young broccoli
1 tablespoon wine vinegar
3 tablespoons dry sherry
salt and pepper
9 tablespoons oil
1 egg yolk
1 teaspoon mild tarragon or
wholegrain mustard
¼ teaspoon mustard powder
1½ tablespoons lemon juice
dash Worcestershire sauce
100 g/4 oz mushrooms

Wash and trim the broccoli, cut away any tough stalks and blanch the broccoli in boiling salted water for 3 minutes. Drain and leave to cool. Beat together the vinegar, sherry, salt, pepper and 3 tablespoons oil. Separate the broccoli into small florets, place in a bowl and pour over the dressing. Cover and leave to stand for 1 hour.

Beat the egg yolk with the

tarragon mustard, mustard powder, 1 tablespoon lemon juice and the Worcestershire sauce, and add salt to taste. Gradually whisk in the remaining oil, a little at a time, until the mixture becomes creamy. Clean, trim and finely slice the mushrooms, and sprinkle with the remaining lemon juice. Arrange the broccoli salad with the mushrooms on a flat dish. Serve the mayonnaise separately. *Serves 4*

Salads as Main Meals

Smoked Salmon Platter

350 g/12 oz frozen French beans
4 tomatoes
1 small lettuce
1 head red endive
1 onion
100 g/4 oz baby gherkins
1 (169-g/6-oz) can crabmeat
100 g/4 oz thinly sliced smoked salmon
1 clove garlic
3 tablespoons wine vinegar
6 tablespoons olive oil
½ teaspoon hot mustard
½ teaspoon dried oregano
1 tablespoon chopped fresh parsley
salt and black pepper

Cook the frozen beans according to the instructions on the packet, drain and leave to cool. Peel the tomatoes, cut each into eight and remove the seeds. Wash the lettuce and red endive, separate the leaves and allow to drain. Peel the onion and cut into rings. Drain the gherkins and cut into strips. Drain the crabmeat, break up with a fork and remove any bones. Roll up the slices of smoked salmon. Line a salad dish with the lettuce and endive leaves, and arrange all the other salad ingredients in spoonfuls on top.

Peel and crush the garlic. Beat the vinegar with the oil, mustard, garlic, oregano, parsley, salt and pepper and sprinkle the dressing over the salad. *Serves 4*

Fish and Pea Salad

350 g/12 oz frozen young peas
1 tablespoon lemon juice
3 tablespoons water
3 tablespoons white wine
¼ teaspoon salt
450 g/1 lb frozen white fish fillets
2 eggs
3 sticks celery
2 medium gherkins
1 lettuce
2 tablespoons mayonnaise
½ (150-g/5.3-oz) carton natural yogurt
1 (142-ml/5-fl oz) carton soured cream
2 drops Tabasco sauce
1 tablespoon chopped fresh parsley

Cook the peas following the instructions on the packet, drain and sprinkle with the lemon juice. Bring the water, white wine and salt to the boil in a shallow pan and add the frozen fish. Cover and simmer for 20 minutes. Take the pan off the heat and leave the fish to cool in the liquid. Hard-boil the eggs for 10 minutes, plunge into cold water, shell and leave to cool. Wash the celery and cut into strips, together with the gherkins. Wash and drain the lettuce, and line a salad bowl with the leaves. Strain the fish, reserving the stock on one side, separate into pieces and arrange on the lettuce with the peas, celery and gherkin.

Beat the mayonnaise with the yogurt, soured cream, 2 tablespoons of the fish stock and the Tabasco. Taste and adjust seasoning, then pour the dressing over the salad. Slice the eggs and arrange on the salad. Sprinkle with parsley before serving. *Serves 4*

Vegetable Salad Platter

1 small cauliflower
2 medium carrots
175 g/6 oz frozen peas
175 g/6 oz frozen beans
4 small boiled potatoes
100 g/4 oz mushrooms
bunch radishes
1 hard-boiled egg
small bunch parsley
1 onion
8 tablespoons oil
3 tablespoons wine vinegar
1 tablespoon mild French
    mustard
salt and white pepper
pinch sugar
GARNISH
6 stuffed olives
4 canned anchovy fillets

Wash the cauliflower and
break into florets. Peel and
slice the carrots. Bring a little
salted water to the boil in a
pan, add the cauliflower and
carrot and blanch for 5
minutes, then drain. Cook the
peas and beans following the
instructions on the packet.
Rinse all the cooked vegetables
in cold water, drain and leave
to cool.

Peel and slice the cold
potatoes. Clean, trim and
finely slice the mushrooms and
radishes. Shell and slice the
egg. Arrange all the vegetables
in spoonfuls on a flat serving
dish and top with the sliced
egg.

Wash and drain the parsley,
and chop finely. Peel and dice
the onion. Beat the oil with the
vinegar, mustard, salt, pepper,
sugar, diced onion and parsley,
and pour over the salad. Slice
the olives, roll up the anchovy
fillets and sprinkle both over
the salad. Serve with garlic
bread straight from the oven
(see page 197). *Serves 4*

Chanterelle Salad

450 g/1 lb chanterelle
   mushrooms
2 sprigs thyme
4 basil leaves
4 canned anchovy fillets
1 clove garlic
juice of 1 lime or lemon
1 egg yolk
150 ml/¼ pint olive oil
bunch parsley

Clean and trim the
chanterelles. Bring 450 ml/¾
pint salted water to the boil in
a pan with the thyme, and
continue boiling for 5 minutes.
Add the chanterelles, cover
and simmer over a moderate
heat for 5 minutes. Drain and
leave to cool.
   Finely chop the basil leaves
and anchovy fillets. Peel and
crush the garlic. Mix the basil,
anchovy and garlic into the
lime or lemon juice. Whisk the
egg yolk in a bowl and

gradually beat in the oil, a few
drops at a time, until creamy.
Stir in the anchovy and lime or
lemon mixture. Place the
chanterelles in a large bowl
and pour over the mayonnaise.
Cover and leave to stand at
room temperature for 30
minutes. Wash, drain and chop
the parsley. Sprinkle the salad
with parsley and serve with
freshly toasted white bread and
butter. *Serves 4*

Cook's Tip
You can also make this
salad using ordinary
field mushrooms, in
which case, fry the
mushrooms in 2
tablespoons olive oil for
5 minutes instead of
stewing them. Sprinkle
with thyme whilst
cooking.

Rice and Mackerel Salad

225 g/8 oz rice
4 tomatoes
2 (125-g/4.4-oz) cans mackerel
   fillets
small bunch each chives and
   parsley
1 tablespoon wine vinegar
1 teaspoon mild French mustard
salt and black pepper
3 tablespoons oil
1 (49-g/1¾-oz) can anchovy
   fillets

Cook the rice following the
instructions on the packet,
rinse through with cold water
and drain. Dip three tomatoes
into boiling water, remove the
skins and dice the flesh,
scooping away the seeds.
Drain the mackerel fillets and
break into pieces. Mix the rice,
tomato and mackerel together
in a bowl.

Wash the chives and parsley,
drain and chop finely. Beat the
vinegar with the mustard, salt,
pepper, herbs and oil and pour
the dressing over the rice salad.
Cover and leave to stand at
room temperature for 30
minutes. Wash the remaining
tomato and cut it in half.
Drain the anchovies and form
into rolls. Top the salad with
tomato and anchovies before
serving. *Serves 4*

Salads as Main Meals

Riviera Salad Platter

225 g/8 oz frozen or canned
    prawns
1 lettuce
½ punnet mustard and cress
2 avocados
juice of ½ lemon
6–8 tablespoons bottled
    Thousand island salad
    dressing
4 slices white bread

Place frozen prawns in a bowl,
cover and leave to thaw, then
drain. Rinse canned prawns in
cold water and allow to drain.
Wash the lettuce, separate the
leaves and leave to dry. Then
use to line a salad platter.

Snip the cress with kitchen
scissors, rinse under cold water
and leave to drain. Peel and
halve the avocados, remove the
stones and thinly slice the flesh.
Arrange the slices in a ring on

the bed of lettuce, sprinkle
with lemon juice to prevent
discoloration, and top with the
prawns. Spoon the Thousand
island dressing over the salad
and garnish with the mustard
and cress. Lightly toast the
bread, cut the slices in half
diagonally and serve with the
salad. *Serves 4*

Asparagus and Cress Salad

450 g/1 lb asparagus
½ teaspoon salt
1 cube sugar
3 tablespoons oil
1 tablespoon wine vinegar
few lettuce leaves
2 hard-boiled eggs
1 punnet mustard and cress
4 tablespoons natural yogurt
6 tablespoons mayonnaise
GARNISH
1 hard-boiled egg yolk, chopped
1 tablespoon chopped fresh
    mixed herbs

Wash the asparagus, and
lightly scrape the bases of the
stalks. Divide into two or three
bundles, and bind each with
thread. Bring 2 litres/3½ pints
water to the boil in a tall pan
with the salt and sugar, place
the bundles of asparagus
upright in the pan and simmer

over a low heat for 20–30
minutes until the shoots are
tender. Then drain the
asparagus bundles and leave to
cool. Remove the threads. Beat
the oil and vinegar together
and sprinkle over the
asparagus. Cover and leave to
marinate for 15 minutes.

Wash and drain the lettuce
leaves and use to line a large
flat dish. Remove the
asparagus from the marinade
and arrange on the lettuce.
Shell and quarter the eggs.
Snip the cress, rinse in cold
water, drain and arrange on
the dish with the quarters of
egg. Beat the yogurt with the
mayonnaise and spoon over
the asparagus. Garnish with
the chopped egg yolk and fresh
herbs. *Serves 4*

Salads as Main Meals

Summerhouse Salad

½ head endive
100 g/4 oz corn salad or
    watercress
1 lettuce
1 small cucumber
1 avocado
2 tomatoes
100 g/4 oz blue cheese (Stilton,
    Dolcelatte, Roquefort)
1 tablespoon double cream
1 tablespoon lemon juice
5 tablespoons mayonnaise
pinch each salt and sugar
5 drops Tabasco sauce
2 tablespoons chopped fresh
    chives

Wash the endive, cut into thin strips and leave to drain. Trim the corn salad or watercress, wash thoroughly and drain. Remove the dark green outer leaves of the lettuce and retain for use in another salad. Wash the lighter green inner part of the lettuce, separate the leaves and allow to drain. Peel the cucumber, cut in half lengthways and remove the seeds. Thinly slice the cucumber halves. Peel and halve the avocado, remove the stone and cut the flesh into thin slices. Wash and halve the tomatoes. Arrange all the ingredients together on a salad platter.

Pass the cheese through a sieve and beat with the cream, lemon juice and mayonnaise. Season the dressing with salt, sugar and Tabasco sauce and spoon onto the centre of the salad. Sprinkle the chives over the top. *Serves 4*

Chef's Salad Platter

3 tomatoes
1 small cucumber
2 hard-boiled eggs
100 g/4 oz Emmental or Edam
    cheese, sliced
225 g/8 oz ham
2 small red onions
few round lettuce leaves
1 small head endive, or
    1 Iceberg lettuce
coarsely ground black pepper
5 tablespoons oil
3 tablespoons vinegar
1 tablespoon chopped fresh
    mixed herbs, or 1 teaspoon
    dried mixed herbs
salt and white pepper

Wash, dry and thinly slice the tomatoes and cucumber. Shell and finely dice the eggs. Cut the cheese and ham into fine strips. Peel the onions and slice into rings. Wash the round lettuce leaves and drain thoroughly. Wash the endive or the Iceberg lettuce, cut into strips and leave to drain.

Mix together the sliced tomato and cucumber, arrange on one side of a salad dish and strew the diced egg over the top. Place the round lettuce leaves on another part of the dish and top with the ham and onion. Sprinkle with coarsely ground black pepper. Cover the rest of the dish with the endive or Iceberg lettuce, and sprinkle with the cheese. Beat together the oil, vinegar, herbs, salt and white pepper, and pour over the salad just before serving. *Serves 4*

Chicken and Vegetable Salad

½ cauliflower
1 roast chicken
1 leek
½ root celeriac
½ red pepper
½ green pepper
1 carrot
1 (142-ml/5-fl oz) carton
    soured cream
1 (150-g/5.3-oz) carton natural
    yogurt
juice of 1 lemon
salt and pepper
2 tablespoons chopped fresh
    mixed herbs (optional)
1 teaspoon powdered brewer's
    yeast (optional)

Wash the cauliflower, break
into florets and blanch in
boiling salted water for 4–5
minutes. Plunge into ice-cold
water, drain and leave to cool.
Take the chicken off the bone,
remove the skin and carve the
meat into small slices. Trim
and wash the leek and slice
into thin strips. Peel and wash
the celeriac and cut also into
thin strips. Blanch the leek and
celeriac in a little boiling salted
water for 4 minutes, rinse in
cold water, drain and leave to
cool. Wash and quarter the
peppers, remove the seeds and
pith, and cut the flesh into
strips. Peel the carrot and grate
finely.

  Beat the soured cream with
the yogurt, lemon juice, salt
and pepper, and add the herbs
and brewer's yeast, if used.
Mix all the salad ingredients
together in a large bowl and
spoon the dressing on top.
Serves 4

Chicken and Asparagus Salad

450 g/1 lb asparagus
350 g/12 oz frozen peas
1 roast chicken
4 hard-boiled eggs
bunch parsley
4 slices canned pineapple
5 tablespoons mayonnaise
2 tablespoons single cream
3 tablespoons canned pineapple
    juice
1 teaspoon lemon juice
generous pinch salt and sugar

Wash the asparagus and lightly
scrape the bases of the stalks.
Place upright in a pan
containing boiling salted water
and simmer over a low heat for
20–30 minutes, until tender.
Cook the peas following the
instructions on the packet.
Bone the chicken, remove the
skin, and cut the meat into
pieces. Drain the asparagus
and peas and leave to cool,
then cut the asparagus into
equal lengths. Shell and finely
chop the eggs. Wash and chop
the parsley. Drain the sliced
pineapple and cut into chunks.
Beat the mayonnaise with the
cream, pineapple juice, lemon
juice, salt and sugar. Place the
chicken, asparagus, peas and
pineapple together in a bowl
and pour over the dressing.
Sprinkle the chopped egg and
parsley over the top. Serves 4

Italian Salad

1 red pepper
1 green pepper
1 medium onion
¼ lettuce
2 small oranges
225 g/8 oz cooked chicken
12 stuffed olives
1 (142-g/5-oz) can prawns
1 (113-g/4-oz) can mussels
3 tablespoons remoulade sauce
  (see page 197)
2 tablespoons single cream
salt and white pepper
1–2 tablespoons lemon juice
GARNISH
2 hard-boiled eggs

Wash and halve the peppers, remove the seeds and pith, and slice into strips. Peel and dice the onion. Wash the lettuce, separate into leaves, drain and tear into pieces. Peel the oranges, remove the skin from the segments and dice the flesh. Cut the chicken into strips and

slice the olives. Drain the prawns, rinse in cold water and leave to dry. Drain the mussels. Mix the prawns, mussels, peppers, lettuce, onion, orange, chicken and olives together in a bowl. Beat the remoulade sauce with the cream, salt, white pepper and lemon juice, stir into the salad and leave to stand for a few minutes. Shell the eggs, cut into eight wedges and use to garnish the salad. *Serves 4*

Fetta Cheese Salad

350 g/12 oz fetta cheese
5 tablespoons olive oil
2 tablespoons wine vinegar
½ teaspoon coarsely ground
  black pepper
2 sticks celery
½ head endive
¼ teaspoon salt
25 g/1 oz shelled pecan nuts

Slice the cheese and place in a bowl. Beat 3 tablespoons oil with 1 tablespoon vinegar and the pepper, and sprinkle over the cheese. Cover and leave to stand at room temperature for 40 minutes.

Wash, trim and slice the celery. Wash the endive, drain well and cut into strips. Place the celery and endive in a bowl. Mix together the remaining oil and vinegar, add the salt and pour over the salad. Carefully

add the cheese and top with the pecan nuts. *Serves 4*

Cook's Tip

For a variation, substitute stoned black olives for the pecans and sprinkle the salad with a few freshly chopped leaves of mint.
Walnuts can also be substituted for pecans.

Danish Macaroni Salad

225 g/8 oz frozen peas
225 g/8 oz frozen carrots
225 g/8 oz macaroni
450 g/1 lb ham sausage, unsliced
1 pickled cucumber
1 large onion
225 g/8 oz mayonnaise
1 (150-g/5.3-oz) carton natural
   yogurt
1 tablespoon lemon juice
salt and pepper
½ teaspoon sugar
2 tablespoons chopped fresh
   mixed herbs, (dill, parsley,
   chives)
GARNISH
2 hard-boiled eggs
2 firm tomatoes

Bring a little salted water to
the boil in a pan, add the
frozen peas and carrots and
simmer over a low heat for 6
minutes. Drain and leave to
cool. Simmer the macaroni in
plenty of salted water,
following the instructions on
the packet, until cooked but
still firm. Rinse through with
cold water and drain. Remove
the skin from the ham sausage
and cut the meat into 1-cm/
½-inch cubes. Slice the pickled
cucumber into strips. Peel the
onion and cut into rings, and
place all the salad ingredients
together in a bowl. Beat the
mayonnaise with the yogurt,
lemon juice, salt, pepper, sugar
and chopped herbs. Stir the
dressing into the salad, cover
and leave to stand at room
temperature for 30 minutes.
   Shell and slice the eggs. Cut
the tomatoes into eight.
Garnish the macaroni salad
with tomato and egg. *Serves 4*

Meat and Vegetable Salad

350 g/12 oz frozen mixed
   vegetables
225 g/8 oz cold roast pork
1 red onion
4 strips canned pimiento
2 tablespoons wine vinegar
1 teaspoon hot mustard
5 drops Tabasco sauce
¼ teaspoon salt
pinch sugar
4 tablespoons oil
100 g/4 oz Wensleydale or
   Stilton cheese
2 tablespoons chopped mixed
   fresh herbs (optional)

Cook the frozen vegetables
following the instructions on
the packet, drain and leave to
cool. Slice the roast pork into
strips. Peel the onion and cut
into rings. Drain and dice the
canned pimiento. Mix all the
salad ingredients in a bowl.
   Beat the wine vinegar with
the mustard, Tabasco, salt,
sugar and oil. Stir the dressing
into the salad, cover and leave
to stand at room temperature
for 15 minutes. Crumble the
cheese and sprinkle over the
salad just before serving,
together with the chopped
herbs, if used. *Serves 4*

Cheese and Salami Salad

1 clove garlic
5 tablespoons oil
3 tablespoons wine vinegar
salt and black pepper
¼ teaspoon sugar
pinch dried rosemary
1 bay leaf
100 g/4 oz green noodles
100 g/4 oz thinly sliced salami
225 g/8 oz Emmental cheese
2 onions

Peel and finely chop the garlic. Beat the oil with the vinegar, garlic, salt, pepper and sugar. Crush the rosemary and bay leaf between finger and thumb and add to the dressing. Cover and leave to stand at room temperature for 2 hours.

Cook the noodles in plenty of salted water following the instructions on the packet. Take care that you do not over-cook them. Rinse through with cold water, drain and leave to cool. Cut the salami and cheese into thin strips. Peel the onions and cut into rings. Mix all the salad ingredients together, cover and leave to stand in a cool place. Strain the dressing and sprinkle over the salad just before serving. *Serves 4*

Pepper and Herring Salad

250 ml/8 fl oz milk
8 pickled herring fillets
1 green pepper
1 red pepper
2 tomatoes
1 small onion
4 tablespoons oil
2 tablespoons wine vinegar
few lettuce leaves
GARNISH
2 hard-boiled eggs
bunch dill or parsley

Mix the milk with 100 ml/ 4 fl oz water. Rinse the herring fillets in cold water, place in the mixture and leave to soak for 1 hour. Wash the peppers, cut them in half and remove the seeds and pith, then slice into rings. Dip the tomatoes into boiling water, plunge into cold water, remove the skins and cut each into eight wedges.

Take the herrings out of the milk, drain and cut into strips. Peel the onion and cut into rings. Beat the oil with the vinegar. Place the herring, pepper, tomato and onion in a bowl, pour over the dressing, cover and leave to stand for 10 minutes.

Wash the lettuce leaves, allow to drain and use to line a salad dish. Arrange the herring and pepper salad on the bed of lettuce. Shell and dice the eggs. Wash and chop the parsley or dill, and sprinkle over the salad before serving, together with the diced egg. *Serves 4*

71

Party Specials

Salad Supreme

2 heads chicory
100 g/4 oz corn salad or
    watercress
1 yellow pepper
2 firm tomatoes
1 small honeydew melon
1 onion
100 g/4 oz Edam cheese
100 g/4 oz smoked or boiled
    ham
50 g/2 oz canned tuna fish
2 smoked trout fillets
50 g/2 oz canned prawns
1–2 spring onions
bunch fresh mixed herbs
    (optional)
4 tablespoons oil
1 tablespoon wine vinegar
1 tablespoon fresh lime juice
½ teaspoon sugar
salt and coarsely ground black
    pepper
generous pinch ground ginger
10 black olives

Wash the chicory and separate
the leaves. Trim, wash and
drain the corn salad or
watercress. Cut the stalk off
the pepper, slice the pepper
into rings and remove the
seeds. Wash and dry the
tomatoes and cut into eight.
Slice the melon in half, remove
the seeds and scoop out the
flesh with a melon baller or
teaspoon. Peel the onion and
cut into rings. Cut the cheese
and ham into strips. Drain the
tuna and break up with a fork.
Skin and flake the trout fillets.
Drain the prawns, rinse
through with cold water and
allow to dry. Wash the spring
onions, and the herbs, if used,
drain well and chop finely.
Beat the oil with the vinegar,
lime juice, sugar, salt, pepper
and ginger. Arrange the salad
ingredients in four individual
cocktail glasses or dishes,
sprinkle with the dressing and
garnish with olives. *Serves 4*

Camembert Cocktail

2 medium carrots
1 (269-g/9½-oz) jar mixed
  pickled vegetables
4 strips canned pimiento
2 small onions
½ (396-g/14-oz) can artichoke
  hearts
350 g/12 oz Camembert cheese
100 g/4 oz mushrooms
2 tablespoons tarragon vinegar
1 teaspoon lemon juice
¼ teaspoon sugar
½ teaspoon salt
5 tablespoons oil
small bunch parsley

Trim, wash and scrape the
carrots. Blanch in a little
boiling salted water for 2
minutes, then drain and cut
into slices. Drain the mixed
pickled vegetables and canned
pimiento and cut into pieces.
Peel the onions and slice into

very thin rings. Drain and
halve the artichoke hearts. Cut
the Camembert into thick
slices. Clean, trim and finely
chop the mushrooms. Mix all
the salad ingredients gently
together in a large bowl. Beat
the vinegar with the lemon
juice, sugar, salt and oil,
sprinkle over the salad, cover
and leave to stand at room
temperature for 30 minutes.
  Wash, drain and finely chop
the parsley. Arrange the
Camembert cocktail in four
individual glasses and sprinkle
each with parsley. Serve with
fresh wholemeal or
pumpermickel bread and
butter. *Serves 4*

Corned Beef and Cheese Salad

2 eggs
175 g/6 oz frozen peas
2 (198-g/7-oz) cans corned beef
100 g/4 oz Cheddar or
  Emmental cheese
2 green peppers
4 tomatoes
100 g/4 oz canned sweet corn
20 stuffed olives
small bunch parsley
1 clove garlic
5 tablespoons oil
3 tablespoons vinegar
salt and pepper

Hard-boil the eggs for 10
minutes, plunge into cold
water, shell and leave to cool.
Cook the frozen peas following
the instructions on the packet,
rinse under cold water and
leave to drain. Cut the corned
beef and cheese into strips.
Wash, dry and quarter the

peppers, remove the seeds and
pith, and slice. Cut the eggs
into eight segments. Wash
the tomatoes and cut also into
eight. Drain the sweet corn.
Slice the olives. Wash, drain
and finely chop the parsley.
Peel and crush the garlic, and
beat with the oil, vinegar, salt
and pepper. Mix the dressing
into the salad ingredients,
cover and leave to stand for 15
minutes. Sprinkle with parsley
before serving. *Serves 4*

Apple and Celery Salad

1 head celery
3 small red dessert apples
1 teaspoon lemon juice
50 g/2 oz shelled hazelnuts
100 g/4 oz fetta or cottage
  cheese
200 ml/7 fl oz single cream
salt and white pepper

Wash the celery, break into sticks and cut off the green leaves. Chop the celery very finely. Wash the apples, cut into quarters and remove the cores. Slice thinly and sprinkle with lemon juice. Coarsely chop the nuts. Mix the celery and apple with half the nuts and arrange on a flat serving dish.

Crush the Fetta or cottage cheese in a bowl with a fork and mix with the cream, salt and pepper. Stir the remaining nuts into the dressing and serve separately with the salad.
Serves 4

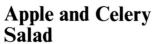

Cook's Tip
Blue cheese dressing also goes very well with this salad. Substitute 75–100 g/3–4 oz to taste Gorgonzola or Danish Blue for the fetta or cottage cheese and proceed as above.

Potato and Apple Salad

450 g/1 lb new potatoes
1 Iceberg or Webb's Wonder
  lettuce
1 small cucumber
2 crisp dessert apples
2 onions
1 (340-g/12-oz) can sweet corn
bunch dill (optional)
2 tablespoons wine vinegar
1 tablespoon lemon juice
2 tablespoons apple juice
1 teaspoon mild French mustard
salt and pepper
¼ teaspoon sugar
5 tablespoons oil

Wash the potatoes, plunge into boiling salted water and simmer for 20–25 minutes. Pour off the water and remove the potato skins. Leave to cool, then slice and place in a large bowl.

Wash and trim the lettuce, allow to drain and tear the leaves into strips. Cut the cucumber in half lengthways and scoop out the seeds. Thinly slice the cucumber halves. Wash, dry and quarter the apples, remove the cores and cut into thin slices. Peel the onions and cut into rings. Drain the sweet corn, and add all the salad ingredients to the potatoes.

Wash and chop the dill, if used. Beat the vinegar with the lemon juice, apple juice, mustard, salt, pepper, sugar and oil. Pour the dressing over the salad and mix well. Sprinkle with dill, if used, before serving. *Serves 4*

Party Specials

For Autumn

White Cabbage Salad
1 small white cabbage
100 g/4 oz streaky bacon, sliced
*   thickly*
1 large onion
5 tablespoons wine vinegar
5 tablespoons oil
1 teaspoon sugar
1 teaspoon caraway seeds

Wash and trim the cabbage, remove the stalk and cut the cabbage into quarters. Shred into thin strips and blanch in boiling salted water for 5–8 minutes. Drain well and leave to cool. Remove the rind from the bacon, cut the bacon into small pieces and fry in a pan until crisp. Peel and finely chop the onion. Beat the vinegar with the oil and sugar. Place the cabbage, bacon and onion in a bowl and pour over the dressing. Sprinkle with caraway seeds, cover and leave to stand in a cool place for 20 minutes before serving.
Serves 4

Red Cabbage Salad
1 small red cabbage
1 large or 2 small crisp dessert
*   apples*
1 onion
5 tablespoons oil
3 tablespoons wine vinegar
1 tablespoon lemon juice
1 tablespoon sugar
3 tablespoons orange juice
grated rind of ½ orange
1 (142-ml/5-fl oz) carton
*   soured cream*

Wash the cabbage, cut into quarters and remove the stalk. Shred the quarters into fine strips. Blanch in boiling salted water for 5–8 minutes and drain. Peel and quarter the apple, remove the core and slice thinly. Peel and finely dice the onion. Beat the oil with the vinegar, lemon juice, sugar, orange juice, orange rind and diced onion. Place the red cabbage and sliced apple in a large bowl, pour over the dressing and mix well. Leave to stand in a cool place for 20 minutes and top with the soured cream before serving.
Serves 4

Savoy Cabbage Salad
1 small Savoy cabbage
1 onion
5 tablespoons wine vinegar
4 tablespoons oil
1 teaspoon sugar
¼ teaspoon salt
pinch white pepper
generous pinch curry powder
25 g/1 oz each shelled almonds,
*   hazelnuts and cashew nuts*

Wash, trim and quarter the cabbage, and remove the stalk. Shred the cabbage into fine strips. Blanch in boiling salted water for 5–8 minutes and drain.

Peel and finely dice the onion. Beat the vinegar with the oil, sugar, salt, pepper, curry powder and diced onion. Mix the dressing thoroughly into the cabbage, cover and leave in a cool place for 20 minutes. Stir in the nuts before serving. *Serves 4*

Strawberry and Radish Salad

bunch large radishes
1 crisp dessert apple
100 g/4 oz strawberries
1 tablespoon lemon juice
½ teaspoon salt
½ teaspoon sugar
generous pinch cayenne pepper
2 tablespoons oil

Wash the radishes, top and tail them and grate into thin strips. Wash, dry and quarter the apple, remove the core and cut into thin slices. Hull the strawberries and cut each in half or into quarters.

Beat the lemon juice with the salt, sugar, cayenne pepper and oil, mix all the salad ingredients together in a large bowl and sprinkle with the dressing. *Serves 4*

Cook's Tip

You may prefer to grate the apple as well as the radishes. If so, peel the apple first as it is difficult to grate with the peel.

Chicory Boats

1 large head chicory
1 (150-g/5-oz) can prawns
6 stuffed olives
8 black olives
1 tablespoon wine vinegar
3 tablespoons oil
1 teaspoon mild French mustard
salt and pepper
GARNISH
2 hard-boiled eggs (optional)
small bunch dill or parsley

Break off four large chicory leaves, wash in cold water and leave on one side to drain. Wash and trim the rest of the chicory, separate into leaves and cut into thin strips. Drain the prawns, rinse through with cold water and leave to dry. Cut the stuffed olives in half and stone the black olives. Place all the salad ingredients together in a bowl. Beat the vinegar with the oil, mustard, salt and pepper and mix into the salad.

Shell the eggs and cut each into eight wedges. Wash the dill or parsley, allow to drain and break into sprigs. Arrange the four large chicory leaves on a flat dish and fill each with salad. Garnish the platter with the egg wedges, if used, and the chicory boats with dill or parsley sprigs. *Serves 4*

Avocado and Ham Salad

4 avocados
juice of 1 lemon
100 g/4 oz smoked or boiled
ham, thinly sliced
1 (312-g/11-oz) can mandarin
segments
3 tablespoons oil
1 tablespoon brandy
generous pinch salt
3–4 lemon balm leaves
(optional)

Cut the avocados in half and remove the stones. Scoop out the flesh with a melon baller, place in a bowl and sprinkle with a little lemon juice. Slice the ham into very fine strips. Drain the mandarin segments, retaining the juice on one side, and mix the mandarin, avocado and ham together. Beat the remaining lemon juice with 1 tablespoon canned mandarin juice, the oil, brandy and salt. Stir into the salad, cover and leave to stand for a few minutes.

Wash the lemon balm, if used, drain well and cut into strips. Arrange the salad on a serving dish and sprinkle with the lemon balm. *Serves 4*

Angelo's Chicken Salad

3 cooked chicken breasts
¼ cucumber
4 tomatoes
1 apple
juice of ½ lemon
1 tablespoon mild or wholegrain
mustard
5 tablespoons mayonnaise
bunch dill or parsley
1 tablespoon castor sugar
2 tablespoons wine vinegar
3 tablespoons orange juice
grated rind of ½ orange

Skin the chicken breasts, if necessary, and carve the meat into thin slices. Wash and dry the cucumber, cut in half lengthways and scoop out the seeds with a spoon. Slice the cucumber very finely. Peel and quarter the tomatoes, remove the seeds and dice the flesh. Peel, quarter, core and slice the apple, and sprinkle with the lemon juice. Mix all the salad ingredients together in a bowl.

Beat the mustard into the mayonnaise. Wash, drain and finely chop the dill or parsley. Mix the sugar thoroughly into the vinegar, and orange juice, and stir into the mayonnaise together with the dill, or parsley, and grated orange rind. Arrange the salad in four individual glasses and top each with a tablespoon of the dressing. *Serves 4*

Fruit Salads

Grapefruit Salad

2 grapefruit
50 g / 2 oz sugar
3 tablespoons Grand Marnier
  liqueur
1 tablespoon clear honey
8 fresh or maraschino cherries

Peel the grapefruit, removing all the pith, and slice thinly. Discard any pips. Sprinkle with the sugar and Grand Marnier, cover and leave to stand in the refrigerator for 2 hours.
  Strain the grapefruit, collecting the juice in a bowl, and beat the juice with the honey. Divide the grapefruit between four individual plates, pour the syrup over the top and decorate each portion with two fresh or maraschino cherries. *Serves 4*

Orange Salad

4 oranges
75 g / 3 oz sugar
4 tablespoons water
6 tablespoons Grenadine syrup
1 tablespoon Cointreau liqueur
1 tablespoon fresh mint leaves
  (optional)

Wash the oranges, rub dry and peel very thinly, taking care that you do not peel the pith with the rind. Place the rind in a pan with the sugar and water, bring to the boil and simmer over a low heat for 5 minutes. Strain the syrup, add the Grenadine and bring to the boil again. Remove the liquid from the heat. Stir in the Cointreau, and the mint, if used, retaining a few leaves on one side, and leave to cool.
  Remove all the pith from the oranges and thinly slice the flesh. Pour over the syrup and leave to stand in the refrigerator for 2 hours. If mint leaves are used, strain the oranges before serving, collecting the syrup in a jug. Discard the marinated mint leaves, pour the syrup over the orange salad and decorate with the remaining fresh mint leaves. *Serves 4*

Jamaican Fruit Salad

1 pineapple
2 limes
1 coconut
1-2 tablespoons sugar
2 tablespoons coconut milk
1 tablespoon white rum
2 tablespoons lime juice
GARNISH
4 sprigs mint (optional)

Slice the pineapple and cut the tough outer peel off each slice. Cut the flesh into strips, discarding any hard parts of the core. Wash and dry the limes and slice very finely. Puncture three holes into the three indentations at the top of the coconut and pour the milk out into a jug. Break the coconut open with a cleaver or hammer, cut out the flesh with a sharp knife and grate.

Arrange the slices of lime in a semi-circle on four individual plates. Place the pineapple in the centre and top with the grated coconut. Beat the sugar with the coconut milk, rum and lime juice and sprinkle over the salad. Garnish each portion with a sprig of mint, if liked. *Serves 4*

Cook's Tip

If you are unable to obtain fresh coconut, you can make this salad with desiccated coconut, replacing the coconut milk with 4 tablespoons low-fat milk mixed with 1 tablespoon rosehip syrup.

Kiwi Fruit Salad with Orange Cream

6 kiwi fruit
6 tablespoons orange juice
1-2 tablespoons sugar
1 tablespoon Curaçao liquer
6 tablespoons double cream
grated rind of 1 orange
generous pinch ground ginger
1 teaspoon pickled pink or
  green peppercorns (optional)

Thinly peel and slice the kiwi fruit. Beat 2 tablespoons orange juice with the sugar and Curaçao until the sugar has completely dissolved, and sprinkle the dressing over the kiwi fruit. Cover and leave to marinate in the refrigerator for 2 hours.

Arrange the kiwi fruit on four individual plates. Whip the cream with the remaining orange juice, half the grated orange rind and the ground ginger. Spoon the orange cream onto the fruit. Sprinkle the rest of the orange rind over the top, together with the pickled pink or green peppercorns, if used. *Serves 4*

Cook's Tip

If the idea of a hot, spicy garnish to kiwi fruit does not appeal to you, use chopped pistachio nuts instead of the peppercorns.

Fruit Salads

Melon Salad

1 small honeydew melon
1 large Spanish onion
3 tablespoons oil
1 tablespoon wine vinegar
¼ teaspoon each salt, paprika
    pepper and white pepper
6 tablespoons port

Slice the melon into eight
wedges, remove the seeds and
cut the flesh into cubes. Peel
and halve the onion, and slice
or grate as thinly as possible.
Place the melon and onion
together in a bowl.
    Beat the oil with the wine
vinegar, salt, paprika and
pepper, and pour over the
melon and onion. Cover and
leave to stand in the
refrigerator for 20 minutes.
Before serving, pour the port
over the salad.

Cook's Tip

If the unusual
combination of melon
and onion does not
appeal to you, you can
replace the onion with
½ head fennel, cut into
fine strips.

Banana and Tomato Salad

4 medium tomatoes
2 bananas
juice of 1 lemon
3 tablespoons oil
salt and black pepper
¼ teaspoon curry powder
½ teaspoon pink peppercorns
    (optional)

Wash and dry the tomatoes
and cut into thin slices.
Arrange the tomato in a fan-
shape on a salad dish, or on
four individual plates. Peel and
slice the bananas, arrange over
the tomato slices and sprinkle
immediately with 1 teaspoon
lemon juice to prevent
discolouring. Beat the oil with
the remaining lemon juice, the
salt, pepper and curry powder.
Pour the dressing over the
salad. Crush the pink
peppercorns, if used, with a
mortar and pestle, and sprinkle
over the salad. *Serves 4*

Cook's Tip

This salad tastes even
better if you replace one
of the bananas with
100 g/4 oz canned
bamboo shoots. In this
case you should peel and
dice the tomatoes and
banana, mix in a bowl
with the bamboo shoots
and stir in the dressing.

Spicy Fruit Salad

2 crisp dessert apples
1½ tablespoons lemon juice
3-4 sticks celery
225 g/8 oz canned mandarin
  segments
100 g/4 oz black grapes
25 g/1 oz shelled walnuts
25 g/1 oz shelled almonds
1 (142-ml/5-fl oz) carton
  soured cream
2 tablespoons mayonnaise
1 tablespoon chilli sauce
pinch each salt and sugar
1 small lettuce

Peel, quarter, core and thinly slice the apples. Sprinkle with ½ tablespoon lemon juice to prevent discolouring. Wash, trim and dice the celery. Drain the mandarin segments and cut them in half. Wash and halve the grapes and remove the pips. Chop the walnuts and almonds, and mix all the salad ingredients together in a bowl.

Beat the soured cream with the mayonnaise, chilli sauce, the remaining lemon juice, the salt and sugar. Pour the dressing over the salad, cover and leave to stand in the refrigerator for 15 minutes. Wash the lettuce, separate the leaves and allow to drain. Line a salad bowl with lettuce and arrange the fruit salad on top. *Serves 4*

Apple Salad with Rum Dressing

450 g/1 lb dessert apples
225 g/8 oz green grapes
juice of ½ lemon
100 ml/4 fl oz white wine
3 tablespoons sugar
1 tablespoon honey
generous pinch each ground
  cinnamon and ginger
2 tablespoons white rum
4 tablespoons fresh grated
  coconut or desiccated coconut
GARNISH
4 dates

Peel, quarter, core and finely dice the apples. Wash and peel the grapes, cut in half and remove the pips. Mix the apple and grapes with the lemon juice, white wine and sugar. Cover the fruit and leave to stand at room temperature for 2 hours.
  Strain the salad marinade

into a pan, placing the fruit in a bowl on one side. Bring the marinade to the boil and simmer gently over a low heat until half the liquid has evaporated. Stir in the honey and leave to cool, then add the cinnamon, ginger and rum, and pour over the fruit salad. Arrange in four individual salad bowls or empty coconut shells, and sprinkle the coconut over the top. Garnish each portion with a date. *Serves 4*

Fruit Salads

Apple and Orange Salad

3 medium dessert apples
juice of 1 lemon
450 g/1 lb oranges
50 g/2 oz marzipan
1 tablespoon honey
2 tablespoons Bénédictine
*   liqueur*
6 tablespoons single cream
50 g/2 oz shelled walnut halves

Peel the apples, cut into eight wedges and remove the cores, then slice finely. Sprinkle with lemon juice to prevent discolouring. Peel and slice the oranges, taking care to remove all the pith. Cut each slice into eight and remove the pips. Mix the apple and orange together in a large bowl.

Beat the marzipan thoroughly with the honey, Bénédictine and cream. Stir the mixture into the fruit, cover and leave to stand for 15 minutes. Arrange the salad in a serving bowl, cut the walnuts in half again and sprinkle over the salad.
Serves 4

Plum and Ginger Salad

450 g/1 lb sweet ripe dessert
*   plums*
4 pieces preserved stem ginger
6 tablespoons double cream
1-2 tablespoons brandy
1½ tablespoons icing sugar
generous pinch ground ginger

Scald the plums briefly in boiling water, plunge into cold water, then drain and remove the skins. Halve and stone the plums and place in a bowl. Drain the preserved ginger, cut into thin strips and stir into the plums. Whip the cream with the brandy, icing sugar and ground ginger and pour the dressing into the centre of the plums. Cover and leave to stand in the refrigerator for 30 minutes. Mix the dressing thoroughly into the plums at the table.

Cook's Tip

You can add extra spice to the dressing by beating 1 tablespoon of the preserved ginger syrup into the cream and brandy. The syrup will sweeten the dressing, so the icing sugar can then be omitted, or stirred in, according to taste.

Autumn Fruit Salad

2 crisp dessert apples
2 pears
2 teaspoons lemon juice
100 g/4 oz green grapes
100 g/4 oz black grapes
225 g/8 oz sweet dessert plums
50 g/2 oz shelled walnut halves
2 tablespoons sugar
juice of 2 oranges
1-2 tablespoons Kirsch liqueur

Wash, dry and quarter the apples and pears. Remove the cores, and slice the quarters into thin wedges, then sprinkle with the lemon juice. Wash and dry the grapes and plums. Cut the plums into quarters and remove the stones. Halve the walnut halves again, and mix all these ingredients together in a bowl.

Beat the sugar into the orange juice, bring to the boil

in a pan and simmer over a low heat until the liquid begins to form a syrup, stirring continuously. Allow to cool, then add the Kirsch and pour over the salad. *Serves 4*

Cook's Tip

This makes an excellent fruit salad for a children's party if you leave out the alcohol.

Grape and Walnut Salad

450 g/1 lb sweet white grapes
4 tablespoons sweet sherry
1 small lettuce
50 g/2 oz chopped walnuts
3 tablespoons fresh lime juice
generous pinch salt
4 tablespoons walnut or
    sunflower oil
1-2 tablespoons castor sugar
GARNISH
½ teaspoon pickled pink or
    green peppercorns (optional)

Peel the grapes, place in a large bowl and pour over the sherry. Cover and leave to stand in the refrigerator for 2 hours.

Remove the outer leaves from the lettuce, retaining them for use in another salad. Wash the light green leaves from the centre of the lettuce in cold water, drain well and cut into fine strips. Add the lettuce

and chopped walnuts to the grape marinade and stir in gently. Beat the lime juice with the salt and walnut or sunflower oil, add sugar to taste and pour the dressing over the salad. Crush the peppercorns, if used, in a mortar and sprinkle over the salad before serving. *Serves 4*

Fruit Salads

Raspberry and Kiwi Fruit Salad

225 g/8 oz raspberries
2 tablespoons sugar
1 William pear
juice of $\frac{1}{2}$ lemon
1 tablespoon Poire William or
   Kirsch liqueur
2 canned peach halves
4 canned apricot halves
4 kumquats, or 3 tablespoons
   drained canned mandarin
   segments
2 kiwi fruit
150 ml/$\frac{1}{4}$ pint double cream
1 tablespoon icing sugar
few drops vanilla essence

Place the raspberries in a large bowl and sprinkle with sugar. Peel, quarter and core the pear, cut into thin wedges and place on a dish. Sprinkle with the lemon juice and the Poire William or Kirsch, and leave to stand for 10 minutes.

Drain the peach and apricot halves and cut into slices. Wash, dry and slice the kumquats, if used. Mix the pear, peach, apricot, and kumquats or mandarins with the raspberries. Thinly peel and slice the kiwi fruit, arrange in a ring on each of four individual plates and top with the fruit salad. Whip the cream with the icing sugar, add vanilla essence to taste and spoon onto the salad portions before serving. *Serves 4*

Chinese Fruit Salad

225 g/8 oz strawberries
2 tablespoons sugar
225 g/8 oz canned lychees
225 g/8 oz canned mandarin
   segments
1 tablespoon lemon juice
2 tablespoons arrack or
   Cointreau liqueur
3 tablespoons double cream
1 teaspoon icing sugar
1 tablespoon chopped pistachio
   nuts (optional)

Place the strawberries in a bowl and sprinkle with sugar. Drain the lychees and mandarins and mix with the strawberries. Sprinkle the fruit with the lemon juice and 1 tablespoon arrack or Cointreau, cover and leave to stand for 15 minutes. Then arrange the fruit in a serving dish or on individual plates.

Whip the cream with the icing sugar until creamy and stir in the remaining arrack or Cointreau. Spoon the cream over the fruit salad before serving and top with chopped pistachio nuts, if used. *Serves 4*

Fruit Salads

Sicilian Salad

*1 small Ogen melon
2 persimmons
2 prickly pears
2 oranges
juice of 1 lemon
100 ml/4 fl oz white Corvo
   (Sicilian wine), or dry white
   wine of your choice
4 tablespoons sugar*

Cut the melon into wedges, scoop away the seeds and remove the rind from each wedge. Cut the flesh into long, thin slices. Peel and slice the persimmons, prickly pears and oranges, removing all the skin from the orange. Place all the fruit in a bowl. Sprinkle with lemon juice, cover and chill for 1 hour. Place the wine and sugar together in a pan, bring to the boil and simmer until the liquid is reduced by half. Cool and pour over the fruit. *Serves 4*

Caribbean Salad

*1 small pineapple
1 papaya
2 fresh guavas, or 4 canned
   guava halves
2 limes
100 g/4 oz sugar
juice of 1 orange
½ cinnamon stick, or ½
   teaspoons cinnamon
1 vanilla pod, or a few drops
   vanilla essence
a little grated nutmeg
generous pinch ground ginger
1 tablespoon white rum*

Slice the pineapple. With a sharp knife cut all around each slice just inside the skin, remove the skin and discard. Peel the papaya and fresh guavas, if used, cut into pieces and remove the pips. Drain and slice canned guavas. Wash the limes and slice very finely. Place all the fruit in a bowl.

Bring the sugar to the boil in a pan with the orange juice, cinnamon and vanilla and simmer over a low heat, stirring continuously, until the sugar has dissolved. Then strain and leave to cool. Season the syrup with nutmeg and ginger and stir in the rum. Pour the syrup over the fruit and chill for 1 hour. Serve the salad ice-cold. *Serves 4*

Fruit Salads

Summer Fruit Salad

1 honeydew melon
1 banana
juice of 1 lemon
1 apple
225 g/8 oz green grapes
1 peach
2 apricots
100 g/4 oz cherries
100 g/4 oz strawberries
100 g/4 oz raspberries
4 tablespoons castor sugar
150 ml/¼ pint Malaga or
    Madeira wine, or port

Slice off one end of the melon, scoop the flesh out of the slice and discard the rind. Carefully scoop the flesh out of the rest of the melon, and dice, removing the seeds. Cut a zigzag pattern around the edge of the melon shell. Peel and slice the banana and sprinkle immediately with a little lemon juice. Peel, core and slice the apple, and sprinkle with the remaining lemon juice. Wash the grapes. Dip the peach briefly into hot water, and peel away the skin. Wash the apricots. Cut both peach and apricots in half, remove the stones and finely dice the flesh. Wash and stone the cherries and hull the strawberries. Mix all the fruit, including the raspberries, together in a bowl.

Beat the sugar with the Malaga, Madeira or port, pour over the fruit salad and leave to stand in the refrigerator for 1 hour. Then transfer the salad to the melon shell and serve on a bed of crushed ice cubes, with hot Sweet wine sauce (see page 235), if liked. Serves 4

Fruit Salad in Pineapple

1 pineapple
3 kiwi fruit
100 g/4 oz strawberries
100 g/4 oz grapes
100 g/4 oz cherries
225 g/8 oz canned mandarin
    segments
juice of 1 lemon
5 tablespoons castor sugar
1 tablespoon maraschino or
    Kirsch liqueur
150 mml/¼ pint double cream
few drops vanilla essence
1 maraschino cherry

Slice a wedge out of the pineapple lengthways, leaving a gap measuring about one third of the pineapple. Peel this wedge, discard any hard parts of the core and dice the flesh. Scoop the rest of the flesh out of the pineapple, and dice, again removing the core, if tough. Peel and thinly slice the kiwi fruit. Hull the strawberries and cut them in half. Wash the grapes and cherries. Stone the cherries and halve, together with the grapes. Drain the mandarin segments. Gently mix all the fruit together in a bowl.

Bring the lemon juice to the boil in a pan with 3 tablespoons sugar and simmer, stirring continuously, until the sugar dissolves. Leave the lemon juice to cool, beat in the maraschino or Kirsch and sprinkle over the salad. Cover and leave to stand in the refrigerator for 1 hour.

Whip the cream with the remaining sugar and the vanilla essence until stiff. Transfer the fruit salad to the pineapple shell and spoon or pipe the whipped cream over the top. Decorate with the maraschino cherry. Serves 4

Stuffed Watermelon

1 small watermelon
3 oranges
juice of ½ lemon
50 g / 2 oz sugar
1 tablespoon white rum
1 tablespoon clear honey
4 scoops vanilla ice cream
1 teaspoon chopped pistachio
  nuts (optional)

Slice one third off the watermelon and scoop the flesh out of the slice. Scoop the flesh out of the rest of the melon with a tablespoon, discard the seeds and cut the flesh into strips. Peel 2 oranges, removing all the pith, and separate the segments. Peel the fine skin from the segments and cut the flesh into pieces. Mix the orange and melon in a bowl. Cut a decorative arched pattern around the top of the melon shell and fill the melon with the fruit salad.

Squeeze the juice from the remaining orange. Bring the orange and lemon juice and sugar to the boil in a pan, and simmer, stirring continuously, until the sugar has completely dissolved. Leave to cool and beat in the rum and honey. Pour the syrup over the fruit salad and top with scoops of vanilla ice cream. Sprinkle with chopped pistachios, if used. *Serves 4*

Avocado Fruit Salad

2 avocados
juice of ½ lemon
4 small yellow tomatoes
3 peaches
100 g / 4 oz strawberries
3 tablespoons sugar
2 teaspoons fresh lime juice
1 tablespoon port
1 teaspoon port
1 teaspoon pickled green
  peppercorns (optional)

Wash and dry the avocados, cut in half lengthways and remove the stones. Scoop out the flesh with a melon baller or a coffee spoon, place in a large bowl and sprinkle with lemon juice. Wash and dry the tomatoes and cut into thin wedges. Dip the peaches briefly in hot water, remove the skin, and cut the peaches in half, discarding the stones. Slice into equally thin wedges. Mix the tomato and peach gently with the avocado balls.

Hull the strawberries and crush them with a fork. Beat the strawberry purée with the sugar, lime juice and port and stir in the pickled green peppercorns, if used. Transfer the fruit salad to the avocado halves and top with the strawberry dressing. *Serves 4*

Simple Salad Buffet

Salad Buffet with Assorted Dressings

For a large buffet you will need between six and eight different salad ingredients. Choose any of the following, depending on what is in season, and bearing texture and colour in mind: round and cos lettuces, Iceberg or Webb's Wonder lettuce, corn salad, chicory, red endive, curly endive, young spinach, dandelion leaves, watercress, sliced tomatoes and cucumber, radishes, onion rings, green and black olives, hard-boiled eggs, canned sweet corn, green, red and yellow peppers sliced into rings, celery, chopped fresh herbs, cooked peas and diced fruit. Wash and thoroughly drain all salad ingredients, arrange separately in bowls or on platters as liked,

and serve with the following dressings:

Blue Cheese Dressing
100 g/4 oz blue cheese (Stilton, Roquefort, Dolcelatte)
1 tablespoon single or soured cream
1 tablespoon white wine vinegar
2 tablespoons mayonnaise
salt and white pepper

Crush the cheese with a fork and mix with the cream, vinegar, mayonnaise, salt and pepper. Blue cheese dressing goes especially well with all varieties of lettuce.

Egg and Herb Dressing
4 hard-boiled eggs
3 tablespoons oil
1 tablespoon wine vinegar
salt and pepper
2 tablespoons chopped fresh mixed herbs

Shell and finely dice the eggs. Beat the oil with the vinegar, salt and pepper. Stir in the egg and herbs, and serve with tomato or cucumber salad.

French Dressing
3 tablespoons lemon juice
salt and pepper
¼ teaspoon sugar
¼ teaspoon mustard powder
8 tablespoons olive oil

Beat the lemon juice with the salt, pepper, sugar and mustard powder. Gradually mix in the oil, beating continuously. French dressing goes well with chicory, red endive and all kinds of lettuce.

Simple Salad Buffet

Yogurt Dressing

1 (150-g/5.3-oz) carton natural
  yogurt
2 tablespoons lemon juice
1 tablespoon oil
salt and pepper
2 tablespoons chopped fresh
  mixed herbs

Mix the yogurt with the lemon
juice and oil and whisk until
creamy. Stir in the salt, pepper
and herbs. Yogurt dressing
goes well with chicory, lettuce
and hard-boiled eggs.

Thousand Island Dressing

2 strips canned pimiento
225 g/8 oz mayonnaise
3 tablespoons tomato ketchup
1 teaspoon finely chopped green
  pepper
1 teaspoon grated onion
¼ teaspoon salt
generous pinch paprika pepper

Drain the pimiento and dice
finely. Mix the mayonnaise
with the pimiento, ketchup,
green pepper, grated onion,
salt and paprika. Serve with all
kinds of lettuce, and chicory,
tomato or dandelion salad.

Sherry Dressing

1 egg
2 tablespoons sugar
2 tablespoons dry sherry
¼ teaspoon salt
15 g/½ oz melted butter
4 tablespoons orange juice
2 tablespoons lemon juice
4 tablespoons double cream

Beat the egg. Whisking
continuously, gradually add
the sugar, sherry, salt, butter,
orange and lemon juice and
transfer the mixture to a pan.
Heat very gently, stirring
continuously, until it begins to
thicken, but do not allow to
boil. Remove from the heat
and leave to cool. Then whip
the cream and fold it into the
dressing. Sherry dressing goes
well with celery, red endive,
canned sweet corn and any
kind of fruit salad.

Cook's Tip

You can make your
salad buffet a more
substantial meal by
serving diced Cheddar,
Edam, Emmental or
other kinds of cheeses,
cold ham, beef, chicken
or pork, rolled
anchovies, rollmop
herrings, shrimps or any
kind of smoked fish.
Serve with a selection of
different kinds of bread.

Seafood Moulds

Shrimps in Aspic

350 g/12 oz frozen or canned
   shrimps
300 ml/½ pint clarified fish stock
   (see page 201)
150 ml/¼ pint dry white wine
salt and pepper
15 g/½ oz gelatine
large bunch dill or parsley
150 ml/¼ pint mayonnaise
1 teaspoon lemon juice
1 teaspoon curry paste
1 teaspoon chopped fresh dill or
   parsley
generous pinch white pepper
2 tablespoons single cream

Place frozen shrimps in a bowl,
cover and leave to thaw. Drain
canned shrimps. Rinse the
thawed or canned shrimps in
cold water and drain.

Heat the stock gently in a
pan with the wine and season
with salt and pepper. Pour
2 tablespoons of the hot liquid
into a bowl and stand in a pan

of hot water. Sprinkle with
the gelatine and stir until the
gelatine has dissolved, then
return to the stock. Pour a thin
layer of the gelatine liquid into
a 1.15-litre/2-pint ring mould.
Place the mould in the
refrigerator to set.

Wash and chop the dill or
parsley. Place alternate layers
of dill or parsley and shrimps
in the mould, pouring gelatine
liquid between the layers and
allowing each layer to set in
the refrigerator or freezer
before adding another. When
the layers are complete, stand
the mould in the refrigerator
for 2–4 hours until completely
set.

Before serving, dip the
mould into hot water for a few
seconds, then turn out onto a
plate. Beat the mayonnaise
with the lemon juice, curry
paste, chopped dill or parsley,
pepper and cream, and serve
with the aspic. *Serves 4*

Tomato and Fish Mould

1 small onion, peeled
2 tablespoons lemon juice
½ teaspoon salt
4 white peppercorns
1 small bay leaf
225 g/8 oz white fish fillets
175 ml/6 fl oz tomato juice
75 ml/3 fl oz white wine
2 teaspoons vinegar
¼ teaspoon each celery salt and
   dried tarragon
¼ teaspoon paprika pepper
15 g/½ oz gelatine
50 g/2 oz peas, cooked
GARNISH
lettuce, lemon slices, dill

Bring 450 ml/¾ pint water to
the boil in a pan with the
onion, lemon juice, salt,
peppercorns and bay leaf. Add
the fish and poach gently for
10 minutes. Remove from the
heat and allow the fish to cool

in the water. Then take it out
and cut into large chunks,
trimming away any skin and
bones. Strain the liquid,
measure out 75 ml/6 fl oz and
pour this back into the pan.
Add the tomato juice, wine,
vinegar, celery salt, tarragon
and paprika and heat, but
do not allow to boil. Pour
2 tablespoons warm water into
a bowl, and stand in a pan of
hot water. Sprinkle with the
gelatine, stir until dissolved,
then add to the hot stock. Pour
a thin layer of the gelatine
liquid into a 600-ml/1-pint fish
mould and place in the
refrigerator until set. Fill the
mould with alternate layers of
fish and peas, pouring gelatine
liquid between the layers and
allowing each layer to set
before adding another. Finally
place the mould in the
refrigerator to set completely.
Before serving, turn out onto a
plate and garnish with lemon,
lettuce and dill. *Serves 4*

Seafood in Aspic

Salmon in Riesling

10 peppercorns
juice of 1 lemon
4 (150-g/5-oz) fresh salmon
   cutlets
450 g/1 lb fresh or canned
   asparagus
25 g/1 oz gelatine
20 g/¾ oz truffles (optional)
6 small tomatoes
1 egg white, whisked
500 ml/17 fl oz dry Riesling

Bring 750 ml/1¼ pints salted water to the boil in a pan with the peppercorns and lemon juice. Add the salmon cutlets and poach very gently for 10 minutes. Remove the salmon from the water, dry and wrap in cooking foil.

   Lightly scrape the lower stems of the fresh asparagus; cut into 2-cm/1-inch lengths. Simmer in the salmon stock until the asparagus is soft.

Lift out of the stock, drain and allow to cool. Drain the canned asparagus, if used. Unwrap the salmon cutlets, place each on a plate and sprinkle with asparagus and chopped truffle, if used. Cut the tomatoes in half and place three halves on each plate. Clarify the salmon stock with the whisked egg white by bringing the stock to the boil, adding the egg white and simmering for 2 minutes. Take off the heat and leave to stand until the egg white gathers on top of the stock. Strain through a piece of clean muslin or a sieve lined with a treble thickness of absorbent kitchen paper. Measure out 750 ml/ 8 fl oz of stock into a bowl and stand in a pan of hot water. Sprinkle with the gelatine and stir until dissolved. Add the wine and pour the gelatine liquid into the individual soup plates. Place in the refrigerator until set. *Serves 4*

Haddock Mould

450 g/1 lb white fish (coley,
   whiting) and fish trimmings
¼ teaspoon salt
juice of 1½ lemons
a selection of fresh vegetables in
   season, chopped
800 g/1¾ lbs haddock fillet
1 (177-g/6¼-oz) can shrimps
3 hard-boiled eggs
200 g/7 oz carrots
150 g/5 oz cooked peas
1 egg white, whisked
100 ml/4 fl oz dry white wine
20 g/¾ oz gelatine
few dill or parsley sprigs

For the stock, place the white fish and the fish trimmings in a large pan and cover with 2 litres/3½ pints water. Add the salt, half the lemon juice, and chopped vegetables and simmer for 20-30 minutes.

   Sprinkle the haddock with the remaining lemon juice and poach in 1 litre/1¾ pints salted water for 10 minutes. Drain the haddock and leave to cool, then remove the skin and cut the fish into large pieces.

   Rinse the shrimps and dry. Shell the eggs and cut each into six wedges. Cut the carrots into fine strips, blanch in a little boiling water for 2 minutes, then drain. Mix together the haddock, shrimps, egg, peas and carrots and divide between four soup plates. Strain the fish stock, clarify with the egg white (see Salmon in Riesling) and strain again, then boil until reduced to 750 ml/1¼ pints. Take the pan off the heat and pour in the wine. Pour 2 tablespoons warm water into a bowl and stand in a pan of hot water. Sprinkle with the gelatine and stir until dissolved, then add to the stock. Pour the liquid into the four soup plates and place in the refrigerator to set. Garnish with dill or parsley. *Serves 4*

91

Chicken and Vegetable Mould

1 onion
2 large raw carrots
1 (1.25-kg/2½-lb) boiling
    chicken
1 teaspoon salt
20 g/¾ oz gelatine
2 tablespoons vinegar
¼ teaspoon Worcestershire
    sauce
pinch pepper
100 g/4 oz canned asparagus
    tips
50 g/2 oz canned sliced
    mushrooms
2 hard-boiled eggs
2 tomatoes
1 large cooked carrot
1 large gherkin
150 g/5 oz peas, cooked

Peel the onion and cut it in half. Wash and trim the carrots. Place the chicken in a large saucepan, cover with water and add the onion halves, carrots and salt. Bring to the boil, cover and simmer for an hour. Remove the chicken, strain the stock and leave both to cool.

Reheat 1 litre/1¾ pints chicken stock, but do not allow to boil. Pour 2 tablespoons of the hot stock in a bowl and stand in a pan of hot water. Sprinkle with the gelatine and stir until dissolved, then return to the rest of the stock. Add the vinegar, Worcestershire sauce and pepper. Rinse out a 1.15-litre/2-pint soufflé or gratin dish with a little of the gelatine liquid and place in the refrigerator to set.

Remove the skin and bones from the chicken and cut the meat into small pieces. Drain the asparagus tips and sliced mushrooms. Shell and slice the eggs. Wash, dry and slice the tomatoes, together with the cooked carrot and the gherkin. Mix all the ingredients together, add the cooked peas and place in the dish on top of the layer of jelly. Pour over the remaining jelly and leave to set in the refrigerator. *Serves 4–6*

Ham and Vegetable Mould

*275 g/10 oz frozen mixed
   vegetables*
3–4 large carrots
1 tablespoon bone marrow jelly
*generous pinch each salt and
   grated nutmeg*
20 g/¾ oz gelatine
*250 ml/8 fl oz fat-free meat
   stock*
250 ml/8 fl oz white wine
3 tablespoons vinegar
1 hard-boiled egg, sliced
few chives and celery leaves
225 g/8 oz sliced ham

Bring 450 ml/¾ pint salted
water to the boil in a pan, add
the frozen vegetables and cook
for 12 minutes. Remove the
vegetables from the water and
allow to cool.

Wash, trim and peel the
carrots, place together with the
bone marrow jelly in the
vegetable water and simmer
for 20 minutes. Drain the
carrots, blend in the liquidiser
and season with the salt and
nutmeg. Heat the carrot purée
gently and sprinkle with a
quarter of the gelatine, stirring
until the gelatine has dissolved.

Heat the meat stock, wine,
and vinegar together in a pan.
Pour 2 tablespoons of the hot
liquid in a bowl and stand in a
pan of hot water. Sprinkle
with the remaining gelatine,
stir until dissolved and return
to the rest of the stock. Line a
1.15-litre/2-pint mould with
a thin layer of the meat aspic
and allow to set. Arrange the
egg slices, chives and celery
leaves on top. Pour over
another layer of aspic and
leave to set. Spread this layer
with the carrot purée and allow
to set. Build up the rest of the
mould in layers of mixed
vegetables and slices of ham,
pouring aspic between the
layers and allowing each layer
to set before adding the next.
Place the finished aspic in the
refrigerator to set completely.

Prawns in Aspic

350 g/12 oz frozen or canned
    prawns
1 tablespoon lemon juice
1 small cauliflower
175 g/6 oz frozen peas
175 g/6 oz frozen carrots
550 ml/18 fl oz fat-free stock
25 g/1 oz gelatine
450 ml/¾ pint white wine
generous pinch each salt, white
    pepper, sugar and cayenne
    pepper
1 (312-g/11-oz) can sweet corn
200 g/7 oz canned asparagus
    tips
lettuce leaves

Place the frozen prawns, if used, in a bowl, sprinkle with lemon juice, cover and leave to thaw for 1 hour at room temperature. Drain canned prawns, rinse in cold water and allow to dry. Wash the cauliflower and break into florets, trimming off any excess stalk. Place the florets in a steamer. Bring some unsalted water to the boil in a pan, place the steamer over the boiling water, cover and steam the cauliflower for 10–15 minutes. Remove the steamer, plunge into cold water and drain the cauliflower. Leave to cool. Bring 250 ml/8 fl oz salted water to the boil in another pan. Add the frozen peas and carrots, cover and simmer over a low heat for 8 minutes. Then turn the peas and carrots out into a sieve, plunge into cold water, drain and leave to cool.

Heat 4 tablespoons of the stock, pour into a large bowl and stand in a pan of boiling water. Sprinkle with the gelatine and stir until the gelatine has dissolved. Add the remaining stock, the white wine, salt, pepper, sugar and cayenne. Taste and adjust seasoning, adding a few drops lemon juice if liked. Rinse out a 1.4-litre/2½-pint ring mould with cold water and fill with gelatine liquid up to 1 cm/½ inch high. Place the mould in the refrigerator until set. Drain the sweet corn and asparagus tips, and mix with the cauliflower, peas and carrots. Take the mould out of the refrigerator and fill with alternate spoonfuls of prawns and vegetables. Pour some gelatine liquid into the mould in between spoonfuls and return to the refrigerator each time until set. Continue this process until the mould is full, then place it in the refrigerator for a few hours and allow to set completely.

Just before serving, wash the lettuce, drain thoroughly and use to cover a flat dish. Stand the mould in hot water for a few seconds, then turn the aspic out onto the lettuce.

Cook's Tip
For full instructions on making and using an aspic see page 201.

94

Summer Salad Mould

8 white peppercorns
large bunch fresh mixed herbs
(parsley, sage, chervil,
tarragon, thyme)
small bunch dill or chives
bunch parsley
1 small cauliflower
225 g/8 oz frozen peas
25 g/1 oz gelatine
450 ml/¾ pint white wine
generous pinch each salt, white
pepper and sugar
few drops lemon juice
2 hard-boiled eggs
½ red or yellow pepper
few mint sprigs

Bring 250 ml/8 fl oz salted
water to the boil in a pan and
add the peppercorns. Wash
and dry all the herbs. Place the
mixed herbs in the boiling
water, cover the pan, and
simmer over a low heat for

10 minutes. Strain the liquid
and transfer to another pan.
Wash the cauliflower and
break into florets, cutting off
any excess stalk. Place the
florets in the herb stock, cover
and simmer over a low heat for
15 minutes. Take the florets
out of the pan, plunge into
cold water, drain and cool.

Place the peas in the stock,
cover and cook over a low
heat for about 3 minutes.
Remove from the pan, plunge
into cold water, drain and
leave to cool. Take the pan off
the heat, sprinkle with the
gelatine and stir until
thoroughly dissolved. Add
enough white wine to make the
stock up to 750 ml/1¾ pints,
topping up with water if
necessary. Season with the salt,
pepper, sugar and lemon juice
and leave to cool.

Rinse out a 1.4-litre/2½-pint
jelly mould with cold water
and pour 'aspic' into it up to
5 mm/¼ inch high. Place in the

refrigerator to set. Shell and
slice the eggs. Wash the
pepper, remove the seeds and
cut into thin strips. Finely
chop all but a few of the
chives, if used. Arrange the
egg, strips of pepper, dill sprigs
or chopped chives on top of
the mould, keeping back a few
dill sprigs or chives for the
garnish. Pour over a little more
'aspic' and return to the
refrigerator to set, then add
half the peas followed by all
the cauliflower. Cover with
more 'aspic' and return to the
refrigerator to set. Remove the
parsley sprigs from the stems,
keeping a few sprigs on one
side for the garnish. Place the
parsley on top of the
cauliflower layer, top with the
remaining peas and pour on
the remaining gelatine liquid.
Return to the refrigerator for
3-4 hours to set completely.
Before serving, loosen the
edges with a sharp knife. Dip
the mould in hot water for a

few seconds and turn out the
salad mould onto a plate.
Garnish with the remaining
parsley, dill or chives, and the
mint sprigs.

Stuffed Eggs

Party Eggs

10 hard-boiled eggs

Fillings for 4 egg halves at a time:

*2 tablespoons full fat cream
     cheese
1 tablespoon chopped fresh
     mixed herbs
2 tablespoons milk
pinch salt*

*2 tablespoons cottage cheese
1 tablespoon finely grated
     carrot
1 teaspoon ground hazelnuts
pinch each salt and pepper*

*2 tablespoons full fat cream
     cheese
1 teaspoon mild curry powder
1 teaspoon crushed avocado
1 teaspoon lemon juice
1 tablespoon milk
pinch salt*

*2 tablespoons curd cheese
1 teaspoon chopped fresh dill or
     parsley
grated lemon rind
pinch salt*

*2 tablespoons curd cheese
1 tablespoon tomato purée
½ teaspoon paprika pepper
pinch salt*

SUGGESTED GARNISHES
*canned baby sweet corn cobs
     and pickled green
     peppercorns
chillies and parsley
black olives and parsley
rolled anchovies, diced tomato
     and capers
sliced kiwi fruit and maraschino
     cherries
sliced lemon, prawns, and dill or
     parsley
smoked salmon rolls and dill or
     parsley
lumpfish roe and mustard and
     cress
gherkins and sliced mild chillies
stuffed olives and mustard and
     cress*

Shell the eggs and halve
lengthways. Take out the
yolks, mix four yolk halves at a
time with one of the suggested
sets of ingredients for the
fillings, and spoon or pipe the
different fillings into the egg
whites. Garnish as shown.
(A choice of two garnishes is
shown for each of the four
basic fillings.)

Piquant Eggs with Bean Salad

FOR THE EGGS
4 hard-boiled eggs
2 tablespoons mayonnaise
50 g/2 oz soft butter
*salt and freshly ground black
    pepper*
1 tablespoon brandy
*1 teaspoon pickled green
    peppercorns (optional)*
FOR THE SALAD
225 g/8 oz young French beans
3 tablespoons oil
225 g/8 oz calf's liver
2 shallots
small bunch parsley
1 tablespoon tarragon vinegar
GARNISH
sprig corn salad or watercress

Shell the eggs and cut in half
widthways. Take out the yolks,
pass through a sieve and beat
with the mayonnaise, butter,
salt, pepper and brandy.

Transfer the mixture to a
piping bag fitted with a star-
shaped nozzle and pipe the
filling into the egg whites.
Garnish with the pickled green
peppercorns, if used.
　To make the salad, trim and
wash the beans, and place in
boiling salted water. Cover and
simmer for 10 minutes, then
drain and leave to cool. Heat
1 tablespoon oil in a pan. Slice
the liver into thin strips and fry
in the oil for 2-3 minutes. Peel
and finely chop the shallots.
Wash, dry and chop the
parsley. Beat the remaining oil
with the vinegar, shallot and
parsley and season to taste.
Place the beans and liver
together in the centre of a
serving platter, sprinkle with
salad dressing and arrange the
eggs all round. Wash the corn
salad or watercress sprig,
shake dry and use to garnish
the platter.

Party Egg Platter

10 hard-boiled eggs
6 tablespoons mayonnaise
salt and pepper
1 tablespoon chopped parsley
juice of ½ lemon
2 tablespoons oil
SUGGESTED GARNISHES
*few lettuce leaves, sprigs of corn
salad or watercress, small
onion rings, anchovy fillets,
ham slices, smoked salmon
slices, prawns, bottled or
canned mussels, olives, sliced
cooked carrot, sliced
radishes, capers, pickled
green peppercorns, chillies,
canned baby sweet corn cobs,
lemon slices, parsley and dill*

Shell the eggs and halve
lengthways. Remove the yolks,
pass through a sieve and beat
with the mayonnaise, salt and
pepper. Divide the mixture in
half and stir the chopped
parsley into one of the

portions. Place the portions
separately into piping bags
fitted with star-shaped nozzles,
and fill ten egg whites with
plain mayonnaise and the
other ten with the parsley
mayonnaise. Arrange the eggs
on a serving platter and
garnish with any of the
suggested toppings, as shown
in the photograph.
　Tear the lettuce leaves into
strips and place in a bowl with
any left-over garnishes. Beat
the lemon juice with the oil,
season to taste and stir into the
salad ingredients. Arrange the
salad in the centre of the
platter.

Egg Specialities

Hard-boiled Eggs with Sauces

Allow two eggs per person

Russian sauce
1 red pepper
1 green pepper
1 yellow pepper
large bunch chives
1½ (142-ml/5-fl oz) cartons soured cream
1 teaspoon paprika pepper
dash Tabasco sauce
1 teaspoon horseradish sauce
1 (58-g/2-oz) jar lumpfish roe

Wash, dry and halve the peppers, remove the seeds and pith, and dice. Wash the chives and chop finely. Mix the soured cream with the diced pepper, chives, paprika, Tabasco, horseradish sauce and half the lumpfish roe. Spoon the remaining lumpfish roe on top.

Mushroom sauce
225 g/8 oz mushrooms
2 leeks
2 onions
100 g/4 oz streaky bacon
15 g/½ oz butter

Clean, trim and slice the mushrooms. Wash and slice the leeks. Peel and finely dice the onions. Remove the rinds from the bacon rashers, cut the bacon into pieces and fry until the fat runs. Add the butter, leek and onion and cook for 4-5 minutes. Lastly add the mushroom and continue cooking for 6 minutes. Cool and serve.

Cheese sauce
100 g/4 oz cottage cheese
50 g/2 oz Stilton cheese
juice of 1 lemon
salt
1 teaspoon red currants or cranberry sauce (optional)

Sieve the cottage cheese and

Stilton into a bowl and beat with the lemon juice until creamy. Season to taste with salt and serve garnished with red currants or cranberry sauce, if liked.

Capri Sauce
large bunch fresh mixed herbs
2 canned anchovy fillets
1 tablespoon capers
10 stuffed olives
2 egg yolks
1 teaspoon strong mustard
3 tablespoons wine vinegar
salt and pepper
6 tablespoons oil
2 tomatoes

Wash and drain the herbs and chop finely, together with the anchovy fillets, capers and olives. Beat the egg yolks with the mustard, vinegar, salt and pepper. Gradually beat in the oil, a few drops at a time, and finally stir in the chopped ingredients. Peel, quarter and

chop the tomatoes and mix into the sauce.

Cook's Tip

Cottage Cheese with Herbs spread and Cottage Cheese Salad spread (see page 23) also make delicious sauces to go with eggs, and are illustrated above.

Egg Tartlets with Liver Pâté

4 hard-boiled eggs
bunch fresh mixed herbs (sage, parsley, dill, chives, lovage), or 2 teaspoons dried mixed herbs
50 g/2 oz soft butter
2 tablespoons mild French mustard
salt and pepper
8 small savoury pastry tartlet cases (bought ready-made)
100 g/4 oz smooth liver pâté
GARNISH
2 slices canned truffles (optional)
8 small sprigs dill (optional)

Shell the eggs, slice in half widthways and take out the yolks. Place the yolks in a bowl. Wash, drain and finely chop the fresh herbs, if used. Beat the egg yolks with the butter, mustard, salt, pepper and herbs until smooth and creamy, transfer to a piping bag fitted with a star-shaped nozzle and pipe the mixture into the tartlet cases. Place one egg white half in the centre of each. Beat the liver pâté until light and fluffy and spoon it into the egg whites. Finely dice the truffles, if used, and sprinkle over the pâté. Garnish each tart with a sprig of dill, if liked. *Serves 8*

Egg Tartlets with Ham Salad

225 g/8 oz cooked ham
1 crisp dessert apple
1 banana
2 teaspoons lemon juice
3 tablespoons mayonnaise
2 tablespoons single cream
2-3 teaspoons mild curry powder
pinch each salt and sugar
8 small savoury pastry tartlet cases (bought ready-made)
4 hard-boiled eggs
4 slices smoked salmon
few tarragon leaves (optional)

Finely dice the ham. Peel and halve the apple, remove the core and cut the flesh into strips. Peel and dice the banana and mix the ham, apple and banana together in a bowl. Sprinkle with 1 teaspoon lemon juice.

Beat the mayonnaise with the cream, the remaining lemon juice, the curry powder, salt and sugar, taste and adjust seasoning. Mix the dressing into the salad ingredients, and spoon the salad into the tartlet cases. Shell the eggs, halve lengthways and place one half on top of each tartlet. Cut the slices of smoked salmon in half lengthways and roll up. Top each egg half with a roll of salmon, and garnish with the tarragon leaves, if used. *Makes 8*

Egg Specialities

Pickled Eggs

450-600 ml/¾-1 pint vinegar
1 teaspoon mustard seeds
1 teaspoon black peppercorns
3 cloves
1 stick cinnamon
2 bay leaves
12 small hard-boiled eggs

Pour the vinegar into a pan
with the mustard seeds,
peppercorns, cloves, cinnamon
and bay leaves, and bring to
the boil. Cover and simmer
over a low heat for 10 minutes.
Shell the eggs and place in a
tall screwtop jar. Take the pan
off the heat, allow to stand for
a few moments, then pour the
juice over the eggs and leave to
cool. Cover the jar with a piece
of cling-film, held in place with
an elastic band, and seal. Place
in the refrigerator and allow to
marinate for 2-3 days. By this
time the eggs will have
absorbed the taste of the
marinade and will be delicious
sliced in sandwiches, or
served with a sauce (see page
98).

Cook's Tip
Only very fresh eggs
should be pickled. Do
not attempt this recipe
unless you are sure the
eggs you are using are
no more than a week
old.

Eggs in Brine with Tomato Chutney

CHUTNEY
450 g/1 lb tomatoes
2 medium red peppers
3 onions
150 ml/¼ pint red wine vinegar
175 g/6 oz brown sugar
¾ teaspoon salt
1 teaspoon mild French mustard
1 teaspoon ground allspice
½ teaspoon paprika pepper
EGGS
3 tablespoons salt
12 eggs

Peel and quarter the tomatoes. Wash the peppers, slice them in half, remove the seeds and pith, and chop the flesh. Peel and dice the onions. Place the vegetables in a pan with the vinegar, bring to the boil and simmer gently over a low heat until the mixture is pulpy and nearly all the liquid has evaporated. Stir in the sugar, salt, mustard, allspice and paprika, and cook the chutney over a high flame, stirring continuously, for a further 8 minutes. Rinse out two 450-g/1-lb jam jars in boiling water, dry well and pour in the chutney. Cover each jar with a preserving pot cover or a piece of cellophane, held in place with a rubber band.

Bring 1.25 litres/2¼ pints water to the boil in a large pan with the salt, carefully add the eggs and boil for 10-12 minutes. Remove the eggs from the salt water, plunge into cold water and drain. Lightly tap the shells. Leave the salt water to cool. Place the eggs in a large jar and pour over the cooled brine, cover and leave to stand in the refrigerator for 2-3 days. Serve the eggs with the chutney.

Eggs with Orange Chutney

CHUTNEY
450 g/1 lb cooking apples
2 oranges
100 g/4 oz raisins
225 g/8 oz brown sugar
¼ teaspoon salt
1 teaspoon ground ginger
¼ teaspoon ground nutmeg
150 ml/¼ pint red wine vinegar
100 g/4 oz cranberry sauce
EGGS
8 eggs
40 g/1¾ oz tea
1 tablespoon salt
1 tablespoon ground mixed spices

Peel, core and dice the apples. Finely grate the orange rind. Peel the oranges and finely slice, removing the pips. Place the fruit and orange rind in a pan with the raisins, sugar, salt, ginger, nutmeg and vinegar, bring to the boil and simmer over a low heat, stirring frequently, for 20-30 minutes until reduced to a pulp. Stir in the cranberry sauce. Rinse out two 450-g/1-lb jam jars with boiling water, dry well and fill with the hot chutney. Cover each jar as for the previous recipe.

Simmer the eggs in boiling salted water for 12 minutes. Drain the eggs, plunge briefly into cold water, then place on a wooden board. Roll the eggs over the board until the shells have cracked all over. Bring 1 litre/1¾ pints fresh water to the boil in a pan and add the tea, salt and spices. Place the eggs in the water, cover the pan and simmer over a low heat for a further 10 minutes until all the eggs have turned brown. Take the pan off the heat and leave the eggs to stand in the water for 30 minutes. Drain, allow to dry and serve with the chutney.

Stuffed Vegetables

Stuffed Cucumber

1 large cucumber
175 g/6 oz canned golden plums
¾ root celeriac
1 large red dessert apple
*225 g/8 oz freshly cooked or
    canned asparagus tips*
1 small lettuce
3 tablespoons mayonnaise
3 tablespoons natural yogurt
1 teaspoon lemon juice
¾ teaspoon salt
pinch sugar

Wash and dry the cucumber
and cut out a wedge running
down the centre lengthways,
leaving a gap measuring a third
of the whole cucumber. Scoop
the seeds out of both parts and
discard. Take out the
cucumber flesh and cut into
pieces. Drain, halve and stone
the plums. Peel and wash the
celeriac, and dice as finely as
possible. Wash, quarter, core
and dice the apple. Drain the
canned asparagus tips, if used.
Wash the lettuce, separate the
leaves and allow to dry. Mix
the cucumber, plums, celeriac,
apple and canned or fresh
asparagus tips together in a
bowl. Beat the mayonnaise
with the yogurt, lemon juice,
salt and sugar and stir the
dressing into the salad
ingredients. Line the hollowed
out cucumber with lettuce and
arrange the salad inside.

Chicken Salad Tomatoes

100 g/4 oz frozen or canned
prawns
8 tomatoes
salt and white pepper
1 fresh peach or 2 canned peach
halves
1 roast chicken breast
2 tablespoons mayonnaise
1 tablespoon soured cream
1 tablespoon tomato purée
dash Worcestershire sauce
pinch cayenne pepper
1 teaspoon brandy

Place frozen prawns, if used, in a dish, cover and leave to thaw, then drain. Rinse through canned prawns with cold water and leave to dry. Wash and dry the tomatoes and cut a third off the bottom of each to make a lid. Scoop the seeds out of the tomatoes with a teaspoon and discard.

Sprinkle the insides of the shells with salt and pepper. Peel, halve and stone the fresh peach, if used. Drain canned peach halves, and dice the fresh or canned peach. Remove any skin from the chicken breast and chop the meat into small pieces. Mix the peach, chicken and prawns together in a bowl.

Beat the mayonnaise with the soured cream, tomato purée, Worcestershire sauce, cayenne and brandy and stir into the mixed ingredients. Cover and leave to stand at room temperature for 15 minutes, then fill the tomatoes with the mixture and place the lids on top. *Makes 8*

Cheese and Peppers on Tomato

2 medium green peppers
175 g/6 oz full fat cream cheese
or curd cheese
1-2 tablespoons soured cream
salt and white pepper
1 small onion
4 tomatoes
½ teaspoon paprika pepper

Wash and halve the green peppers and remove the seeds and pith. Finely dice two of the halves. Beat the cheese with the soured cream to a smooth, creamy paste, add the diced green pepper and season with salt and white pepper to taste. Fill the two remaining pepper halves with the cheese mixture and place the halves together. Wrap in cling-film and stand in a cool place for 30 minutes.

Peel and finely dice the onion. Wash and dry the tomatoes and cut into thick slices. Place the tomato slices individually on a kitchen board and sprinkle each with salt, pepper and diced onion. Unwrap and separate the pepper halves, cut into slices and place each slice on top of a slice of tomato. Sprinkle with paprika before serving.

103

Avocado with Shrimps

350 g/12 oz frozen shrimps
2 avocados
2 tablespoons lemon juice
3 tablespoons mayonnaise
3 tablespoons single cream
1 tablespoon whisky
salt and white pepper
bunch fresh mixed herbs (dill,
tarragon, salad burnet)
GARNISH
few sprigs dill (optional)

Place the shrimps in a bowl, cover and leave to thaw at room temperature, then drain. Wash, dry and halve the avocados lengthways. Remove the stones and scoop the flesh out of each half to within 1 cm/½ inch of the shell. Brush the avocado halves with a little lemon juice and leave in a cool place.

Finely dice the avocado

flesh, place in a bowl with the shrimps and sprinkle with more lemon juice. Beat the mayonnaise with the cream, whisky, the remaining lemon juice and the salt and pepper. Wash, drain and finely chop the herbs and stir into the mayonnaise sauce. Mix the mayonnaise sauce into the avocado and shrimps, spoon the mixture into the avocado halves and garnish each portion with a sprig of dill, if used. *Serves 4*

Stuffed Aubergines

50 g/2 oz rice
2 aubergines
salt and white pepper
1 shallot
2 tablespoons oil
225 g/8 oz minced beef
¼ teaspoon curry powder
generous pinch garlic salt
½ teaspoon grated lemon rind
1 tablespoon orange juice
GARNISH
fresh mint leaves (optional)

Cook the rice following the instructions on the packet, drain and leave to cool. Wash and dry the aubergines, cut in half lengthways and scoop out the flesh to within 1 cm/½ inch of each shell. Sprinkle the insides with salt and place in an ovenproof dish.

Peel the shallot and chop finely, together with the

aubergine flesh. Heat the oil and fry the shallot and aubergine until soft. Add the minced beef and continue cooking until all the ingredients are cooked through, stirring frequently. Stir in the rice, curry powder, garlic salt, lemon rind, orange juice, and salt and pepper to taste. Cook for a further 1 minute, then transfer the mixture to the aubergine halves. Bake in a moderately hot oven (2000 C, 400 F, Gas Mark 6) for 10-20 minutes. Leave to cool and garnish with mint, if used, before serving. *Serves 4*

Fennel with Blue Cheese Dressing

2 heads fennel
1 tablespoon lemon juice
bunch dill
1 tablespoon capers
2 tomatoes
50 g/2 oz soft blue cheese
*   (Roquefort, Dolcelatte)*
100 g/4 oz cottage cheese
3 tablespoons double cream
salt and black pepper
pinch garlic salt
dash vinegar

Wash and trim the fennel,
keeping the tender leaf shoots
on one side. Bring 250 ml/
8 fl oz salted water to the boil
in a pan with the lemon juice.
Place the fennel in the pan,
cover and simmer for
15 minutes, then drain and
leave to cool.

Wash the dill and chop
finely, together with the fennel

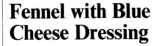

leaves. Drain and chop the
capers. Peel and halve the
tomatoes, remove the seeds
and dice the flesh. Crumble the
blue cheese into a bowl. Pass
the cottage cheese through a
sieve and add to the blue
cheese, followed by the cream,
salt, pepper, garlic salt,
vinegar, chopped capers, dill
and fennel leaves. Blend all the
ingredients well together.

Place the fennel flat on a
kitchen board, and slice each
in half horizontally along the
length of the head. Top each
half with blue cheese cream
and garnish with diced tomato.
Serves 4

Stuffed Artichokes

8 canned artichoke bottoms
1 (198-g/7-oz) can tuna
2 hard-boiled eggs
3 tablespoons mayonnaise
salt and pepper
few drops lemon juice
generous pinch cayenne pepper
1 (142-g/5-oz) can prawns
few lettuce leaves
GARNISH
1 (58-g/2-oz) jar lumpfish roe
few small lemon slices

Drain the artichoke bottoms
and tuna. Shell and finely dice
the eggs. Work the egg into the
tuna with a fork, or blend
together in the liquidiser.
Gradually add the mayonnaise
and season with salt, pepper,
lemon juice and cayenne.

Drain the prawns, rinse
through with cold water and
leave to dry. Wash the lettuce,

drain thoroughly and use to
line a flat serving dish. Arrange
the artichoke bottoms on the
bed of lettuce, and spoon the
tuna mayonnaise into the
centre of each. Top the
artichokes with the prawns and
garnish each with a lemon slice
and some lumpfish roe.
Makes 8

Stuffed Leeks

2 large leeks
1 tablespoon lemon juice
2 hard-boiled eggs
5 canned anchovy fillets
50 g/2 oz canned baby sweet
   corn cobs, or canned sweet
   corn
1 tablespoon chopped parsley
3 tablespoons oil
1 tablespoon wine vinegar
pinch salt
dash Tabasco sauce

Wash and trim the leeks and
slice each into two 10-cm/
4-inch lengths. Bring 450 ml/
¾ pint salted water to the boil
in a pan and blanch the leeks
for 10 minutes. Remove from
the pan, plunge into cold water
and drain thoroughly. Leave to
cool.

Slice the leek pieces in half
lengthways and sprinkle with
the lemon juice. Cut a 1-cm/
½-inch strip off the end of each

leek piece and finely slice the
strips. Shell and dice the eggs.
Rinse the anchovy fillets in
cold water, allow to dry and
dice finely. Drain the sweet
corn cobs, or sweet corn, and
cut the cobs, if used, into thin
slices. Mix the strips of leek,
diced egg, anchovy, sweet corn
and parsley together in a bowl.
Beat the oil with the vinegar,
salt and Tabasco and pour
over the salad ingredients.
Cover and leave to stand at
room temperature for 10
minutes, then divide the salad
between the leek halves.
Makes 8

Carrot Boats

4 large carrots
¼ teaspoon salt
½ teaspoon sugar
1 tablespoon lemon juice
2 large crisp dessert apples
10 baby gherkins
225 g/8 oz ham
small bunch parsley
4 tablespoons soured cream
4 tablespoons mayonnaise

Wash the carrots, peel thinly
and cut in half lengthways.
Bring 750 ml/1¼ pints water to
the boil in a pan with the salt
and sugar, add the carrot
halves and simmer over a low
heat for 15-20 minutes. Drain
the carrots, plunge into cold
water and leave to dry.
Carefully hollow out a channel
along each carrot half with a
teaspoon, dice the scooped out
flesh and place in a bowl.
Sprinkle the carrot halves with
lemon juice.

Wash, quarter, core and
finely dice the apples. Drain
the gherkins and chop as finely
as possible, together with the
ham. Wash, drain and chop
the parsley. Mix the apple,
ham, gherkin and parsley with
the diced carrot, fill each carrot
half with the salad and leave to
stand in the refrigerator for
10-15 minutes.

Whip the soured cream with
the mayonnaise, season to
taste and serve separately with
the carrot boats. *Makes 8*

Stuffed Chicory

2 large heads chicory
1¼ tablespoons lemon juice
2 fresh mandarins, or 2
*   tablespoons canned mandarin*
*   segments*
10 stuffed olives
4 tomatoes
salt and black pepper
generous pinch sugar
2 tablespoons oil

Wash the chicory, discard any damaged outer leaves and trim the stalks. Slice the chicory heads in half lengthways and leave to drain, then sprinkle the inside of each half with a little lemon juice. Peel the fresh mandarins, if used, divide into segments, and remove the skin from the segments. Drain canned mandarins. Slice the olives. Peel and quarter the tomatoes, scoop out the seeds and finely dice the flesh. Mix the mandarin, olive slices and tomato together in a bowl.
Beat the remaining lemon juice with the salt, pepper, sugar and oil and pour over the mixed ingredients. Cover and leave to stand at room temperature for 10 minutes, then arrange the filling in the chicory halves. *Makes 4*

Celery Rolls

4 sticks celery
225 g/8 oz full fat cream cheese
*   or curd cheese*
3 tablespoons single cream
1 tablespoon brandy
1 teaspoon paprika pepper
pinch celery salt
generous pinch each white
*   pepper and ground ginger*
GARNISH
2 baby gherkins
4-8 chillies

Wash and trim the celery and cut each stick to 7.5 cm/ 3 inches in length. Beat the cheese with the cream, brandy, paprika, celery salt, pepper and ginger, transfer to a piping bag fitted with a small star-shaped nozzle and pipe the mixture into the sticks of celery. Drain and slice the gherkins and arrange on the celery rolls, together with the chillies. Cover with cling-film and leave in a cool place for 15-20 minutes. *Makes 4*

Cook's Tip

You can serve celery rolls as a starter, as cocktail canapés, or with wine and cheese after dinner. If you are serving them as canapés, make them half the length as they will then be easier to eat.

Classic Oysters

For each:
12–16 oysters
2–3 wedges lemon

Clean the oysters under cold
running water and dry them.
Hold one oyster at a time in a
damp cloth with the domed
side of the shell in the palm of
your hand and, with a sharp
movement of the oyster opener
or a strong knife, open the
pointed edge or 'hinge' of the
oyster. Make sure that any sea
water trapped inside the shell
does not escape, as this adds to
the flavour. With a kitchen
knife, loosen the muscle all
round the edge inside the shell.
Remove the top half of the
shell, leaving the oyster in the
bottom half, and place all the
half-shells containing oysters
on a dish. If you do not have a
special oyster plate, sprinkle a
layer of rock salt 1 cm/½ inch
thick over an ordinary plate
and arrange the oysters on this.
It will prevent the oysters
tipping and losing any of their
precious liquid. Eat the oysters
directly from the shells,
seasoned to taste with a little
lemon juice or freshly ground
pepper. Serve with fresh white
bread or caraway bread and a
dry white wine.

Mussels with Saffron Sauce

1 onion
1 small leek
250 ml/8 fl oz white wine
250 ml/8 fl oz water
2.25 litres/2 quarts mussels
2 tablespoons olive oil
1 shallot
¼ teaspoon powdered saffron
3 tablespoons single cream
2 lettuce hearts
1 tablespoon lemon juice
GARNISH
1 stick celery
2 teaspoons chopped chives
few tarragon leaves (optional)

Peel and dice the onion. Wash,
trim and cut the leek into fine
strips. Pour the wine and water
into a large pan, add the
chopped vegetables and bring
to the boil. Scrub the mussels
under cold, running water, cut
away the 'beards' and add the
mussels to the boiling liquid.
Cover the pan and simmer
over a high heat for 10 minutes
until all the shells have opened.
Remove the mussels from the
liquid, discarding any that have
not opened fully; drain and
leave to cool. Shell the mussels
and place in an ovenproof bowl.

Strain the mussel juice,
retaining 250 ml/8 fl oz on one
side. Heat the oil in a pan. Peel
and dice the shallot and brown
in the oil. Add the saffron,
cream and mussel juice. Boil
for 1 minute. Pour over the
mussels and leave to cool.

Wash the celery, slice into
thin strips and blanch for
2 minutes in a little boiling
water. Drain and leave to cool.
Place half a lettuce heart on
each of four plates and
sprinkle with the lemon juice.
Arrange the mussel salad
around the lettuce and garnish
each plate with celery, chopped
chives and tarragon, if used.
Serves 4

Mussels with Mayonnaise

1 small onion
1 small leek
250 ml/8 fl oz white wine
250 ml/8 fl oz water
2.5 litres/2 quarts mussels
225 g/8 oz mayonnaise
1 teaspoon lemon juice
pinch each salt, white pepper
  and sugar
3 tablespoons double cream
chopped parsley

Peel and chop the onion. Wash the leek thoroughly, trim and cut into small pieces. Pour the wine and water into a large pan, add the chopped vegetables and bring to the boil. Prepare the mussels and cook in the boiling liquid for 10 minutes (discard any that do not open fully). Then lift out the mussels, drain and leave to cool. Remove the empty mussel shells and arrange the halves containing the flesh on four individual plates.

Continue boiling the mussel juice until it is reduced to about 100 ml/4 fl oz, then strain and allow to cool. Beat the mayonnaise with the mussel juice, lemon juice, salt, pepper and sugar. Whip the cream and fold into the mixture. Spoon the mayonnaise dressing over the plates of mussels, and sprinkle with chopped parsley.
Serves 4

Lobster Tartlets

4 tablespoons mayonnaise
2 tablespoons double cream
few drops lemon juice
pinch each salt and sugar
4 savoury shortcrust pastry tart
  cases (bought ready-made)
350 g/12 oz fresh lobster meat,
  or 1½ (227-g/8-oz) cans
  lobster
100 ml/4 fl oz white wine aspic
  (see page 202)
4 lettuce leaves
4 teaspoons lumpfish roe
GARNISH
few dill sprigs (optional)

Beat the mayonnaise with the cream, lemon juice, salt and sugar and pour into the tart cases. Drain the canned lobster, if used. Slice the lobster meat and arrange over the mayonnaise. Pour the white wine aspic over the tartlets and leave them to set in the refrigerator.

Wash the lettuce, drain thoroughly and arrange on four individual plates. Place the tartlets on the lettuce. Top the aspic on each tartlet with 1 teaspoon lumpfish roe. Garnish with dill, if used.
Serves 4

Scampi with Aniseed Cream

16 fresh or frozen scampi
1 teaspoon aniseed
¼ teaspoon salt
20 ml/1 fl oz Pernod
6 tablespoons clear meat stock
2 teaspoons wine vinegar
2 egg yolks
100 g/4 oz unsalted butter
GARNISH
1 teaspoon pickled red or green
*   peppercorns (optional)*

Rinse fresh scampi in cold running water and leave to drain. Place frozen scampi in a dish, cover and leave to thaw, then drain. Crush a quarter of the aniseed and leave on one side. Bring 450 ml/¾ pint water to the boil in a pan, together with the remaining aniseed and the salt. Add the fresh scampi and simmer over a very low heat for 5 minutes. If frozen scampi are used, place in the boiling water, remove the pan immediately from the heat and leave to stand for 5 minutes. Drain the scampi in a sieve and allow to cool, then remove the shells from the fresh scampi.

Bring the Pernod, stock and vinegar to the boil in a pan and simmer until reduced to 40 ml/1½ fl oz (two tablespoons) liquid. Leave to cool. Beat the egg yolks into the cooled liquid. Reheat the pan over a very low heat and gradually stir in the butter to form a thick cream. Stir in the crushed aniseed. Taste and adjust seasoning. Crush some ice cubes, place on a large dish and arrange the scampi on top. Sprinkle the aniseed cream with red or green peppercorns, if used, and serve separately.
Serves 4

Marinated Dublin Bay Prawns with Sole Fillets

675 g/1½ lb sole fillet
1–2 tablespoons flour
1 tablespoon cooking oil
1 tablespoon currants
2 onions
4 tablespoons olive oil
250 ml/8 fl oz white wine vinegar
1 bay leaf
salt and pepper
25 g/1 oz pine kernels or flaked
*   almonds*
8 cooked Dublin Bay prawns

Wash and dry the sole fillet, cut into four portions and dip each in flour. Heat the cooking oil and fry the sole until golden brown on both sides. Drain on absorbent kitchen paper.

Soak the currants in lukewarm water. Peel the onions and cut into rings. Heat the olive oil and fry the onion rings until golden brown. Add the vinegar and bay leaf, and season with salt and pepper. Bring to the boil and simmer gently for 2 minutes. Drain the currants. Place the sole fillets, pine kernels or almonds, currants and prawns together in a bowl. Take the oil and vinegar marinade off the heat, allow to cool slightly and pour over the fish mixture. Leave to stand in the refrigerator for 5–6 hours. Then strain the marinade, arrange the prawns and sole mixture on a flat dish, and sprinkle with a little of the marinade before serving.
Serves 4

Fish Mousse with Shrimps

*250 ml/8 fl oz white wine aspic
  (see page 234)*
*100 g/4 oz steamed white fish
  (pike, whiting, haddock)*
100 ml/4 fl oz white sauce
pinch each salt and white pepper
5 tablespoons hot meat stock
7 g/¼ oz gelatine
100 ml/4 fl oz double cream
1 (198-g/7-oz) can shrimps
few lettuce leaves
GARNISH
*few dill or parsley sprigs
  (optional)*

Line four dariole moulds with a thin layer of wine aspic and leave to set. Blend the fish and white sauce together in the liquidiser, strain and season with salt and pepper. Pour the meat stock into a large bowl and stand in a pan of hot water. Sprinkle with the gelatine and stir until dissolved. Whip the cream until stiff and stir into the stock, followed by the fish purée. Spoon the fish mixture into the moulds and stand in the refrigerator until set.

Drain the shrimps, rinse in cold water and leave to dry. Wash the lettuce, allow to dry and divide the leaves between four plates. Dip the moulds into hot water for a few seconds, then turn out the mousses onto the beds of lettuce. Top with the shrimps. Pour the remaining wine aspic over each portion and return the mousses to the refrigerator until the aspic has set. Before serving, wash the dill or parsley, if used, drain thoroughly and garnish each mousse with a sprig. *Serves 4*

Prawn and Mango Cocktail

2 mangoes
1 red pepper
1 (150-g/5-oz) can prawns
2 tablespoons mayonnaise
4 tablespoons cream
1 teaspoon sugar
1 teaspoon lemon juice
*a few pickled green
  peppercorns, or freshly
  ground black pepper*
*1 tablespoon freshly grated
  horseradish, or bottled
  creamed horseradish*
GARNISH
few mint leaves (optional)

Wash and dry the mangoes and cut in half lengthways. Remove the stones. Scoop out the flesh to within 5 mm/¼ inch of the shells and dice finely. Wash and dry the pepper, cut in half and place the halves under the grill until the skin breaks. Peel away the skin, remove the seeds and slice the pepper into thin strips.

Drain the prawns, rinse in cold water and leave to dry. Mix together the mayonnaise, diced mango, cream, sugar, lemon juice, green peppercorns or black pepper, horseradish and prawns. Spoon the cocktail into the mango halves and top with strips of pepper. Garnish with mint leaves, if liked *Serves 4*

Fish Specialities

Gravad Lax

1¼ kg/3 lb fresh salmon
large bunch dill or parsley
1 tablespoon coarse salt, or
  1½ teaspoons table salt
1 teaspoon sugar
2 teaspoons white pepper

Scrape away the scales from
the salmon, slice it in half
lengthways and remove the
centre bone. Rinse and dry
both halves. Place one fillet,
skin-side down, in a large dish.
Wash, drain and coarsely chop
the dill or parsley, and sprinkle
over the salmon fillet. Mix the
salt, sugar and pepper
together. Sprinkle the
seasoning over the fish and top
with the second fillet, skin side
uppermost. Cover the fish with
cooking foil and weight it
down with a kitchen board and
two full preserving jars. Leave
the salmon to marinate in the
refrigerator for 3 days. Turn

the fillets every 12 hours and
baste both sides with the juice
produced by the fish.

To serve, place the salmon
fillets separately on a wooden
board. Scrape away the herbs
and seasoning and cut the fish
into very thin slices. Serve with
wedges of lemon, freshly
toasted white bread and a
green salad. *Serves 6*

Smoked Fish with Gourmet Sauce

½ lettuce
450 g/1 lb sliced smoked fish
150 ml/¼ pint single cream
1 tablespoon freshly grated
  horseradish or 1½ tablespoons
  bottled horseradish
6 tablespoons mayonnaise
¼ teaspoon salt
2 teaspoons sugar
3 tablespoons lemon juice
GARNISH
small bunch parsley
½ lime or lemon

Wash the lettuce, separate the
leaves, and drain thoroughly.
Place the lettuce on a flat
serving dish and arrange the
sliced smoked fish on top.

Beat the cream with the
horseradish, mayonnaise, salt,
sugar and lemon juice until
creamy. Transfer the sauce to a
scallop shell or glass bowl and

place on the serving dish.
Wash and drain the parsley.
Wash the lime or lemon, rub
dry and cut into slices. Garnish
the serving dish with the
parsley and lime or lemon
slices. *Serves 4*

Marinated Plaice Fillets

450 ml/¾ pint dry white wine
100 ml/4 fl oz lemon juice
1 teaspoon salt
1 teaspoon green or black
  peppercorns
3 sage leaves, or a sprinkling
  dried sage
3 bay leaves
800 g/1¾ lb plaice fillets

Bring the white wine, lemon juice, salt, peppercorns, sage and bay leaves to the boil in a pan, remove from the heat and leave to cool. Rinse the plaice fillets in cold water, allow to dry and cut them in half lengthways. Place in a bowl and pour over the cooled liquid. Cover the bowl and leave the plaice to marinate in the refrigerator for 1–2 days.

Remove the fish from the refrigerator 2 hours before serving. Lift the fillets out of the marinade, drain and arrange on a flat dish. Sprinkle with some of the peppercorns and herbs from the marinade. Serve with horseradish and apple cream (see page 172) and freshly toasted white bread. *Serves 4*

Cook's Tip
Sole fillets can be marinated in the same way – but remember that only fresh fish is suitable for marinating. Never use frozen fish.

Trout Fillets with Tomato Sauce

1 kg/2 lb fresh trout fillets
juice of 2 lemons
100 ml/4 fl oz wine vinegar
salt and white pepper
2 shallots
4 tomatoes
1 clove garlic
1 teaspoon oil
⅓ teaspoon dried basil
1 tablespoon tomato purée
100 ml/4 fl oz red wine
pinch sugar
1 teaspoon grated lemon rind
freshly ground black pepper
GARNISH
few lemon slices

Wash and dry the trout fillets and cut into very thin slices with a sharp knife. Arrange the fillets on a flat dish and sprinkle with lemon juice, vinegar, salt and pepper. Cover and leave to marinate in the refrigerator overnight.

Peel and dice the shallots. Cut a cross into the base of each tomato, dip in boiling water for a few seconds and remove the skin. Cut the tomatoes in half, scoop away the seeds and dice the flesh. Peel and crush the garlic clove. Heat the oil in a pan and fry the diced shallots, then add the diced tomato, garlic, basil, tomato purée and red wine. Simmer for 1 minute, stirring continuously. Season the sauce with salt and sugar and allow to cool.

Remove the trout from the marinade and arrange on a serving dish. Sprinkle with grated lemon rind and black pepper, and garnish with slices of lemon. Serve the tomato sauce separately with the trout fillets. *Serves 4*

Fish Specialities

Salmon Trout Niçoise

575 g/1¼ lb fresh cleaned salmon trout
pinch salt and pepper
1 teaspoon kelp (optional)
450 ml/¾ pint white wine
5 peppercorns
250 ml/8 fl oz fish aspic (see page 201)
1 tablespoon chopped parsley
1 slice stuffed olive
1 slice cooked carrot
6 thin round slices truffle, or 3 black grapes
1 hard-boiled egg white
175 ml/6 fl oz single cream
1 teaspoon lemon juice
1 tablespoon chopped fresh mixed herbs, or 1 teaspoon dried mixed herbs

Wash the trout and season with salt and pepper. Bring the kelp, if used, to the boil in a pan with the wine, 250 ml/ 8 fl oz water and the peppercorns. Add the trout and simmer over a low heat for 15 minutes. Lift the fish out of the liquid, cut off the fins and remove the skin. Cover the fish with a damp cloth and leave to stand in a cool place for 1 hour.

Pour a thin layer of fish aspic onto a flat serving dish and leave to set. Arrange the trout on the aspic, cover with more aspic and leave to set. Sprinkle the fish's head with parsley, and place the olive slice on top for the eye. Cut the grapes, if used, in half and remove the pips. Arrange the slice of carrot, and rounds of truffle or grapes on the fish. Cut leaf shapes from the egg white and arrange either side of a parsley stalk. Pour the remaining aspic over the fish and allow to set. Beat the cream with the lemon juice and mixed herbs and serve with the fish.

Trout with Dill

4 (225-g/8-oz) prepared trout
large bunch fresh dill, or 2 tablespoons dried dill
100 ml/4 fl oz wine vinegar
1 lemon
100 ml/4 fl oz dry white wine
pinch salt and sugar
7 g/¼ oz gelatine
1 cooked carrot, sliced
175 ml/6 fl oz single cream
grated rind of 1 lemon
1 teaspoon lemon juice
1 tablespoon dry sherry

Wash the fish and the fresh dill, if used. Place half the dill in the stomach cavities of the fish. Bring 250 ml/8 fl oz salted water to the boil in a large pan, together with the vinegar. Cut the lemon in half, squeeze it and add the juice to the liquid, together with a strip of lemon peel. Add the trout and simmer over a low heat for 10–12 minutes. Drain the fish, remove the skin and leave to cool.

Pour the wine into a bowl, add the salt and sugar and stand in a pan of water over a gentle heat. Sprinkle with the gelatine and stir until the gelatine has dissolved. Finely chop the remaining fresh dill, if used, and add the fresh or dried dill to the liquid. Place the fish on a serving dish and decorate with the carrot slices. Pour the aspic over the fish and leave to set in the refrigerator.

Beat the cream with the grated lemon rind, 1 teaspoon lemon juice and the sherry, and season to taste. Serve the sauce separately with the fish.
Serves 4

Salmon with Vegetable Salad

100 ml/4 fl oz white wine
1 tablespoon vinegar
2 white peppercorns
225 g/8 oz cheap fish pieces
  (coley, whiting)
450 g/1 lb salmon fillet
250 ml/8 fl oz fish aspic (see
  page 201)
450 g/1 lb fresh mixed
  vegetables (peas, carrots,
  celery, French beans)
2–3 tomatoes
1½ tablespoons mayonnaise
2 tablespoons single cream
1 teaspoon lemon juice
pinch each salt, white pepper
  and sugar
few lettuce leaves

Bring 250 ml/8 fl oz salted water to the boil in a pan, together with the wine, vinegar, peppercorns and fish pieces, and simmer over a low heat for 15 minutes, then strain. Butter a large piece of cooking foil and wrap the salmon in it, pressing the edges of the foil firmly together. Place the salmon in a roasting tin, pour over the fish stock and bake in a hot oven (220 c, 425 f, Gas Mark 7) for 20 minutes. Take the salmon out of the oven, allow to cool in the foil, then unwrap and place in the refrigerator until completely cold.

Pour a thin layer of the fish aspic over a flat serving dish and leave to set. Cut the salmon into very thin slices, arrange on the dish and top with the remaining aspic. Wash, prepare and dice the mixed vegetables. Bring a little salted water to the boil in a pan, add the vegetables and simmer for 15 minutes. Skin the tomatoes, cut them in half and remove the seeds. Finely dice the flesh and cook with the vegetables for 5 minutes. Drain the vegetables and leave to cool.

Mix together the mayonnaise, cream, lemon juice, salt, pepper and sugar and stir into the vegetables. Wash and dry the lettuce leaves and arrange at one end of the serving dish. Spoon the vegetable salad on top. Garnish the dish with stuffed eggs (suggested fillings page 96). *Serves 4*

Fish Specialities

Herrings with Mixed Peppers

12 pickled herring fillets
1 red pepper
1 green pepper
1 yellow pepper
4 shallots or 2 small onions
3 tablespoons wine vinegar
2 sprigs thyme, or ½ teaspoon
   dried thyme
1 sage leaf, or a pinch dried
   sage
few sprigs basil, or ½ teaspoon
   dried basil
8 tablespoons oil
juice of 1 lemon

If the herrings are very salty,
soak them in cold water for
1–2 hours, changing the water
several times. Less salty fillets
should be washed in cold water
and patted dry.
   Cut the fillets into thick
strips. Wash the peppers,
remove the core and seeds and
cut each into thin rings. Peel
and finely dice the shallots or
onions. Bring the vinegar to
the boil in a pan, add the diced
shallot or onion, cover the pan
and simmer over a low heat for
2 minutes. Leave to cool. Mix
the herring and peppers
together in a large bowl and
pour on the vinegar marinade.
Wash and dry the fresh herbs,
if used, and chop finely. Add
the herbs to the herring salad.
Beat the oil with the lemon
juice and pour over the
mixture. Mix thoroughly.
Cover the salad and leave to
stand for 2 hours in the
refrigerator. *Serves 4*

Herrings in Dill Mayonnaise

8 pickled herring fillets
100 ml/4 fl oz milk (optional)
1 egg
2 tablespoons French mustard
1 teaspoon wine vinegar
generous pinch each salt and
   white pepper
6 tablespoons oil
4 tablespoons single cream
150 g/5 oz pickled cucumbers
bunch fresh dill, or 1 tablespoon
   dried dill

If the herring fillets are very
salty, mix the milk with
3 tablespoons water and leave
the fillets to soak in the
mixture for 12 hours. Then
drain the fillets and cut into
fairly thick strips. Place in a
bowl or earthenware dish.
   Beat the egg with the
mustard, vinegar, salt and
pepper. Gradually add the oil,
a few drops at a time, stirring
continuously. Stir in the cream.
Finely dice the pickled
cucumbers. Wash and drain
the fresh dill, if used. Keep one
sprig on one side and chop the
remainder. Mix the cucumber
and dill into the mayonnaise,
pour the mayonnaise over the
herring and stir in. Cover and
leave to stand in the
refrigerator for 1–2 hours.
Before serving garnish with
the remaining sprig of dill.
Serves 4

Herring Fillets in Red Wine Marinade

8 pickled herring fillets
2 large red onions
250 ml/4 fl oz red wine
100 ml/4 fl oz wine vinegar
175 g/6 oz sugar
4 black peppercorns
1 stick cinnamon
3 cloves

Wash the herring fillets in cold water, place in 450 ml/¾ pint water and leave to soak for 12 hours, then drain. Cut the fillets in half, both lengthways and widthways, and arrange in layers in a deep earthenware dish.

Peel the onions and cut into thin rings. Pour the red wine and vinegar into a pan, add the onion rings, sugar, peppercorns, cinnamon and cloves and bring to the boil.

Simmer over a low heat for 5 minutes and leave to cool. When cold pour over the herring fillets. Cover and leave to stand in the refrigerator for 3 days. *Serves 4*

Cook's Tip

Herring fillets in red wine marinade will keep for two weeks in a firmly closed screw-top jar in the refrigerator. It is worth making double the quantity and having marinated herring fillets on the menu more than once.

Soused Herrings

4 medium onions
100 ml/4 fl oz vinegar
2 tablespoons sugar
1 teaspoon black peppercorns
8 prepared salt herring fillets
GARNISH
2 hard-boiled eggs

Peel the onions and chop coarsely. Stir together the vinegar, sugar, peppercorns and onion. Cut the herrings into equal pieces and place in a deep earthenware dish. Pour the vinegar marinade over the herrings, cover and leave to stand in the refrigerator for 4 days.

Shell the eggs and cut each into eight wedges. Use to garnish the herring dish before serving. *Serves 4*

Cook's Tip

These marinated herrings will keep for two weeks in a firmly closed screw-top jar in the refrigerator. It is therefore worth making double the quantity. As a variation, you could mix diced apple and soured cream into the herrings just before serving (see the buffet on page 171 for an illustration).

Herrings with Apple Salad

1 slice canned pineapple
2 carrots
1 apple
½ teaspoon sugar
juice of 1 small lemon
2 small tomatoes
bunch chives
4 tablespoons mayonnaise
1 tablespoon single cream
generous pinch each salt, black
   pepper, and paprika pepper
8 pickled herring fillets

Drain the pineapple and dice.
Trim and wash the carrots.
Peel and core the apple and
grate into a bowl, together
with the carrots. Beat the sugar
with the lemon juice, add the
pineapple and stir into the
grated apple and carrot.
   Cut a cross in the bases of
the tomatoes, dip them in
boiling water for a few
seconds, then peel them. Cut
the tomatoes in half, remove
the seeds and finely dice the
flesh. Wash, drain and chop
the chives. Beat the
mayonnaise with the cream,
salt, pepper, paprika and
chives. Fold the diced tomato
into the mayonnaise sauce.
Roll up the herring fillets.
Arrange the apple and carrot
salad on a flat dish and top
with the rolled herrings.
Sprinkle with the mayonnaise
dressing. *Serves 4*

Herring Tartare

8 pickled herring fillets
1 large onion
2 tablespoons capers
2 teaspoons caraway seeds
2 teaspoons coarsely ground
   white pepper
1 tablespoon paprika pepper
2 tablespoons chopped parsley
4 egg yolks

If the herrings are very salty,
soak them for a few hours in
cold water, changing the water
frequently. Drain them on
absorbent kitchen paper, dice
coarsely and arrange in the
centres of four individual
plates. Make a well in the
middle of each portion.
   Peel and finely dice the
onion. On each plate, arrange
spoonfuls of diced onion,
capers, caraway seeds, pepper,
paprika and parsley around
the herring. Tip one egg yolk
into the well made in each
herring portion. Each guest
mixes a portion of herring with
seasonings to taste. Serve with
fresh brown bread and butter.
Serves 4

Herring Salad Platter

6 tablespoons wine vinegar
3 tablespoons oil
1 teaspoon sugar
2 tablespoons capers
8 pickled herring fillets
4 hard-boiled eggs
100 g/4 oz red or black lumpfish
  roe
2 small cooked beetroot
4 tablespoons pickled cocktail
  onions
100 g/4 oz cooked carrots

Beat together the vinegar, oil
and sugar. Keep a few capers
on one side and lightly crush
the rest with a fork. Add to the
mixture. Place the herring
fillets in the marinade, cover
and leave to stand in the
refrigerator for 2 hours.

Shell the eggs, cut them in
half lengthways and top each
with 1 teaspoon lumpfish roe.

Peel and dice the beetroot.
Drain the cocktail onions.
Chop the carrots. Remove the
herring fillets from the
marinade and place on a
serving dish together with the
eggs. Arrange spoonfuls of
beetroot, onions and carrot
around the herring and
sprinkle with the remaining
capers. *Serves 4*

Herring Rolls with Sweet Corn Salad

½ small cauliflower
1 (227-g/8-oz) packet frozen
  peas
1 (283-g/10-oz) can sweet corn
2 small onions
salt and black pepper
2 tablespoons wine vinegar
4 tablespoons oil
2 small pickled cucumbers
6-8 strips canned pimiento
2 cooked carrots
8 pickled herring fillets

Wash the cauliflower and
break into florets. Place the
florets in a pan of boiling
salted water, and simmer for
10–15 minutes. Cook the peas
following the instructions on
the packet. Drain the
cauliflower and peas and leave
to cool. Drain the sweet corn.

Peel and dice the onions, and
beat with the salt, pepper,
vinegar and oil in a bowl. Mix
the cauliflower, peas and sweet
corn into the dressing.

Drain the pickled cucumbers
and pimientoes. Slice the
carrots, cucumbers and
pimientoes into thin 5-cm/
2-inch long strips and mix
together. Place a few strips
across each herring fillet, roll
up the fillets and secure with
cocktail sticks. Spoon the pea,
cauliflower and sweet corn
salad into a large serving dish
and arrange the herring rolls
alongside. *Serves 4*

119

Mock Caviare Cream Horns

250 ml/8 fl oz double cream
¼ teaspoon salt
few drops lemon juice
1 (58-g/2-oz) jar lumpfish roe
4–8 puff pastry horns (bought ready-made)

Place the cream and salt together in a bowl and whip until stiff. Fold in the lemon juice and lumpfish roe. Transfer the cream to a piping bag and pipe into the horns. Serve with ice-cold vodka. *Serves 4*

Cook's Tip
You can make your own horns from frozen puff pastry. Roll out the thawed pastry and cut it into 2.5-cm/1-inch wide strips. Make cones from aluminium foil. Coat one side of the pastry strips with beaten egg yolk and twist them, egg-side-down, around the cone so that the coated edges overlap by about ½ cm/¼ inch. Press the edges gently together and coat the whole with more egg yolk. Bake in a moderately hot oven (200 c, 400 f, Gas Mark 6) for 15 minutes. Allow to cool and remove the foil cones.

Sole Mousse with Mock Caviare

100 ml/4 fl oz fish aspic
  (see page 201)
250 ml/8 fl oz double cream
350 g/12 oz cooked sole fillets
200 ml/7 fl oz white sauce
salt and pepper
6 tablespoons hot chicken stock
15 g/½ oz gelatine
½ (58-g/2-oz) jar lumpfish roe
6 limes
GARNISH
few dill sprigs (optional)

Line four (300-ml/½-pint) moulds with a thin layer of fish aspic and leave to set. Whip the cream until stiff. Skin the fish fillets, break into pieces, and blend with the white sauce in the liquidiser until smooth. Season with salt and pepper.

Pour the chicken stock into a bowl and stand in a pan of hot water. Sprinkle with gelatine and stir until dissolved. Fold in half the whipped cream. Allow the aspic to cool slightly, then fold in the remaining cream and the fish purée. Pour half the sole mousse into the lined moulds. Make a small well in the centre of each and fill with lumpfish roe. Top with the remaining mousse and leave to set in the refrigerator.

Wash, dry and thinly slice the limes. Wash and drain the dill, if used. Arrange the lime slices on four individual plates. Dip the moulds in hot water for a few seconds and turn out the mousses onto the plates. Garnish each portion with dill, if liked. *Serves 4*

Trout Toast with Asparagus

4 small slices white bread
4 freshly smoked trout fillets
24 freshly boiled asparagus
  shoots or 24 canned
  asparagus tips
3 tablespoons vinaigrette
  dressing (see page 139)
100 ml/4 fl oz white wine aspic
  (see page 202)
1 lemon
GARNISH
8 leaves lemon balm or mint
  (optional)

Toast the bread until golden brown and cut the slices in half. Remove any skin from the fish with a sharp knife and cut the fillets in half widthways. Top each slice of toast with half a trout fillet.

Drain the fresh asparagus shoots, if used, and cut them in half, retaining the bottom

halves for use in a salad. Drain the canned asparagus tips. Place the asparagus on a flat dish, pour the vinaigrette dressing over the tops of the shoots, cover and leave to marinate for 15 minutes. Then drain the asparagus tips and place three tips on each trout fillet. Pour the wine aspic over the asparagus and leave to set.

Wash the lemon, rub dry and cut three slices from the centre. Cut each slice of lemon into five or six segments. Place two lemon segments on each slice of toast and garnish each with a lemon balm or mint leaf, if used. *Makes 8*

Smoked Salmon Vols-au-Vent

1 (150-g/5-oz) can prawns
¼ teaspoon lemon juice
100 g/4 oz smoked salmon
250 ml/8 fl oz double cream
pinch each salt and white pepper
generous pinch gelatine
8 (5-cm/2-inch) puff pastry
  vol-au-vent cases (bought
  ready made)
GARNISH
8 thin slices truffle (optional)

Drain the prawns, rinse in cold water and allow to dry thoroughly. Chop them coarsely and sprinkle with the lemon juice. Cut the smoked salmon into small pieces and blend with the chopped prawns in the liquidiser. Whip the cream until stiff and season with salt and pepper. Gradually fold the prawn and salmon purée by spoonfuls

into the whipped cream.

Bring 3 tablespoons water to the boil in a small pan, remove the pan from the heat, allow to cool slightly and sprinkle with the gelatine. Stir until the gelatine has dissolved. Leave to cool, then stir into the smoked salmon cream. Cover and stand in a cool place for 30 minutes. Transfer to a piping bag fitted with a round nozzle and pipe into the vols-au-vent. Garnish each vol-au-vent with a slice of truffle, if used. *Makes 8*

Cook's Tip

The vols-au-vent can be garnished with lemon or cucumber segments, or sliced mushrooms, instead of sliced truffle.

Fish Specialities

Party Trout Platter

8 freshly smoked trout fillets
250 ml/8 fl oz white wine aspic
   (see page 202)
250 ml/8 fl oz double cream
pinch salt
1 tablespoon freshly grated
   horseradish or 1½ tablespoons
   bottled horseradish
4 hard-boiled eggs
½ (58-g/2-oz) jar lumpfish roe
2 lemons
1 (241-g/8½-oz) can asparagus
   tips
4 thin slices smoked salmon
½ cucumber
few lettuce leaves
100 g/4 oz hard butter
8 slices white bread
small bunch dill or parsley

Arrange the trout fillets in a ring on one side of a large flat dish. Pour over the white wine aspic and leave to set. Whip the cream with the salt until stiff and fold in the horseradish. Transfer to a glass dish or bowl and place on the serving dish.

Shell and slice the eggs. Place a slice of egg on each trout fillet and garnish with a spoonful of lumpfish roe. Wash the lemons, rub them dry and cut four thin slices from the centre of each. Cut through to the centre of each lemon slice, twist it and arrange between the trout fillets.

Drain the asparagus tips. Roll a few asparagus tips at a time in each slice of smoked salmon. Wash, dry and thinly slice the cucumber, and arrange in a ring on the dish next to the trout fillets. Top with the salmon rolls.

Wash and drain the lettuce and place on the serving dish. Shave the butter into curls with a butter curler and arrange on the lettuce. Toast the bread, cut the slices in half diagonally and place on the far side of the serving dish. Wash and drain the dill or parsley and use to garnish the platter. *Serves 8*

Cook's Tip

If you are serving the trout platter when asparagus is in season, fill the smoked salmon rolls with steamed fresh asparagus tips. The stems of the asparagus shoots can be reserved and used in a salad.

Smoked Fish Platter

100 g/4 oz smoked eel
100 g/4 oz smoked conger eel
225 g/8 oz smoked salmon,
*   sliced*
1 smoked mackerel
2 smoked trout fillets
100 g/4 oz canned anchovies
few dill and parsley sprigs
1 tomato
1 lime

Cut the eel into 2.5-cm/1-inch pieces, and slice the conger eel. Arrange both kinds of eel on a large serving dish, together with the salmon, mackerel and trout fillets. Drain the anchovies and place on the dish. Wash and dry the dill and parsley and use to garnish the fish. Slice the tomato and lime, and arrange on the serving dish. Decorate the dish with stuffed eggs (recipes pages 96

and 97). Serve with horseradish cream (see Party Trout Platter opposite) and the following fish salads:

Sweet and Sour Sardines
½ (113-g/4-oz) can sardines
1 slice fresh or canned pineapple
1 small mild-flavoured onion
1 large tomato
1 Ogen melon
1 tablespoon lemon juice
2 tablespoons oil
pinch each salt and pepper
generous pinch mustard powder

Drain the sardines, and the canned pineapple, if used. Slice the sardines and the pineapple. Peel the onion and slice into rings. Peel and dice the tomato. Cut the melon in half widthways with a zig-zag motion, and using a melon baller, scoop out all the flesh.

   Beat the lemon juice with the oil, salt, pepper and mustard. Place the sardine, pineapple, onion, tomato and melon

together in a bowl and pour over the dressing. Mix well and arrange the salad in one of the melon halves, retaining the other for the Bean Salad.

Herring Fillets with Pepper Cream
225 g/8 oz pickled herring fillets
½ red pepper
few lettuce leaves
2 tablespoons soured cream
pinch each salt and white pepper
few drops each Worcestershire
*   sauce and lemon juice*
1 teaspoon pickled green
*   peppercorns, or ½ teaspoon*
*   freshly ground black pepper*

Cut the herring fillets into pieces. Wash the red pepper, remove the seeds and cut into strips. Mix the pepper and herring together. Wash and drain the lettuce and place on the serving dish. Arrange the herring salad on top.

   Beat the soured cream with the salt, pepper, Worcester-

shire sauce, lemon juice and peppercorns or pepper. Spoon over the herring salad.

Bean Salad
½ (283-g/10-oz) can green
*   beans*
1 (250-g/8¾-oz) can mussels
1 (142-g/5-oz) can prawns
1 tablespoon wine vinegar
2 tablespoons oil
pinch each salt and white pepper
1 teaspoon chopped fresh chives
*   (optional)*

Drain and chop the beans. Drain the mussels and prawns, and mix the mussels, prawns and beans together. Beat the vinegar with the oil, salt, pepper, and stir into the salad. Arrange the salad in the second Ogen melon half. Sprinkle with chives, if used.

Roast Meats

Roast Beef Platter with Remoulade Sauce

1 kg/2¼ lb sirloin of beef
1 teaspoon salt
½ teaspoon black pepper
generous pinch each onion salt
*   and garlic salt*
1 teaspoon strong mustard
2 tablespoons oil
1 (269-g/9½-oz) jar mixed
*   pickled vegetables*
REMOULADE SAUCE
1 canned anchovy fillet
1 onion, peeled
2 baby gherkins
1 tablespoon capers
bunch chives
small bunch parsley
3 sprigs each fresh chervil and
*   dill, or ½ teaspoon each dried*
*   chervil and dill*
225 g/8 oz mayonnaise
1 teaspoon strong mustard
salt and pepper

Rinse the beef in cold water, wipe dry and cut a lattice pattern into the thin layer of fat surrounding the joint. Mix together the salt, pepper, onion salt and garlic salt, and rub the mixture into the meat. Brush all over with a very thin layer of mustard. Pour the oil into a roasting tin, add the sirloin and roast in a hot oven (220 C, 425 F, Gas Mark 7) for 40–45 minutes, basting from time to time with the juices that have collected round the joint. Leave the sirloin to cool. Drain the pickled vegetables. Cut half the sirloin into very thin slices and arrange on a large serving dish, together with the rest of the joint and the pickled vegetables.

To make the remoulade sauce, soak the anchovy fillet in water for 10 minutes, drain and chop finely, together with the onion. Finely dice the gherkins. Crush the capers with a fork. Wash, drain and

chop the chives and parsley with the fresh chervil and dill, if used. Beat the mayonnaise with the mustard, salt and pepper, and stir in the chopped ingredients. Taste and adjust seasoning, and serve separately with the roast beef, accompanied by white bread and wholemeal bread and butter. *Serves 6*

Cook's Tip

Instead of mixed pickled vegetables and remoulade sauce, you could serve the roast beef with the vegetable salad given in the recipe for Russian Salad Platter (see page 167). Make double the quantity and omit the ham sausage.

Stuffed Ham and Curry Sauce

50 g/2 oz dried apricots
1 kg/2¼ lb collar joint of ham or
  gammon, cooked
225 g/8 oz sausagemeat
½ onion, peeled and finely
  chopped
3 tablespoons chopped parsley
½ teaspoon each dried thyme
  and marjoram
salt and white pepper
2 tablespoons oil
1 teaspoon paprika pepper
4 tablespoons mayonnaise
2–3 teaspoons curry powder
4 tablespoons single cream
pinch sugar

Soak the apricots for 2–3
hours in warm water. Using a
long, thin knife, carefully cut a
hole 3 cm/1½ inches in diameter
horizontally through the centre
of the ham joint, but do not
cut right through to the other
end. Scoop out the meat and
mince it. Mix together the
sausagemeat, onion,
1 tablespoon parsley, herbs,
salt and pepper. Fry in half the
oil, stirring continuously, until
well browned. Remove from
the heat and stir in the minced
ham. Stuff the joint, brush the
outside with the remaining oil
and sprinkle with paprika.
Cover the opening at one end
of the meat with a piece of foil.
Roast in a moderately hot
oven (200 c, 400 f, Gas
Mark 6) for 20 minutes, and
5 minutes before the end of
cooking time, sprinkle with the
remaining parsley. Leave to
cool.
  Drain the apricots, blend in
the liquidiser and beat with the
mayonnaise, curry powder,
cream, sugar, and pepper to
taste. Serve with the ham.
Serves 6
  Note: this recipe goes well
with fillet of pork (shown on
page 180).

Glazed Fillet of Beef

1 kg/2¼ lb fillet of beef
3 tablespoons oil
½ teaspoon paprika pepper
pinch dried thyme
pinch white pepper
½ teaspoon salt
100 g/4 oz carrots
225 g/8 oz canned artichoke
  hearts
2 tablespoons vinaigrette
  dressing (see page 139)
100 ml/4 fl oz cool Madeira
  aspic (see page 202)
4 tablespoons mayonnaise
6 tablespoons single cream
½ teaspoon strong mustard
2 tablespoons chopped fresh
  mixed herbs, or 2 teaspoons
  dried mixed herbs

Remove any skin from the
beef. Mix the oil with the
paprika, thyme and pepper
and rub the mixture into the
meat. Wrap the meat in
cooking foil and leave to
marinate in the refrigerator for
12 hours, then remove the foil,
sprinkle with salt and roast in
a hot oven (220 c, 425 f, Gas
Mark 7) for 30–45 minutes.
The meat should be rare.
  Wash, scrape and trim the
carrots and cut into strips.
Drain the artichoke hearts and
cut them in half. Take the fillet
out of the oven, allow to cool,
and cut into thick slices.
Arrange the slices on a flat
serving dish. Mix together the
carrot and artichoke, sprinkle
with the vinaigrette dressing,
and arrange on the dish
alongside the meat. Pour the
Madeira aspic over the beef
and leave to set. Beat the
mayonnaise with the cream,
mustard and herbs, season to
taste, and serve separately with
the fillet. *Serves 6*

Spit Roast Pork with Herb Mayonnaise

*1 kg/2¼ lb neck end of pork,
   boned and rolled, or boned
   knuckle of pork*
½ clove garlic
2 tablespoons oil
1 teaspoon salt
1 tablespoon strong mustard
*½ teaspoon each dried thyme
   and marjoram*
225 g/8 oz mayonnaise
1 gherkin
bunch chives
bunch parsley
*small bunch fresh dill, or
   1 teaspoon dried dill*
2 hard-boiled eggs
GARNISH
*1 tablespoon chopped onion
asparagus (optional)*

Wash the meat in cold water
and wipe dry. Peel and crush
the garlic clove. Beat the oil
with the salt, garlic, mustard,
thyme and marjoram and rub
the mixture well into the meat.
Preheat the grill to moderate
(180 C, 350 F, Gas Mark 4).
Thread the joint onto the spit
and grill for up to 1 hour
40 minutes, until cooked right
through. Remove the pork
from the spit and leave to cool,
then arrange on a flat serving
dish.

Pour the mayonnaise into a
bowl. Finely chop the gherkin.
Wash, dry and finely chop the
chives and parsley, and the
fresh dill, if used. Shell and
chop the eggs. Mix all the
chopped ingredients into the
mayonnaise and serve with the
pork, together with freshly
cooked asparagus, if liked.
Garnish the dish with chopped
onion. *Serves 6*

Braised Veal 'Mostarda'

1 kg/2¼ lb fillet of veal
1 teaspoon salt
*¼ teaspoon each white pepper,
   dried rosemary and dried
   sage*
½ teaspoon paprika pepper
1 onion
*a selection of fresh vegetables in
   season (carrots, celery, leek)*
4 tablespoons oil
100 ml/4 fl oz hot meat stock
100 ml/4 fl oz white wine
225 g/8 oz crystallised fruits

Rinse the meat in cold water
and wipe dry. Mix together the
salt, pepper, herbs and
paprika, and rub the mixture
into the meat. Peel the onion
and cut into quarters. Wash
and trim the fresh vegetables,
allow to drain and chop
coarsely. Heat the oil in a
flameproof casserole, add the
meat and brown in the oil for
10 minutes, turning from time
to time. Add the onion and the
chopped mixed vegetables and
continue frying for a few
minutes. Pour the meat stock
and white wine into the
casserole, cover with a tightly
fitting lid, and place in a hot
oven (220 C, 425 F, Gas
Mark 7). Braise the veal for
60–70 minutes, basting often
during cooking. Remove from
the casserole and leave to cool.

Before serving, carve the
meat into thin slices and
arrange on a platter. Serve the
crystallised fruits separately.
Serves 6

Game

Roast Breast of Pheasant

2 young pheasants, dressed
salt and pepper
bunch fresh mixed herbs
(parsley, rosemary, thyme,
marjoram), or 1 tablespoon
mixed dried herbs
50 g/2 oz canned truffles
(optional)
8–10 streaky bacon rashers
2 tablespoons oil
20 ml/1 fl oz brandy
GARNISH
100 ml/4 fl oz Madeira aspic
(see page 202)
sprig watercress

Rinse the pheasants under cold
running water and wipe dry.
Rub the insides of the birds
with salt and pepper. Wash the
fresh herbs, if used, allow to
drain and divide the bunch in
half. Place one half of the fresh
or dried herbs in the cavity of

each pheasant. Slice the
truffles, if used, very thinly.
Loosen the skin over the breast
of each pheasant with a sharp
knife and insert the truffle
slices underneath, then cover
the breasts with the bacon
rashers, to protect the meat
from drying out. Rub the
pheasants all over with oil.
Place in a roasting tin and
roast in a hot oven (220 C,
425 F, Gas Mark 7) for 40–45
minutes, basting often. Ten
minutes before the end of
cooking time, remove the
bacon rashers and pour the
brandy over the pheasants.
When they are done, take the
pheasants out of the oven and
slice the breast off each. Allow
to cool, then cut into thick
slices. Arrange the slices on a
dish and garnish with diced
Madeira aspic and watercress.
Serves 4

Glazed Saddle of Venison

1.5 kg/3 lb saddle of venison
3 juniper berries
1 bay leaf
salt and pepper
generous pinch each allspice,
ground ginger and thyme
1 teaspoon paprika pepper
4 tablespoons oil
100 ml/4 fl oz port
4 shallots
25 g/1 oz butter
100 g/4 oz liver sausage
100 ml/4 fl oz port aspic
(see page 202)
GARNISH
5 glacé cherries
6 kumquats, or 1 (312-g/11-oz)
can mandarin segments,
drained

Wash the meat in cold water
and wipe dry. Crush the
juniper berries and bay leaf
and mix with the salt, pepper,

allspice, ginger, thyme, paprika
and oil. Rub the mixture into
the meat, cover, and leave to
marinate for 3 hours. Transfer
to a roasting tin and roast in a
moderately hot oven (200 C,
400 F, Gas Mark 6) for 1 hour
20 minutes. After 30 minutes
of cooking, pour the port over
the meat. When the meat is
cooked, remove from the pan,
allow to cool and carve into
thick slices. Do not discard the
saddle carcass.

Peel and dice the shallots,
then fry in the butter until soft.
Bring the roasting juices to the
boil in the tin, and simmer for
a few minutes until the liquid
thickens. Mix the liver sausage
and diced shallot into the
liquid. Brush the saddle carcass
all over with the mixture and
arrange the meat slices on top.
Pour over the cooled port aspic
and allow to set. Serve
garnished with the glacé
cherries and kumquats or
canned fruits. *Serves 6*

Turkey Legs with Broccoli

2 (350-g/12-oz) turkey legs
salt and pepper
5 tablespoons oil
1 carrot
1 stick celery
1 onion
1½ tablespoons chopped parsley
generous pinch dried thyme
450 ml/¾ pint chicken stock
100 ml/4 fl oz wine vinegar
100 ml/4 fl oz sherry
450 g/1 lb broccoli
2 teaspoons lemon juice
pinch sugar
GARNISH
tomato quarters

Heat 3 tablespoons oil in a large pan and brown the turkey all over. Wash, trim and chop the carrot and celery. Peel and dice the onion, and add all the chopped vegetables to the pan, together with ½ tablespoon parsley, and the thyme. Continue frying for a few minutes, then pour in the chicken stock, vinegar, sherry and salt and pepper to taste. Cover the pan and cook gently for 30–40 minutes. Remove the turkey legs and leave to cool. Continue boiling the stock until reduced to 250 ml/8 fl oz, and allow to cool.

Place the broccoli in a pan, add enough boiling salted water to cover the stalks, and simmer gently for 10–15 minutes, then drain. Beat the lemon juice with the sugar and remaining oil, add salt to taste and pour over the broccoli. Cover and leave to stand. Arrange the turkey legs on a flat serving dish and sprinkle with the rest of the parsley. Skim the fat from the cold stock and pour over the meat. Allow to set, then arrange the broccoli salad on the serving dish, and garnish with the tomato quarters. *Serves 4*

Poulet-Bresse

2 (1-kg/2¼-lb) spring chickens
1 tablespoon oil
50 g/2 oz butter
2 onions
1 carrot
1 stick celery
250 ml/8 fl oz wine vinegar
2 sprigs each fresh thyme and parsley, or ½ teaspoon each dried thyme and parsley
salt and pepper
1.5 litres/2¾ pints chicken stock
15 g/½ oz plain flour
juice of 1 lemon
12 shallots
2 tablespoons finely chopped chives

Joint the chickens. Heat the oil and butter together in a large pan, and brown the chicken joints. Peel and dice the onions. Wash, trim and chop the carrot and celery, and brown the vegetables in the pan with the chicken. Pour over the vinegar, followed by 250 ml/8 fl oz water. Add the herbs, season with salt and pepper, then cover the pan and simmer gently for 25 minutes. Remove the chicken and continue boiling the liquid until it is reduced to one third. Add the chicken stock and simmer for a further 30 minutes. Strain the stock, cool slightly and chill in the refrigerator.

Mix the flour and lemon juice together in a pan, add 750 ml/1¼ pints salted water and bring to the boil. Add the peeled shallots and cook gently in the liquid for 8 minutes, then drain and leave to cool. Skim the fat from the chilled stock. Arrange the chicken joints and shallots on a flat serving dish. Pour over a layer of stock and allow to set. Add another layer every 30 minutes until all the stock is used up. Chill until set, and serve sprinkled with chives. *Serves 6*

Stuffed Turkey Breast

100 g/4 oz carrots
100 g/4 oz bacon rashers
1.5 kg/3 lb boned turkey breast
¼ teaspoon each salt and white
* pepper*
1 teaspoon paprika pepper
1 tablespoon oil
100 g/4 oz butter
GARNISH
250 ml/8 fl oz Muscatel aspic
* (see page 202)*
few leaves red endive and
* 1 fresh or canned whole peach*

Wash, trim and scrape the carrots. Remove the rind from the bacon. Cut the carrots and bacon into long strips and freeze solid.

Using a long skewer, pierce several holes running right through the meat near the sides, and, with the aid of a trussing needle, insert frozen carrot and bacon strips alternately into the meat. Mix together the salt, pepper and paprika, and rub this mixture into the turkey breast. Place in a roasting tin. Heat the oil and pour all round the turkey, then place the tin in a moderately hot oven (200 C, 400 F, Gas Mark 6) and roast for 65–70 minutes. Fifteen minutes before the end of the cooking time, melt the butter and sprinkle it over the meat. Allow the turkey to cool, then wrap in cooking foil and leave in the refrigerator until cold.

Dice the Muscatel aspic. Carve the turkey into thin slices, arrange on a flat plate and sprinkle with the diced aspic. Garnish the platter with a salad of red endive and chopped peaches, if liked.
Serves 6

Stuffed Quails

8 dressed quails
salt and pepper
¼ teaspoon dried basil
75 g/3 oz butter
1 tablespoon oil
250 ml/8 fl oz Madeira aspic
* (see page 202)*
½ head endive
STUFFING
100 g/4 oz chicken livers
1 tablespoon Madeira wine
25 g/1 oz butter
25 g/1 oz bacon
pinch each salt, white pepper
* and dried basil*
100 ml/4 fl oz double cream
8 slices canned truffle
* (optional)*
GARNISH
fresh or canned mandarin
* segments*

Rub the quails inside and out with salt, pepper and basil. Heat the butter and oil together in a pan, and brown two quails at a time for 10–15 minutes. Leave the birds to cool.

To make the stuffing, trim the chicken livers, sprinkle with Madeira wine and marinate for 30 minutes. Melt the butter in a pan and fry the bacon until soft. Add the livers and continue frying for 4 minutes. Season with salt, pepper and basil, and leave to cool, then blend the liver and bacon together in the liquidiser. Whip the cream and stir into the purée. Transfer to a piping bag fitted with a round nozzle and half-fill each quail with purée. Add a slice of truffle, if used, and pipe the remaining purée on top. Coat the quails several times with the Madeira aspic, leaving each layer to set before adding the next. Wash the endive, cut into strips and arrange on a large serving dish with the stuffed quails. Garnish with mandarin segments. *Serves 8*

129

Party Tournedos

675 g/1½ lb fillet of beef
salt and white pepper
¼ teaspoon paprika pepper
3 tablespoons oil
250 ml/8 fl oz sherry aspic
    (see page 202)

GARNISHES
1 hard-boiled egg
7 g/¼ oz soft butter
2 teaspoons single cream
pinch each salt, pepper and
    paprika pepper
1 teaspoon chopped fresh mixed
    herbs, or pinch dried mixed
    herbs
2 wedges tomato

½ (340-g/12-oz) can asparagus
    tips
3 tablespoons white wine
1 teaspoon lemon juice
pinch each salt, sugar and white
    pepper
few drops Worcestershire sauce
3 slices cooked carrot

3 canned artichoke bottoms
2 teaspoons lemon juice
3 tablespoons white wine
3 teaspoons mayonnaise
few dill or parsley sprigs
1 teaspoon pickled red or green
    peppercorns (optional)

2 slices liver pâté
6 grapes
2 tablespoons brandy

Remove any skin from the
beef, rinse in cold water and
wipe dry. Beat together the
salt, pepper, paprika and oil.
Rub the meat all over with the
seasoned oil, wrap in cooking
foil and leave to marinate in
the refrigerator for 3 hours.
Open the foil, place the beef,
still in the foil, in a hot oven
(220 C, 425 F, Gas Mark 7) and
roast for 25–30 minutes until
tender but still rare. Leave the
meat to cool, and when cold
carve into ten thick slices.
Garnish the tournedos as
follows:

Shell the egg, cut in half
lengthways and remove the
yolk. Mix the yolk with the
butter, cream, salt, pepper,
paprika and herbs. Pipe the
mixture into the egg whites and
top each with a wedge of
tomato. Arrange the eggs on
two of the tournedos.

Drain the asparagus tips.
Beat the white wine with the
lemon juice, salt, sugar, pepper
and Worcestershire sauce.
Pour the mixture over the
asparagus and leave to
marinate for 1 hour. Then
drain, and arrange the
asparagus on three of the
tournedos. Garnish with the
slices of cooked carrot.

Drain the artichoke
bottoms. Mix the lemon juice
with the white wine, pour over
the artichoke bottoms and
leave to marinate for 1 hour.
Then drain, arrange the
artichokes on three more
tournedos and spoon the
mayonnaise into the centres.

Garnish the tournedos with dill
or parsley sprigs, and a few
pickled red or green
peppercorns, if liked.

Place the liver pâté on the
two remaining tournedos.
Peel the grapes, soak in the
brandy for about 10 minutes,
drain and use to garnish the
pâté.

Arrange all the tournedos on
a serving dish, pour over the
sherry aspic and leave to set.
Serves 10

Veal Tournedos with Broccoli Purée

8 thick slices fillet of veal
¼ teaspoon white pepper
pinch paprika pepper
4 tablespoons oil
¼ teaspoon salt
175 g/6 oz broccoli
¼ teaspoon each grated nutmeg,
    dried thyme and basil
3 tablespoons hot meat stock
15 g/½ oz gelatine
250 ml/8 fl oz double cream
250 ml/8 fl oz white wine aspic
    (see page 202)
8 pickled quail's eggs or
    slices of hard-boiled egg

Wipe the veal slices and rub with the pepper and paprika. Heat the oil in a frying pan and fry the slices for 3–4 minutes on each side. Season with salt and leave to cool, then arrange individually on a serving dish.

Wash and trim the broccoli. Bring a little salted water to the boil in a pan, add the broccoli and simmer for 10 minutes, then drain and leave to cool. Blend the broccoli in the liquidiser with the nutmeg, thyme and basil. Taste and adjust seasoning. Pour the meat stock into a bowl and stand in a pan of hot water. Sprinkle with the gelatine and stir until dissolved, then mix the stock into the broccoli purée. Whip the cream until stiff and fold into the purée. Transfer to a piping bag fitted with a star-shaped nozzle and pipe a rosette onto each tournedos. Spoon the wine aspic over all the tournedos, and place the serving dish in the refrigerator to set. Top the tournedos with the quail's eggs or slices of hard-boiled egg before serving.
Serves 8

Vitello Tonnato

1 kg/2¼ lb leg or loin of veal,
    boned and rolled
1 clove garlic
6 canned anchovy fillets
1 onion
2 carrots
1 stick celery
1 litre/1¾ pints meat stock
100 ml/4 fl oz dry white wine
2 bay leaves
5 peppercorns
4 tablespoons single cream
1 egg yolk
1 (198-g/7-oz) can tuna
2 tablespoons lemon juice
175 ml/6 fl oz olive oil
2 tablespoons capers
pinch each salt and pepper
225 g/8 oz crystallised fruits

Pierce the veal all over with the point of a sharp knife. Peel the garlic clove and slice lengthways. Cut the anchovy fillets into pieces. Peel the onion and cut in half. Wash, trim, scrape and coarsely dice the carrots. Wash and chop the celery. Insert the garlic slices and half of the anchovy pieces into the openings in the meat, then place in a pan with cold water to cover, bring to the boil and simmer for 1 minute. Pour away the water and add 250 ml/8 fl oz fresh water, with the onion, carrot, celery, meat stock, wine, bay leaves and peppercorns. Cover and simmer for 1½ hours. Allow the veal to cool in the stock, then take out to dry.

Strain 100 ml/4 fl oz stock and put on one side. Drain the tuna. Blend together the cream, egg yolk, tuna, the remaining anchovies and the lemon juice in the liquidiser, and gradually add the oil. Stir in the capers, salt and pepper, and enough strained stock to give the sauce a thin, creamy consistency. Slice the meat and serve with the sauce, and the crystallised fruits.

The Cheeseboard

Giant Cheese Buffet

There is such an enormous range of cheeses on the market that you should have no difficulty in setting up a cheese buffet with as much variety as possible.

Make sure your cheese is fresh and of good quality, and try to balance your selection by including hard, medium and soft cheeses, whether mild, seasoned or strong. Allow 175 g-225 g/8 oz cheese per person. Arrange your cheeses on platters, as above, slicing only a small amount of each type, as cheese stays fresh longer if kept in one piece. You could add variety to your buffet with a Gorgonzola Dip (see page 141), a Cheese and Sausage Salad or a Cheese and Fruit Salad. Remember to serve plenty of fresh bread and butter, as well as fruits, nuts, pickles and chutnies.

The cheese buffet illustrated above is made up as follows: on the tray to the left are Edam, Leicester, Emmental and Cheshire cheeses, both sliced and in cubes; the cheeseboard in the centre holds Tilsit, Livarot, Pont l'Evêque, Reblochon, Camembert, goat's cheeses and Gorgonzola Dip; and on the board in the background are Samsoe, Jarlsberg, Fontina, Gouda and Danish Blue.

Cheese and Sausage Salad

350 g/12 oz ham sausage
225 g/8 oz Edam cheese
100 g/4 oz Emmental cheese
1 Spanish onion
1 clove garlic
2 tablespoons wine vinegar
salt and white pepper
1 teaspoon mild or wholegrain
  mustard
2 tablespoons chopped fresh
  mixed herbs (parsley, lovage,
  thyme, salad burnet, mint) or
  2 teaspoons dried herbs
6 tablespoons oil

Remove the skin from the ham sausage, and cut the sausage, Edam and Emmental into thick slices. Then cut the slices into strips. Peel the onion and slice into thin rings. Mix the sausage, cheese and onion together in a salad bowl.

Peel and crush the garlic clove. Beat the vinegar with the salt, pepper, mustard, herbs, garlic and oil, and pour over the salad. *Serves 6*

Cheese and Fruit Salad

1 round honeydew melon
350 g/12 oz Gouda cheese
350 g/12 oz diced mixed fresh
  fruit (pears, peaches,
  cherries)
2 tablespoons lemon juice
pinch salt
1 teaspoon sugar
pinch each cayenne pepper and
  ground ginger
1 tablespoon brandy
4 tablespoons oil

Slice one third off the stalk end of the melon and scoop the flesh out of both parts using a melon baller. Dice the Gouda and mix the melon balls, Gouda and diced fruit in a bowl.

Beat the lemon juice with the salt, sugar, cayenne, ginger, brandy and oil, and pour over the salad. Cut a pattern around the rim of the melon shell, if liked, and fill the melon with the cheese and fruit salad. *Serves 6*

The Cheeseboard

Cheese Platter with Gorgonzola Cream

CHEESE PLATTER
*100 g/4 oz Bavarian smoked
cheese with ham
100 g/4 oz Tilsit or Havarti
100 g/4 oz Stilton
225 g/8 oz Emmental
100 g/4 oz Camembert*
GARNISH
*black olives
grapes
shelled walnuts
small salted pretzels*
GORGONZOLA CREAM
*100 g/4 oz Gorgonzola cheese
50 g/2 oz soft butter
1 egg yolk
1 tablespoon single cream
generous pinch cayenne pepper
1 tablespoon chopped fresh
mixed herbs (optional)
100 g/4 oz ham, unsliced*

Cut the Bavarian smoked cheese, the Tilsit or Havarti, the Stilton and half the Emmental into thin slices. Cut the remaining Emmental into cubes and the Camembert into wedges. Arrange the sliced cheese and the Camembert wedges on a cheese board. Thread each Emmental cube onto a cocktail stick, together with an olive or a grape, and place on the board. Arrange the walnuts and pretzels over the cheese.

To make the Gorgonzola cream, place the Gorgonzola in a bowl and mash with a fork. Beat in the butter, egg yolk, cream, cayenne, and the herbs, if used. Finely dice the ham and stir into the mixture, and serve the Gorgonzola cream separately with the platter. *Serves 6*

Country Cheese Board

*100 g/4 oz mature Camembert
cheese
100 g/4 oz Emmental cheese
grated
50 g/2 oz soft butter
1 egg yolk
1 teaspoon paprika pepper
salt and white pepper
1 tablespoon brandy
2 slices pumpernickel bread
3 tablespoons chopped pistachio
nuts
900 g/2 lb assorted cheeses
(such as Limburger, Havarti,
Gouda, Wensleydale,
Cheshire, Rambol Poivre)
1 Spanish onion
bunch radishes*

Place the Camembert in a large bowl and crush it with a fork. Work in the Emmental, butter, egg yolk, paprika, salt, pepper and brandy, and leave to stand in a cool place for 2 hours.

Crumble the pumpernickel very finely. Form the Camembert mixture into balls and dip half the balls in the chopped pistachios and the other half in the pumpernickel crumbs.

Cut your selection of cheeses into thick slices. Peel the onion and cut into rings. Wash the radishes. Arrange the sliced cheese on a large cheeseboard and garnish with the onion rings, radishes and cheese balls. *Serves 6*

Herb Oils and Vinegars

Mixed Herb Oil

*small bunch each parsley and
  chives*
2 sprigs sage
2 teaspoons dried thyme
2 teaspoons dried marjoram
*2 teaspoons dried lovage
  (optional)*
*450-600 ml/¾-1 pint sunflower
  oil*

Wash the parsley, chives and
sage, dry well and chop finely.
Place in a preserving jar
together with the thyme,
marjoram, and lovage, if used.
Pour over enough oil to cover
the herbs, seal the jar and place
in the refrigerator. Leave to
stand for 8-10 days. Shake the
oil well before use and top each
time with fresh oil to keep the
herbs covered.

Rosemary Oil

2-3 sprigs rosemary
*450 ml/¾ pint olive oil or
  sunflower oil*

Wash the rosemary in cold
water and dry thoroughly.
Place in a tall bottle and pour
over enough oil to cover. Cork
the bottle, stand in the
refrigerator and leave to
marinate for 2 weeks. Use the
rosemary oil for salad
dressings, topping up the
bottle each time with fresh oil
to cover the herbs.

Cook's Tip

You can replace the
rosemary with thyme (as
shown in the
illustration), basil,
lavender or sage. But do
not keep any herb oil for
more than 6 weeks.

Herb Oils and Vinegars

Lemon Vinegar

juice and rind of 1 large lemon
250 ml/8 fl oz white wine vinegar
few lemon balm leaves
(optional)

Wash and dry the lemon, and peel very thinly, taking care to remove none of the pith with the rind. Squeeze the lemon, measure 5 tablespoons of the juice and pour this into a bottle. Add the rind and top up the bottle with the vinegar. Wash the lemon balm, if used, dry well and add to the mixture. Cork the bottle and shake well. Place the bottle in the refrigerator and leave to stand for at least 3 weeks. Then strain the lemon vinegar through a muslin cloth, return it to the bottle and use as required. Keep it stored in the refrigerator.

Garlic Vinegar

6 cloves garlic
1 sprig thyme
1 teaspoon white peppercorns
450 ml/¾ pint red wine vinegar

Peel the garlic. Wash the thyme in cold water and dry thoroughly. Place the garlic, thyme and peppercorns in a bottle and top up with the red wine vinegar. Cork the bottle, stand in the refrigerator and leave to marinate for 3 weeks. Strain the garlic vinegar through muslin, return to the bottle and store in the refrigerator until required.

Sage Vinegar

3 sprigs sage
600 ml/1 pint red wine vinegar

Rinse the sage in cold water, dry thoroughly and place in a bottle. Pour over the wine vinegar to cover the sage and seal the bottle with a cork. Place in the refrigerator and leave to stand for at least 3 weeks. Then strain the vinegar through a muslin cloth, return to the bottle and keep in the refrigerator.

Salad Burnet Vinegar

3 small sprigs salad burnet
600 ml/1 pint white wine vinegar

Wash the salad burnet in cold water and dry well. Place in a bottle, pour over the white wine vinegar to cover and cork the bottle. Stand in the refrigerator for at least 3 weeks, then strain the vinegar through muslin and return to the bottle. Replace the cork and store in the refrigerator.

Butters with Herbs and Spices

Savoury Butters

Garlic Butter
1 clove garlic
100 g/4 oz soft butter
1 teaspoon lemon juice
¼ teaspoon white pepper

Peel and crush the garlic clove, and mix with the butter, lemon juice and pepper. Press the butter into a square block and chill before slicing.

Green Butter
100 g/4 oz soft unsalted butter
2 tablespoons cooked spinach juice
¾ teaspoon celery salt
generous pinch white pepper
pinch grated nutmeg
chopped parsley

Beat the butter with the spinach juice, celery salt, pepper and nutmeg. Transfer to a piping bag fitted with a star-shaped nozzle and pipe rosettes onto a sheet of foil. Chill and serve sprinkled with parsley.

Paprika Butter
¾ teaspoon sugar
¼ teaspoon tomato purée
pinch cayenne pepper
100 g/4 oz soft butter
1 tablespoon paprika pepper

Work the sugar, tomato purée and cayenne into the butter. Spread the butter in a 1-cm/½-inch thick layer on a sheet of cooking foil and chill. Then cut the butter into rectangles and coat in paprika.

Truffle Butter
1 (15-g/½-oz) piece truffle
1 teaspoon lemon juice
salt and cayenne pepper
100 g/4 oz soft unsalted butter

Finely chop the truffle. Work the lemon juice, salt, cayenne and truffle into the butter, form in a long roll and wrap in foil. Chill before cutting into slices.

Caper Butter
2 teaspoons capers
100 g/4 oz soft unsalted butter
½ teaspoon each lemon and orange juice
1 (47-g/1¾-oz) can anchovy fillets

Drain the capers and divide into two portions. Crush one portion into the butter, with the lemon and orange juice. Drain and chop the anchovies and mix into the butter. Shape into small balls, chill, and top each butter ball with 3 of the remaining capers.

Orange Butter
1 tablespoon orange juice
1 tablespoon grated orange rind
1 tablespoon pickled green peppercorns (optional)
100 g/4 oz soft unsalted butter

Work the orange juice and rind and peppercorns, if used, into the butter. Spread in a 1-cm/½-inch thick layer on foil, and chill. Cut into rectangles for serving.

Curry Rosettes
1 teaspoon curry paste
¼ teaspoon sugar
100 g/4 oz soft butter

Beat the curry paste and sugar into the butter. Transfer to a piping bag fitted with a star-shaped nozzle and pipe rosettes onto a sheet of foil. Chill until firm.

Cress Butter
½ punnet mustard and cress
100 g/4 oz soft butter
1 teaspoon lemon juice
1 tablespoon soured cream

Snip the cress, wash and drain. Finely chop and work it into the butter, together with the lemon juice and soured cream. Spread the butter in a 1-cm/

Butters with Herbs and Spices

½-inch thick layer on a sheet of foil and chill. Cut into squares or ovals.

Mustard Butter
1 tablespoon strong mustard
6 drops Tabasco sauce
dash Worcestershire sauce
100 g/4 oz soft butter

Beat all the ingredients into the butter until light and fluffy. Transfer to a piping bag fitted with a plain nozzle and pipe three blobs at a time onto a sheet of foil. Chill.

Red Pepper Rounds
100 g/4 oz soft butter
pinch ground ginger
8 drops Tabasco sauce
3 tablespoons finely chopped red pepper
2 tablespoons chopped parsley

Beat the butter with the ginger and Tabasco; mix in the chopped pepper. Wrap the butter in foil, form into a long roll and chill. Unwrap, coat with parsley, and slice.

Pepper Butter
1 teaspoon freshly ground black pepper
¼ teaspoon celery salt
pinch garlic salt
100 g/4 oz unsalted butter

Beat the seasoning into the butter until light and fluffy, shape the butter into a block and wrap in foil. Chill to set then cut into curls.

Herb Balls
100 g/4 oz soft butter
pinch each pepper and sugar
1 teaspoon lemon juice
3 tablespoons chopped fresh mixed herbs

Beat the butter with the seasoning, lemon juice and half the herbs. Shape into balls and chill. Coat with the remaining herbs before serving.

Ham Butter
50 g/2 oz ham, finely chopped
generous pinch each white pepper and grated nutmeg
1 tablespoon finely grated Gouda or Cheddar cheese
100 g/4 oz butter

Work the ham, seasoning and cheese into the butter, shape into balls and chill.

Salmon and Dill Butter
100 g/4 oz soft unsalted butter
generous pinch cayenne pepper
1 tablespoon finely chopped onion
75 g/3 oz smoked salmon
1 tablespoon finely chopped dill

Beat the butter with the cayenne and onion. Chop the salmon very finely and add to the mixture. Spread the butter in a long 1-cm/½-inch thick rectangle on a sheet of foil and chill until firm but not hard. Sprinkle with dill and roll up lengthways as for a swiss roll. Chill thoroughly and slice.

Horseradish Butter
100 g/4 oz soft butter
2 tablespoons freshly grated horseradish, or bottled creamed horseradish
pinch sugar

Beat the butter with the horseradish and sugar, spread in a 1-cm/½-inch thick layer on a sheet of cooking foil and chill. Make patterns with a fork and cut into squares.

Mock Caviare Butter
100 g/4 oz soft butter
1 teaspoon lemon juice
1 small egg yolk
1½ (58-g/2-oz) jars lumpfish roe

Beat the butter with all the other ingredients and spread in a 1-cm/½-inch thick layer on a sheet of cooking foil. Chill and cut into rounds.

137

Ohio Sauce

Serve with meat or fish fondue, cold beef and smoked mackerel.

2 hard-boiled eggs
4 Spanish onions
6 tablespoons oil
6 tablespoons vinegar
salt and pepper
2 garlic cloves
7 tablespoons pickled shredded
 beetroot
1 (142-ml/5-fl oz) carton
 soured cream
2 tablespoons curd cheese, or
 sieved cottage cheese
1½ teaspoons sugar
1 tablespoon chopped chives
1 tablespoon chopped dill
 (optional)
1 tablespoon chopped borage
 (optional)

Shell and quarter the eggs. Finely chop two of the quarters and leave on one side.

Peel the onions and cut into rings. Bring the oil and vinegar to the boil in a pan with 250 ml/8 fl oz water, add the onion rings, salt and pepper and simmer over a low heat for 5 minutes. Leave to cool.
 Peel and crush the garlic. Drain the beetroot and mix with the soured cream, the curd or cottage cheese, sugar, the remaining egg quarters, the garlic and the onion mixture, and blend all the ingredients together in the liquidiser. Mix the chives with the dill and borage, if used, keep 1 teaspoon on one side and stir the remaining herbs into the sauce. Season with salt and pepper to taste, transfer to a sauce boat and sprinkle with the chopped egg and the remaining herbs. *Serves 6*

Frankfurt Green Sauce

Serve with boiled beef, chicken or tongue, all kinds of savoury jellies, and poached eggs.

2 eggs
bunch parsley
bunch chives
large bunch fresh mixed herbs,
 (dill, tarragon, borage, basil)
1 teaspoon sugar
salt and white pepper
2 tablespoons lemon juice
6 tablespoons oil
4 tablespoons mayonnaise
3 tablespoons curd cheese or
 sieved cottage cheese
4 tablespoons soured cream

Hard-boil the eggs for 10 minutes, plunge into cold water, shell and dice, then leave on one side. Wash and drain all the herbs. Place them on a chopping board, sprinkle

with the sugar, salt and pepper and chop finely with a sharp knife, or pound them with a mortar and pestle. Transfer the mixture to a bowl. Beat the lemon juice with the oil, pour over the herbs, cover and leave to stand for 5 minutes.
 In a separate bowl, mix the mayonnaise with the curd or cottage cheese and the soured cream until smooth. Stir in the herb mixture and diced egg and stand the sauce in a cool place. *Serves 6*

Sauce Tartare

Serve with fish, meat fondue and hard-boiled eggs.

2 eggs
225 g/8 oz mayonnaise
4 tablespoons soured cream
bunch parsley
bunch each dill and tarragon
  (optional)
4 gherkins, or 2 gherkins and
  2 tablespoons mixed pickled
  vegetables
25 g/1 oz capers

Hard-boil the eggs for 10 minutes, plunge into cold water, shell and chop finely. Beat the mayonnaise with the soured cream. Wash the herbs, drain well, and chop finely with a sharp knife, or pound with a mortar and pestle. Drain the gherkins, the mixed pickled vegetables, if used, and the capers, and chop finely. Stir all the chopped ingredients into the mayonnaise mixture. Thin the tartare sauce, if necessary, with a little juice from the gherkins. *Serves 6*

Vinaigrette Dressing

Serve vinaigrette dressing with all kinds of salad. It goes particularly well with fresh asparagus.

2 small tomatoes
3 spring onions
large bunch fresh mixed herbs
  (parsley, chives, tarragon,
  lemon balm, salad burnet)
8 tablespoons oil
3 tablespoons wine vinegar
1 teaspoon lemon juice
¼ teaspoon sugar
salt and white pepper

Dip the tomatoes briefly into boiling water, remove the skins and cut them into quarters. Scoop away the seeds and dice the flesh. Wash and trim the spring onions, and chop very finely. Rinse the herbs in cold water, allow to drain and chop finely, or pound with a mortar and pestle. Beat the oil with the vinegar, lemon juice, sugar, salt and pepper and stir the tomato, chopped onion and herbs into the dressing. *Serves 6*

Dips for Vegetables

Serve these dips with strips or slices of raw vegetables, such as fennel, celery, red, green and yellow peppers, chicory and tomatoes.

Tomato Dip
100 g/4 oz tomato purée
1 (150-g/5.3-oz) carton natural yogurt
pinch each salt, cayenne pepper and sugar
1 teaspoon lemon juice
bunch chives
2 tablespoons pickled green peppercorns (optional)

Beat together the tomato purée, yogurt, salt, cayenne, sugar and lemon juice. Wash, drain and finely chop the chives and stir into the mixture. Drain the green peppercorns, if used, crush lightly with a fork and add to the dip.

Herb Dip
1 (150-g/5.3-oz) carton natural yogurt
100 g/4 oz full fat cream cheese
1 tablespoon single cream
½ clove garlic
½ teaspoon celery salt
pinch white pepper
4 tablespoons chopped fresh mixed herbs

Beat the yogurt with the cream cheese and cream until smooth. Peel and crush the garlic and add to the mixture, together with the celery salt, pepper and chopped herbs.

Orange Dip
100 g/4 oz mayonnaise
2 tablespoons double cream
juice and thinly peeled rind of 1 orange
1 tablespoon mild French mustard
pinch each salt, white pepper and sugar

Beat the mayonnaise with the cream, the orange juice and rind (reserving a little for garnishing), the mustard, salt, pepper and sugar. Transfer the dip to a bowl and garnish with the remaining orange rind.

Artichoke Dips

TOMATO DIP
2 tomatoes
100 g/4 oz mayonnaise
3 tablespoons tomato purée
2 tablespoons double cream
5 drops Tabasco sauce
pinch each salt and sugar
1 tablespoon paprika pepper
EGG DIP
3 hard-boiled eggs
8 tablespoons olive oil
3 tablespoons wine vinegar
1 teaspoon mild French mustard
salt and white pepper
1 teaspoon capers
1 tablespoon chopped parsley
1 tablespoon chopped lemon
* balm leaves (optional)*
MAYONNAISE DIP
100 g/4 oz mayonnaise
2 teaspoons lemon juice
3 tablespoons double cream

Peel and quarter the tomatoes,
remove the seeds and finely
dice the flesh. Beat with the

mayonnaise, tomato purée,
cream, and seasonings.
   Shell and halve the eggs.
Take out the yolks, pass them
through a fine sieve and beat
with the oil, vinegar, mustard,
salt and pepper. Drain the
capers, crush lightly with a
fork and stir into the mixture,
followed by the parsley and
lemon balm, if used. Add the
egg whites, chopped very
finely.
   Beat the mayonnaise with
the lemon juice. Whip the
cream until thick and fold in.

Cook's Tip

To cook the artichokes:
cut a slice off the stalk
end of each, place them
in boiling salted water
and simmer over a low
heat for 30 minutes until
tender.

Sausage Dips

GARLIC DIP
4 hard-boiled eggs
2 egg yolks
salt and pepper
juice of 1 lemon
4 cloves garlic
150 ml/¼ pint olive oil
GORGONZOLA DIP
50 g/2 oz soft butter
100 g/4 oz Gorgonzola cheese
1 (150-g/5.3-oz) carton natural
* yogurt*
CREAM DIP
2 hard-boiled eggs
50 g/2 oz butter
1 tablespoon wine vinegar
salt and white pepper
pinch paprika pepper
few drops Worcestershire sauce
2 tablespoons finely chopped
* chives*
150 ml/¼ pint soured cream
150 ml/¼ pint double cream

Shell and halve the hard-boiled
eggs. Take out the yolks, pass

through a fine sieve and mix
with the raw egg yolks, salt,
pepper and lemon juice. Peel
and crush the garlic and add to
the mixture. Gradually beat in
the oil, a little at a time, to
make a creamy mayonnaise.
Chop the hard-boiled egg
whites, stir into the dip and
serve.
   Beat the butter until light
and fluffy. Pass the
Gorgonzola through a sieve and
mix into the butter,
together with the yogurt.
   For the cream dip, shell and
halve the eggs. Pass the yolks
through a sieve and finely chop
the whites. Beat the butter
until light and fluffy, and work
in the vinegar, salt, pepper,
paprika, Worcestershire sauce,
chives, soured cream, egg white
and egg yolk. Lightly whip the
double cream and fold into
the dip.

Fetta Cheese Preserve

450 g/1 lb fetta or chèvre
  cheese
100 g/4 oz black olives
few sprigs fresh rosemary, or
  2 teaspoons dried rosemary
1 large onion
450 ml/¾ pint olive oil

Cut the cheese into 2-cm/
1-inch thick slices and place in
a preserving jar with the olives.
Add the fresh or dried
rosemary. Peel the onion, slice
into rings and arrange these
over the cheese. Pour over
enough olive oil to cover the
cheese, seal the jar, and leave
to marinate in the refrigerator
for at least 24 hours before
serving. Serve with fresh
granary bread and plenty of
coarsely ground black pepper.

Cook's Tip
Preserved cheese will
keep in the refrigerator
for up to 3 months, as
you can keep adding
fresh slices of cheese to
the marinade to replace
the ones taken out. By
the time you have
finished the cheese, the
olive oil will have
absorbed all the delicate
flavours and will make a
delicious addition to any
salad dressing.

Pickled Mushrooms

225 g/8 oz carrots
2 large sticks celery
450 g/1 lb mushrooms
75 g/3 oz shallots
2-4 chillies to taste
salt
2 sprigs dill
750 ml/1¼ pints distilled white
  wine vinegar
1 teaspoon sugar
¾ teaspoon black peppercorns
1 teaspoon mustard seeds
4 bay leaves
1 clove garlic

Wash the carrots, peel if
necessary and slice, using a
decorating knife, if liked. Trim
and wash the celery and cut
into 2-cm/1-inch pieces. Peel
the mushrooms and trim the
stems. Peel and quarter the
shallots. Slice the stalks off the
chillies, cut the chillies in half

and remove any seeds. Place all
the vegetables together in a
colander, sprinkle with salt,
cover and leave overnight.
Then quickly wash away the
salt and leave to drain.

Rinse out two 450-g/1-lb
preserving jars in boiling
water, dry well and fill with the
vegetables. Wash and drain the
dill and place a sprig in each
jar. Bring the vinegar to the
boil in a pan with the sugar,
pepper, mustard seeds and bay
leaves, remove the pan from
the heat and leave to cool. Peel
the garlic, chop finely and add
to the liquid. Pour into the jars
to cover the vegetables, and
seal.

Gooseberry Relish

Serve with roast lamb and cold meats and sausages.

1 kg/2¼ lb gooseberries
450 g/1 lb onions
350 g/12 oz raisins
225 g/8 oz brown sugar
1 teaspoon mustard powder
½ teaspoon cayenne papper
1 teaspoon turmeric
½ teaspoon salt
1 tablespoon powdered ginger
450 ml/¾ pint wine vinegar

Wash, top and tail the gooseberries, and chop into small pieces. Peel and dice the onions. Chop the raisins. Place the gooseberries in a large aluminium pan with the onion, raisins, sugar, mustard powder, cayenne, turmeric, salt, ginger and vinegar, and bring to the boil, stirring continuously. Cover the pan and simmer over a low heat for 45 minutes, stirring from time to time.

Rinse out your preserving jars in boiling water and dry thoroughly. Taste the gooseberry relish, adjust seasoning and pour while still hot into the jars. Seal carefully and leave to cool. Store in a cool, dark place.

Ginger Pears

Serve with game, poultry, roast beef and cold roast pork.

25 g/1 oz root ginger
450 ml/¾ pint distilled vinegar
400 g/14 oz sugar
rind of 1 lemon
1 stick cinnamon
generous pinch grated nutmeg
1.5 kg/3 lb firm pears
10 cloves

Peel and slice the root ginger. Bring 450 ml/¾ pint water to the boil in a pan with the vinegar and sugar and add the lemon rind, sliced root ginger, cinnamon and nutmeg. Remove the pan from the heat. Peel and halve the pears, remove the cores and stud the pear halves with the cloves. Place the pears in the liquid, cover the pan and return it to the boil. Simmer over a low heat for 10 minutes. Rinse two large preserving jars in boiling water and wipe dry. Remove the pears from the liquid and transfer to the prepared jars. Cover the pan again and simmer over a low heat for a further 20 minutes, then pour the liquid into the preserving jars to cover the pears. Seal the jars with greaseproof paper or transparent wrap and store in a cool, dark place.

Vegetable Chutney

Serve with all kinds of cold roast meat, hard-boiled eggs and cheese.

100 g/4 oz pickled cocktail
* onions*
1 gherkin
225 g/8 oz cauliflower
½ cucumber
225 g/8 oz French beans
300 ml/½ pint wine vinegar
generous pinch powdered mace
1 teaspoon white pepper
1 teaspoon mustard powder
1-2 tablespoons curry powder
generous pinch saffron
* (optional)*
100 g/4 oz sugar

Drain the cocktail onions and gherkin and chop finely. Wash, trim and chop the cauliflower, cucumber and French beans. Place all the prepared vegetables in a large, shallow aluminium pan with the vinegar and 250 ml/8 fl oz water. Add the seasonings and sugar, bring to the boil, cover and simmer over a low heat for about 30 minutes, until all the liquid has evaporated, stirring frequently. Rinse out two 450-g/1-lb preserving jars in boiling water and dry well. Taste the chutney and adjust seasoning, transfer it to the preserving jars and seal.

Indian Tomato Chutney

Serve with hard-boiled eggs, cold game, poultry, roast beef and curry.

900 g/2 lb ripe tomatoes
3 medium onions
1 green chilli
1 clove garlic
250 ml/8 fl oz wine vinegar
1 small cinnamon stick
1 teaspoon salt
2 tablespoons chopped parsley
225 g/8 oz brown sugar
1 teaspoon ground ginger
6 cloves
150 ml/¼ pint oil
2 tablespoons mustard seeds

Peel and quarter the tomatoes, remove the seeds and dice the flesh. Peel and finely chop the onions. Trim and chop the chilli, discarding the seeds. Peel and crush the garlic. Bring the vinegar to the boil in a pan with the tomato, onion, cinnamon and salt over a moderate heat, stirring continuously. Add the chopped chilli, parsley, garlic, sugar, ginger and cloves, and simmer over a low heat, stirring continuously, for 5-8 minutes. Heat the oil in a frying pan, add the mustard seeds and fry for 1 minute, stirring all the time. Mix the mustard seeds into the chutney and continue simmering for 30-40 minutes, until the mixture begins to thicken. Rinse out two 450-g/1-lb jam jars in boiling water, dry and fill with the chutney. Seal well.

Sweet and Sour Apple Chutney

Serve with all kinds of poultry dishes, cold roast beef and cheese.

1.5 kg/3 lb cooking apples
450 g/1 lb onions
350 g/12 oz raisins
1 tablespoon mustard seeds
225 g/8 oz brown sugar
350 ml/12 fl oz wine vinegar
1 teaspoon ground ginger
½ teaspoon cayenne pepper

Peel, quarter and core the apples, and cut into wedges. Peel and dice the onions. Wash and drain the raisins. Crush the mustard seeds with a mortar and pestle. Place the apple, onion, raisins and mustard seeds in a large aluminium pan with the sugar, vinegar, ginger and cayenne pepper and bring to the boil, stirring continuously. Simmer over a low heat, stirring frequently, for 30-40 minutes, until the chutney forms a thick liquid. Rinse out four or five 450-g/1-lb jam jars in boiling water and leave to dry. Pour the chutney into the jars while still hot and seal firmly.

Green Bean Chutney

Serve with herring dishes and cold meats.

1 kg/2¼ lb French beans
675 g/1½ lb onions
750 ml/1¼ pints wine vinegar
1 tablespoon cornflour
350 g/12 oz brown sugar
2 teaspoons strong mustard
1 tablespoon turmeric

Wash and top and tail the beans, allow to drain, and slice. Bring 2 litres/3½ pints salted water to the boil in a pan, add the beans, cover and simmer over a low heat for 15 minutes. Drain and leave to cool.

Peel and finely chop the onions. Bring 250 ml/8 fl oz of the vinegar to the boil in a pan, add the onion and simmer very gently until soft. Leave the pan on one side. Beat the cornflour into the remaining vinegar and place in a large aluminium pan with the sugar, mustard and turmeric. Bring the mixture to the boil over a moderate heat, stirring continuously, partially cover the pan, and simmer over a low heat for 8 minutes. Add the beans and the onion and vinegar mixture, and simmer the chutney for a further 15 minutes. Rinse out three 450-g/1-lb preserving jars in boiling water, dry well and transfer the chutney to them while still hot. Seal firmly.

145

Onion Soup

575 g/1¼ lb onions
1 clove garlic
100 g/4 oz butter
¼ teaspoon Tabasco sauce
pinch each cayenne pepper and
    grated nutmeg
1.25 litres/2¼ pints meat stock
250 ml/8 fl oz dry white wine
4 slices French bread
50 g/2 oz grated Emmental or
    Gruyère cheese

Peel the onions and the garlic.
Slice the onions into fine rings
and crush the garlic. Melt the
butter in a large shallow pan,
add the onion and garlic and
fry, stirring continuously, until
golden brown. Add the
Tabasco, cayenne, nutmeg and
stock, cover the pan and bring
to the boil. Simmer over a
moderate heat for 20 minutes.
Pour in the wine, continue
cooking for a few minutes and
take the pan off the heat.

Divide the soup between four
individual flameproof bowls.
 Lightly toast the bread and
place one slice on each portion
of soup. Sprinkle the toast with
the grated cheese and place the
bowls of soup under the grill
until the cheese has melted.
Serves 4

Consommé with Dumplings

150 ml/¼ pint milk
2 dry bread rolls
150 g/5 oz streaky bacon
1 large onion
1 egg
generous pinch each salt and
    grated nutmeg
1 litre/1¾ pints rich, clarified
    meat stock (as for White
    Wine Aspic, page 234)
75-100 g/3-4 oz fresh white
    breadcrumbs
small bunch parsley

Heat the milk in a pan, but do
not allow to boil. Cut the
bread rolls into very thin slices,
place in a bowl and pour over
the hot milk. Leave to stand.
 Remove the rind from the
bacon and dice the bacon as
finely as possible. Peel and
finely chop the onion. Fry the
bacon gently in a non-stick pan

until the fat runs, add the
onion and continue cooking,
stirring all the time, until the
onion becomes transparent.
Beat the egg with the salt and
nutmeg and pour over the
bread and milk mixture. Add
the bacon and onion, mix well
and leave to stand for a few
minutes.
 Bring the stock to the boil in
a pan. Mix enough fresh
breadcrumbs into the bread
and milk mixture to make a
stiff dough. Rinse two
teaspoons in cold water and
scoop eight oval dumplings out
of the dough, using the
teaspoons. Place the dumplings
in the boiling stock and
simmer over a low heat for 10
minutes. Wash, drain and chop
the parsley. Transfer two
dumplings to each of four
individual soup bowls, pour
over the consommé and
sprinkle with parsley. *Serves 4*

Hungarian Goulash Soup

275 g / 10 oz pork fillet
225 g / 8 oz braising steak
4 onions
2 carrots
2 green peppers
1 (227-g/8-oz) can tomatoes
2 tablespoons oil
2-3 teaspoons paprika pepper
generous pinch garlic salt
salt and black pepper
1 litre / 1¾ pints beef stock
150 ml / ¼ pint single cream

Trim the meat and cut into 2-cm/1-inch cubes. Peel the onions and slice into rings. Wash, scrape and slice the carrots. Wash and quarter the green peppers, remove the seeds and pith and cut the flesh into strips. Drain the tomatoes, retaining the juice on one side, and chop the tomatoes coarsely. Heat the oil in a large saucepan or flameproof casserole and fry the onion until transparent. Add the meat and brown it in the oil, then stir in the carrot and green pepper and continue cooking for 1-2 minutes. Add the chopped tomato, followed by the juice from the can, and stir well. Season to taste with the paprika, garlic salt, salt and black pepper. Pour in the beef stock, cover the pan, bring to the boil and simmer the goulash soup over a low heat for 60-80 minutes. Stir in the cream just before serving.
Serves 6-8

Oxtail Soup with Meatballs

1 small onion
150 g / 5 oz minced pork
1 egg, beaten
1-2 tablespoons fresh white
   breadcrumbs
salt and black pepper
pinch dried sage
100 g / 4 oz mushrooms
bunch parsley
2 (425-g/15-oz) cans oxtail soup
150 ml / ¼ pint red wine
100 g / 4 oz frozen peas
2 tablespoons tomato purée
pinch each paprika pepper and
   sugar
few drops Tabasco sauce
4 tablespoons single cream

Peel and finely chop the onion and mix with the minced pork and beaten egg. Add enough breadcrumbs to make the mixture into a stiff dough and season with salt, pepper and sage. Form the dough into meatballs, each the size of a walnut.

Clean and trim the mushrooms and slice as finely as possible. Wash and chop the parsley. Bring the oxtail soup to the boil in a pan with the wine, add the meatballs and simmer over a low heat for 10 minutes. After 5 minutes of cooking add the mushrooms, peas and tomato purée.

Season with the paprika, sugar and Tabasco, take the pan off the heat and stir in the cream. Sprinkle with parsley and serve. *Serves 4*

147

Cold Savoury Soups

Cream of Cucumber Soup

½ cucumber
350 ml/12 fl oz double cream
450 ml/¾ pint milk or buttermilk
½ teaspoon salt
½ teaspoon sugar
juice of 1 lemon
bunch dill

Peel the cucumber, cut in half lengthways and scoop away the seeds with a teaspoon. Finely dice the flesh. Mix together the cream, milk or buttermilk, salt, sugar and lemon juice. Wash the dill, chop finely and stir into the soup, together with the diced cucumber. Chill the soup and serve. *Serves 4*

Chilled Tomato Soup

1 kg/2¼ lb tomatoes
salt and white pepper
generous pinch celery salt
150 ml/¼ pint dry white
    vermouth
225 g/8 oz natural yogurt
50 g/2 oz mushrooms
150 ml/¼ pint single cream
bunch chives

Bring 450 ml/¾ pint water to the boil in a pan. Wash and quarter the tomatoes, place in the boiling water, cover the pan and simmer over a low heat for 10 minutes. Take the pan off the heat and pass the contents through a sieve. Season the tomato purée with the salt, pepper and celery salt and leave to cool.

Stir the vermouth into the yogurt. Clean, trim and finely slice the mushrooms. Beat the yogurt and vermouth mixture, the mushrooms and the cream into the cooled tomato purée and chill the soup in the refrigerator.

Wash and finely chop the chives and sprinkle over the soup before serving. *Serves 4*

Iced Borscht

350 g/12 oz natural yogurt
300 ml/½ pint soured cream
2 pickled cucumbers
1 onion
450 g/1 lb cooked beetroot,
    peeled and diced
salt and white pepper
generous pinch sugar
1 tablespoon orange juice
1 tablespoon lemon juice
2 hard-boiled eggs
GARNISH
few sprigs dill (optional)

Beat the yogurt with all but 2
tablespoons of the soured
cream. Drain and finely dice
the pickled cucumbers. Peel
and chop the onion. Stir the
cucumber, onion and diced
beetroot into the yogurt
mixture, and season with salt,
pepper, sugar and the orange
and lemon juice. Cover and
leave to stand in the
refrigerator for 1 hour.

Fill a soup tureen with ice
cubes and place in the
refrigerator. Shell the eggs and
cut each into eight wedges.
Keep three wedges on one side
and dice the rest. Remove the
ice cubes from the tureen and
fill the tureen instead with the
chilled borscht. Stir in the
diced egg. Whip the remaining
soured cream until stiff and
spoon into the centre of the
tureen. Garnish the borscht
with the remaining three egg
wedges, and a few sprigs dill, if
used. *Serves 4*

Andalusian Gazpacho

450 g/1 lb tomatoes
2 large cloves garlic
3 onions
1 cucumber
1 large green pepper
450 ml/¾ pint fat-free chicken
    or meat stock
2 tablespoons red wine vinegar
2 tablespoons olive oil
50 g/2 oz fresh white
    breadcrumbs
2 teaspoons tomato purée
salt and black pepper
generous pinch sugar
6 slices stale white bread
50 g/2 oz butter

Peel the tomatoes and cut into
quarters. Scoop away the
seeds. Peel and coarsely chop
the garlic and 2 onions. Wash
the cucumber, cut in half
widthways and coarsely dice
one half. Trim and halve the

green pepper, remove the seeds
and pith, and dice. Blend
together the tomato, garlic,
chopped onion, diced
cucumber and green pepper in
the liquidiser. Place the purée
in a bowl and whisk in the
stock, followed by the vinegar,
oil, breadcrumbs and tomato
purée. Season well with salt,
pepper and sugar and chill the
gazpacho in the refrigerator
for 2 hours.

Remove the crusts from the
stale white bread and cut the
bread into cubes. Melt the
butter in a frying pan. Fry the
bread in the butter until golden
brown and leave to cool. Peel
and finely chop the remaining
onion. Finely dice the rest of
the cucumber. Serve the bread
croûtons, onion and cucumber
with the gazpacho. *Serves 4*

Crispy Savouries

Cheese Spirals

350 g/12 oz plain flour
25 g/1 oz fresh yeast, or 15 g/
* ½ oz dried yeast*
150 ml/¼ pint lukewarm milk
100 g/4 oz butter or margarine
1 egg, beaten
1 teaspoon salt
2 egg yolks
100 g/4 oz Emmental or
* Cheddar cheese, grated*
1 teaspoon paprika pepper
1 tablespoon caraway seeds
1 tablespoon coarse salt

Lightly grease a baking tray.
Sift the flour into a mixing
bowl and form a well in the
centre. Cream the fresh yeast
with a little of the milk, add
the remaining milk, and pour
into the well in the flour.
(Whisk dried yeast into the
milk until dissolved and leave
to stand for 5 minutes before
pouring into the well in the
flour.) Sprinkle a little flour

over either yeast mixture, cover
and leave to stand in a warm
place for 15 minutes until
frothy. Melt the butter or
margarine, and add the fat, egg
and salt to the yeast mixture.
Work in the flour and beat
until smooth. Shape the dough
into a ball, cover, and leave to
rise in a warm place for 20–30
minutes. Roll out into a
rectangle 5-mm/¼-inch thick
Beat the egg yolks with 2
.tablespoons water. Coat one
half of the rectangle with egg
yolk and sprinkle with the
grated cheese. Fold over the
other half of the pastry, and
roll out again to 5-mm/¼-inch
thick. Cut into 2.5-cm/1-inch
wide strips, twist into spirals,
and coat with the remaining
egg yolk. Sprinkle the cheese
spirals with paprika, caraway
seeds and salt. Transfer to the
baking tray and bake in a hot
oven (220 C, 425 F, Gas Mark
7) for 15–20 minutes until
golden brown.

Poppy Seed and Cheese Biscuits

1 egg
225 g/8 oz plain flour
50 g/2 oz ground almonds
generous pinch cayenne pepper
½ teaspoon salt
225 g/8 oz Emmental or
* Cheddar cheese, finely grated*
100 g/4 oz butter or margarine
2 tablespoons poppy seeds
2 tablespoons chopped parsley

Lightly grease two baking
trays. Separate the egg. Sift the
flour into a large mixing bowl,
form a well in the centre, and
into it pour the ground
almonds, cayenne, half the salt
and half the grated cheese, and
the egg white. Cut the butter or
margarine into flakes and dot
round the edge of the well.
Work all the ingredients into a
smooth dough. Divide the
dough into two equal portions

and form one into a long roll,
5 cm/2 inches in diameter, and
the other into a ball. Wrap
both portions in foil and
leave to chill for 1–2 hours.
  Beat the egg yolk with
2 teaspoons water. Cut the
pastry roll into 3-mm/⅛-inch
thick slices, and coat the slices
with half the egg yolk. Sprinkle
with poppy seeds and place on
one of the baking trays.
  Roll the ball of dough out
thinly to form a long rectangle,
and coat with more of the egg
yolk. Sprinkle evenly with the
chopped parsley, and the
remaining cheese and salt. Roll
up the pastry rectangle
lengthways. Cut into 3-mm/
⅛-inch thick slices, coat with
the remaining egg yolk and
place the slices on the second
baking tray.
  Bake the poppy seed and
cheese biscuits in a moderately
hot oven (200 C, 400 F, Gas
Mark 6) for 15 minutes, or
until golden brown.

Cheese Tricorns

225 g/8 oz plain flour
generous pinch salt
1 egg
100 g/4 oz butter or margarine
4 (15-g/½-oz) portions
   processed cheese, or 50 g/2 oz
   Bavarian smoked cheese
1 egg yolk
2 tablespoons sesame seeds

Sift the flour and salt into a
large mixing bowl and form a
well in the centre. Tip the egg
into the well. Flake the butter
or margarine and dot around
the edge of the well. Quickly
work all the ingredients into a
dough, wrap in cooking foil or
greaseproof paper and leave to
stand in the refrigerator for
1 hour.

Lightly grease a baking tray.
Roll out the dough on a
floured surface and cut into
5-cm/2-inch rounds. Slice the
processed or smoked cheese
and cut into small cubes,
dipping the knife frequently
into hot water. Place one
cheese cube on each pastry
round and fold in the edges of
the pastry to form a tricorn.
Beat the egg yolk with
2 teaspoons water and use to
coat the tricorns. Sprinkle with
the sesame seeds. Transfer to
the greased baking tray and
bake in a moderately hot oven
(200 C, 400 F, Gas Mark 6) for
15–20 minutes until golden.

Caraway Biscuits

100 g/4 oz plain flour
pinch each salt, sugar and
   grated nutmeg
50 g/2 oz butter or margarine
100 g/4 oz matured Gouda
   cheese, finely grated
1 egg yolk
2–3 tablespoons caraway seeds

Grease a baking tray. Sift the
flour, salt, sugar and nutmeg
into a large mixing bowl and
form a well in the centre. Flake
the butter or margarine and
dot around the edge of the
flour. Tip the grated cheese
into the well, and quickly work
all the ingredients together to a
dough. Divide the dough into
two portions, wrap each in
greaseproof paper or cooking
foil and chill in the refrigerator
for 1 hour.

On a lightly floured surface,
roll out both portions of dough
separately until thin. Using a
pastry cutter, cut the dough
into squares or rectangles. Beat
the egg yolk with 2 teaspoons
water. Coat the biscuits with
egg yolk and sprinkle with
caraway seeds. Transfer to the
greased baking tray and bake
in a moderately hot oven
(200 C, 400 F, Gas Mark 6) for
15 minutes.

Crispy Savouries

Salt Twists with Cheese Dips

1 (370-g/13-oz) packet frozen
*   puff pastry*
1 egg
salt and pepper
DIPS
450 g/1 lb full fat cream cheese
150 ml/¼ pint soured cream
150 ml/¼ pint single cream
1 (35-g/1¼-oz) jar anchovy or
*   sardine paste*
1 tablespoon chopped fresh dill
*   or parsley, or 1 teaspoon*
*   dried dill or parsley*
½ red pepper
1 tablespoon paprika pepper

Allow the puff pastry to thaw, then, without rolling it out, slice horizontally into three. Beat the egg. Coat one side of each piece of pastry with egg. Sprinkle the first piece with salt and pepper and lay the second piece on top, coated side down.

Spread the upper side with more egg, sprinkle it also with salt and pepper and top with the third piece, again coated side down. Sprinkle a large baking tray with cold water. On a lightly floured surface, roll the pastry out into a 10 × 20-cm/4 × 8-inch rectangle and cut into 32 strips, 5 cm/ 2 inches in length. Twist each strip once and place on the baking tray. Leave to stand for 15 minutes, then bake in a moderately hot oven (200 C, 400 F, Gas Mark 6) for 15 minutes until golden.

To make the dips, beat the cream cheese with the soured and single cream and divide into two portions. Mix one portion with the anchovy or sardine paste and dill or parsley. Wash the red pepper, remove the seeds and dice finely. Stir into the remaining cheese portion, together with the paprika. Season both dips with salt and pepper.

Cheese Croissants

225 g/8 oz plain flour
¼ teaspoon salt
2 egg yolks
1–2 tablespoons water
100 g/4 oz butter or margarine
1 (200-g/7-oz) packet sliced
*   processed cheese*
2 tablespoons chopped parsley
1 tablespoon milk
2–3 tablespoons sesame seeds

Sift the flour and salt into a large mixing bowl, form a well in the centre, and tip in one of the egg yolks and the water. Flake the butter or margarine and dot around the edge of the flour. Quickly knead all these ingredients together to form a dough, wrap in cooking foil and leave to stand in the refrigerator for 1 hour.

Grease a baking tray. Roll out the pastry on a lightly

floured surface into a 30 × 40-cm/12 × 16-inch rectangle, and cut into 20 triangles of 7.5 × 15 × 15 cm/3 × 6 × 6 inches each. Cut each cheese slice into four equal triangles and place two triangles on each triangle of pastry. Sprinkle with parsley and roll into croissant shapes. Beat the remaining egg yolk with the milk. Coat the croissants with the mixture and sprinkle with sesame seeds. Transfer the croissants to the baking tray and bake in a hot oven (220 C, 425 F, Gas Mark 7) for 15–20 minutes until golden.

Spicy Cream Cheese Slices

1 (370-g/13-oz) packet frozen
   puff pastry
1 egg yolk
1 tablespoon coarse salt, or
   1 teaspoon table salt
225 g/8 oz full fat cream cheese
225 g/8 oz curd cheese
1 tablespoon brandy
2 tablespoons chopped parsley
2 tablespoons warm water
7 g/¼ oz gelatine
150 ml/¼ pint double cream

Allow the puff pastry to thaw,
then roll out evenly on a
floured surface to a 30 ×
50-cm/12 × 20-inch rectangle.
Leave to stand for 15 minutes.
Sprinkle a baking tray with
cold water. Beat the egg yolk,
and brush over the pastry, then
prick the pastry several times
with a fork and sprinkle one
half with the salt. Transfer to

the baking tray and bake in a
hot oven (220 C, 425 F, Gas
Mark 7) for 12–15 minutes.
Allow to cool, then cut the
pastry in half widthways,
dividing the salted half from
the unsalted. Slice the salted
half into 5 × 10-cm/2 × 4-inch
strips. Place the other half on a
sheet of cooking foil, and turn
up the foil edges all round to
make a 5-cm/2-inch lip.
   Beat together the cream
cheese, curd cheese, brandy
and parsley until smooth, and
season to taste. Pour the warm
water into a bowl and stand it
in a pan of hot water.
Sprinkle with the gelatine and
stir until dissolved, then add to
the cream cheese mixture.
Whip the double cream until
stiff and fold into the mixture.
Spread the cheese thickly over
the pastry base and top with
the strips of pastry. Chill until
the cream cheese is firm. Slice
before serving.

Cheese Boats

225 g/8 oz plain flour
¼ teaspoon salt
1 egg yolk
1–2 tablespoons water
100 g/4 oz butter or margarine
¼ red pepper
100 g/4 oz cooked chicken
1 (200-g/7-oz) packet sliced
   processed cheese
100 g/4 oz canned pineapple
   segments
1 tablespoon canned pineapple
   juice
3 tablespoons mayonnaise
1 teaspoon curry powder
a little mustard and cress

Sift the flour and salt into a
large mixing bowl, form a well
in the centre and tip in the egg
yolk and water. Dot the butter
or margarine around the edge
of the flour. Quickly knead all
the ingredients together to
form a dough, wrap in cooking
foil and leave to stand in the

refrigerator for 1 hour. Roll
out the pastry and use to line
eight boat-shaped pastry
moulds. Prick the pastry with a
fork. Bake the boats in a hot
oven (220 C, 425 F, Gas
Mark 7) for 10–15 minutes,
then leave to cool.
   Wash the red pepper,
remove the seeds and dice,
together with the chicken. Cut
the cheese into strips. Drain
the pineapple segments. Mix
together the pepper, chicken,
cheese and pineapple. Beat the
pineapple juice with the
mayonnaise and curry powder
and pour over the salad. Mix
in gently. Fill the boats with
the salad mixture and garnish
with mustard and cress.

Pies and Pastries

Cheese Puffs

CHOUX PASTRY
200 g/7 oz plain flour
250 ml/8 fl oz water
pinch salt
50 g/2 oz butter or margarine
4 eggs, beaten
FILLING
½ teaspoon salt
pinch each white pepper and
celery salt
575 g/1¼ lb full fat cream cheese
3 tablespoons dry sherry
1 teaspoon paprika pepper

Sift the flour into a bowl. Heat the water in a saucepan with the salt, melt the butter or margarine in it and bring quickly to the boil. Remove from the heat and shoot in the flour all at once, stirring vigorously. Return to the heat and beat for 1 minute until the dough forms a ball and comes clean away from the sides of the pan. Remove from the heat and leave to cool slightly. Grease a large baking tray. Preheat the oven to hot (220 C, 425 F, Gas Mark 7). Gradually beat the egg into the dough, making sure each addition is absorbed before beating in the next. Transfer the mixture to a piping bag fitted with a star-shaped nozzle and pipe dots of dough, each about the size of a cherry, onto the baking tray, leaving a space of 2.5 cm/ 1 inch around each. Bake in the oven for 20 minutes, then slice the puffs in half horizontally while still warm.

To make the filling, beat the salt, pepper and celery salt into the cream cheese, and divide into two portions. Stir the sherry to one portion, and beat the paprika to the other. Pipe the two flavours of cream cheese alternately into the bases of the puffs and arrange the top halves to form lids.

Puff Pastry Cheese Rings

1 (370-g/13-oz) packet frozen
puff pastry
1 egg yolk, beaten
100 g/4 oz Emmental or
Cheddar cheese, grated
pinch each salt and white pepper
225 g/8 oz curd cheese or
cottage cheese
3 tablespoons double cream
¼ teaspoon salt
pinch each white pepper and
caraway seeds, crushed

Allow the puff pastry to thaw. Sprinkle a large baking tray with cold water. On a lightly floured surface roll the pastry out into a 23 × 38-cm/9 × 15-inch rectangle, and using a 6-cm/2½-inch doughnut cutter, cut out 24 rings. Place the rings on the baking tray and coat with beaten egg yolk. Sprinkle with the grated cheese, salt and pepper, and leave the rings to stand on the baking tray for about 15 minutes. Bake in a hot oven (220 C, 425 F, Gas Mark 7) for 12–15 minutes, then transfer the rings to a wire rack and allow to cool.

Sieve the cottage cheese, if used, into a bowl. Beat the cottage or curd cheese with the cream, salt, pepper and caraway until smooth, transfer to a piping bag fitted with a star-shaped nozzle and pipe the mixture around twelve of the rings. Place the remaining twelve rings on top. *Makes 12*

Cook's Tip

If you do not have a doughnut cutter, use a 5-cm/2-inch round plain scone or pastry cutter inside a 6-cm/2½-inch one.

Savoury Cream Cheese Layer

1 (370-g/13-oz) packet frozen
  puff pastry
1 teaspoon pickled green
  peppercorns (optional)
900 g/2 lb full fat cream cheese,
  or curd cheese
2 teaspoons mild French
  mustard
8 drops Tabasco sauce
1 medium onion, grated
1 teaspoon each salt and
  Worcestershire sauce
2 teaspoons tomato purée
1 teaspoon paprika pepper
2 tablespoons chopped fresh
  mixed herbs, or 2 teaspoons
  dried mixed herbs
1 (57-g/2-oz) packet flaked
  almonds
GARNISH
10 chillies
10 pickled cocktail onions
10 thin slices smoked ham

Thaw the puff pastry following
the instructions on the packet.
Sprinkle a large baking tray
with cold water. Roll the
pastry out into three rounds,
each 25 cm/10 inches in
diameter, and place the rounds
individually on the baking
tray. Leave to stand for
15 minutes, then bake in a hot
oven (220 C, 425 F, Gas
Mark 7) for 12–15 minutes and
leave to cool.

Chop the green peppercorns,
if used. Beat the cream or curd
cheese with the mustard,
Tabasco sauce, onion, salt and
Worcestershire sauce until
smooth and divide into three
portions. Stir the tomato
purée and paprika into the
first portion, and the green
peppercorns, if used, and herbs
into the second. Spread the
first pastry round with the
tomato mixture, the second
with the herb mixture and the
third with half the remaining
cream or curd cheese. Stack
the rounds one on top of
another, beginning with the
tomato round, then the herb
round and topping with the
plain cheese round. Lightly
toast the almonds and press
round the edge of the cake.
Transfer the rest of the cheese
to a piping bag fitted with a
star-shaped nozzle and pipe
rosettes round the top of the
cake. Garnish with the chillies,
onions and rolls of ham.

Pies and Pastries

Cheese Pastry Pockets

1 (370-g/13-oz) packet frozen puff pastry
25 g/1 oz butter
100 g/4 oz Cheddar, Gruyère or Edam cheese, grated
2 eggs
2 tablespoons chopped parsley
¼ teaspoon salt
pinch cayenne pepper
juice of 1 lemon
1 egg yolk

Thaw the puff pastry following the instructions on the packet, and roll out on a lightly floured surface. Melt the butter. Mix together the cheese, eggs, parsley, salt, cayenne and lemon juice. Stir the melted butter into the cheese mixture and leave to cool.

Sprinkle a baking tray with cold water. Cut the pastry into large rounds, using a 10-cm/ 4-inch pastry cutter, and place one tablespoon of cheese mixture in the centre of each round. Brush round the edges of the pastry with cold water, fold the rounds in two and press the edges together. Beat the egg yolk with 2 teaspoons water and use to coat the pastry pockets. Transfer to the baking tray and leave to stand for 10 minutes. Bake in a moderately hot oven (200 C, 400 F, Gas Mark 6) for 12 minutes and leave to cool.

Minced Steak Pasties

PASTRY
275 g/10 oz plain flour
½ teaspoon salt
½ teaspoon baking powder
75 g/3 oz soft butter
1 egg
100 ml/4 fl oz soured cream
FILLING
1 onion
50 g/2 oz mushrooms
40 g/1½ oz butter
225 g/8 oz minced fillet steak
¼ teaspoon each salt, pepper and garlic salt
2 hard-boiled eggs
beaten egg yolk to glaze

Sift the flour, salt and baking powder into a mixing bowl. Form a well in the centre, flake the butter into the well and mix with a little of the flour. Add the egg and soured cream and knead all the ingredients together into a smooth dough. Cover and leave to stand in the refrigerator for 1 hour.

To make the filling, peel and finely dice the onion. Clean, trim and chop the mushrooms. Melt the butter and fry the onion and mushroom together. Mix with the minced steak and season with the salt, pepper and garlic salt. Shell and finely dice the eggs and stir into the meat mixture. Roll out the pastry to 3 mm/⅛ inch thick and cut into large rounds, using a 12-cm/4½-inch pastry cutter. Place one tablespoon of filling on each round. Brush all round the edge of the pastry with beaten egg yolk, fold the sides over the filling and press the edges firmly together. Coat the pasties with the remaining egg yolk, transfer to a baking tray and bake in a moderately hot oven (200 C, 400 F, Gas Mark 6) for 15–20 minutes.

Cornish Pasties

PASTRY
225 g/8 oz plain flour
pinch salt
1 egg
100 g/4 oz soft butter
FILLING
1 medium potato
1 shallot
150 g/5 oz stewing beef
4 tablespoons meat stock
1 teaspoon salt
½ teaspoon white pepper
1 teaspoon dried thyme
1 egg yolk

Sift the flour and salt into a mixing bowl, form a well in the centre and tip in the egg. Flake the butter round the edge of the flour and quickly knead all the ingredients together into a dough. Cover in cooking foil and leave to stand in the refrigerator for 1 hour.

To make the filling, peel the potato and shallot and dice

finely. Trim the stewing beef and cut into very small pieces. Mix the potato, shallot and beef with the meat stock, salt, pepper and thyme and divide into four equal portions. Divide the pastry also into four equal portions and roll each into an 18-cm/7-inch round. Beat the egg yolk with 2 teaspoons water. Spoon the filling onto the centres of the rounds and brush all round the edges of the pastry with beaten egg yolk. Fold the rounds in half and press the edges together, making a pattern round the folded edge with a knife, if liked. Coat the tops of the pasties with the remaining egg yolk. Place on a baking tray and bake in a moderately hot oven (190 C, 375 F, Gas Mark 5) for 25 minutes. Turn the oven down to moderate (170 C, 325 F, Gas Mark 3) and bake for a further 20 minutes.

Ham Quiches

PASTRY
225 g/8 oz plain flour
1 egg
1–2 tablespoons cold water
100 g/4 oz soft butter
FILLING
3 medium onions
100 g/4 oz smoked or boiled ham
2 tablespoons oil
100 g/4 oz Parmesan or Cheddar cheese, grated
2 tablespoons chopped parsley
4 eggs
150 ml/¼ pint double cream
¼ teaspoon salt
pinch white pepper

Sift the flour into a mixing bowl and form a well in the centre. Tip the egg and water into the centre, flake the butter round the edge and work all the ingredients together into a dough. Cover in cooking foil and leave to stand in the

refrigerator for 1–2 hours. Then roll the pastry out on a lightly floured surface and use to line eight 10-cm/4-inch tartlet cases. Prick the bases several times with a fork and bake in a hot oven (220 C, 425 F, Gas Mark 7) for 10 minutes. Leave the tart cases to cool.

Peel the onions and dice finely, together with the ham. Heat the oil and fry the onion until soft, then remove from the pan and leave to cool. Mix together the onion, ham, grated cheese and parsley, and spoon the mixture into the tarts. Beat the eggs with the cream, salt and pepper, and pour over the ham and cheese mixture. Return the tartlets to the oven, turn the oven down to moderately hot (200 C, 400 F, Gas Mark 6) and bake for a further 10–12 minutes. Cover with cooking foil, if necessary, to avoid burning.

Asparagus with Smoked Trout

450 g/1 lb fresh asparagus
pinch sugar
2 smoked trout fillets
2 hard-boiled eggs
1 tomato
few sprigs dill (optional)
1 gherkin
1 small onion
3 tablespoons oil
1 tablespoon wine vinegar
1 teaspoon mild French mustard
salt and white pepper
1 tablespoon chopped parsley

Wash the asparagus, lightly scrape the bases of the stalks and tie the shoots into two separate bundles with cotton thread. Bring 1 litre/1¾ pints salted water to the boil in a tall pan, add the sugar and place the asparagus bundles upright in the pan, so that the delicate tips show above the boiling water. Simmer over a low heat for 20 minutes, or until tender, drain and leave to cool. Then untie the asparagus, arrange on two individual plates and top each with a trout fillet.

Shell the eggs and cut one into slices. Finely chop the other and leave on one side. Wash, dry and slice the tomato. Garnish each plate with the egg and tomato slices, and the dill sprigs, if used.

Drain and finely chop the gherkin. Peel the onion and dice as finely as possible, or grate. Beat the oil with the vinegar, mustard, salt, pepper and parsley. Stir in the chopped egg, gherkin and onion and spoon the dressing over the asparagus.

Roquefort Pears with Smoked Ham

150 g / 5 oz smoked ham
1 ripe pear
50 g / 2 oz Roquefort cheese
50 g / 2 oz soft butter
2 teaspoons port
2 shelled walnut halves
2 lettuce leaves
2 teaspoons redcurrant jelly
2 slices brown bread

Arrange the smoked ham on two individual plates. Wash, dry and halve the pear. Remove and discard the core, then, using a teaspoon, carefully scoop the flesh out of each half to within 1-cm/½-inch of the shell. Place the pear flesh in a bowl and crush it with a fork. Work in the Roquefort, then add the butter and port and beat the mixture until smooth and creamy. Transfer to a piping bag fitted with a large star-shaped nozzle and pipe the Roquefort cream into the pear halves. Top each pear half with a shelled walnut and place on the plates next to the ham.

Wash the lettuce, allow to dry and place one leaf on each plate. Top with a spoonful of redcurrant jelly. Lightly toast the bread, cut into fingers and serve with the pears.

Cook's Tip

If you find the Roquefort cream too rich, you can replace the butter with curd cheese, or sieved cottage cheese.

Smoked Eel with Vegetable Salad

¼ small cauliflower
1 carrot
¼ leek
2 tablespoons drained canned sweet corn
1 tablespoon oil
1 teaspoon cider vinegar
pinch each salt and pepper
225 g / 8 oz smoked eel
1 orange
½ punnet mustard and cress
2 teaspoons freshly grated or bottled creamed horseradish
pinch sugar
1 tablespoon double cream
2 slices white bread
4 small lettuce leaves
GARNISH
few sprigs dill (optional)

Wash the cauliflower and break into florets. Wash and trim the carrot and leek and cut each into strips. Wrap the prepared vegetables separately in cooking foil, place the foil packets in boiling water and simmer over a low heat for 15 minutes. Drain the sweet corn. Remove the foil packets from the water, open them and leave the vegetables to cool. Beat the oil with the vinegar, salt and pepper. Mix the cooked vegetables and the sweet corn together in a bowl and stir in the dressing. Cut the eel into four equal slices and remove the skin. Cut two slices from the centre of the orange, place each on an individual plate and top with the cress. Squeeze the juice from the rest of the orange, mix with the horseradish, sugar and cream, and spoon over the cress. Cut the bread slices in half and top with the lettuce leaves. Place the eel pieces on the lettuce, garnish with dill, if liked, and arrange on the plates. Place the vegetable salad on the plates next to the eel.

Chicken Breasts with Melon

½ Iceberg or Webb's Wonder
   lettuce
1 small head red endive
2 medium carrots
½ punnet mustard and cress
2 cooked chicken breasts
¼ honeydew melon
2 tablespoons natural yogurt
3 tablespoons mayonnaise
2 tablespoons French dressing
   (see page 88)

Wash the lettuce and red
endive, separate the leaves and
allow to drain. Line two
individual plates with the
lettuce. Cut the red endive
leaves into strips. Trim and
peel the carrots and cut also
into strips. Snip the cress, rinse
in cold water and leave to
drain. Arrange the red endive,
carrot and cress in portions on
the lettuce.

Slice the chicken and
arrange in a fan shape on the
plates. Cut the melon into four
wedges and scoop away the
seeds. Remove the melon rind
and place two melon wedges
on each plate alongside the
chicken. Beat the yogurt with
the mayonnaise and place in a
small serving bowl. Pour over
the French dressing in a spiral
shape, and serve separately
with the chicken salad.

Chicken Salad

pinch each salt and pepper
1 teaspoon paprika pepper
generous pinch ground ginger
2 chicken legs
2 tablespoons oil
3 large tomatoes
2 sticks celery
4 tablespoons French dressing
   (see page 88)
2 tablespoons mayonnaise
1 teaspoon pickled pink
   peppercorns (optional)

Mix the salt and pepper with
the paprika and ginger and rub
into the chicken legs. Heat the
oil in a frying pan and fry the
chicken over a high heat until
brown all over. Reduce the
heat to moderate and continue
frying for a further 15 minutes.
Drain the chicken on
absorbent kitchen paper and
leave to cool.
   Wash, dry and slice the
tomatoes. Wash the celery, cut

into thin strips retaining the
leaves, and blanch in a little
boiling salted water for 3
minutes. Drain the celery and
arrange on two individual
plates together with the
chicken legs and tomato slices.
Sprinkle the French dressing
over the celery, and top each
plate with 1 tablespoon
mayonnaise. Sprinkle with
pink peppercorns, if used.

Cream Cheese Mousse

225 g/8 oz full fat cream cheese
1 teaspoon lemon juice
200 ml/7 fl oz double cream
salt and white pepper
few drops Worcestershire sauce
1 (150-g/5-oz) can prawns
1 teaspoon chopped dill
7 g/¼ oz gelatine
4-6 lettuce leaves
GARNISH
2 sprigs dill
lemon slices

Beat the cream cheese with the lemon juice, 3 tablespoons cream, salt, pepper and Worcestershire sauce until smooth. Rinse the prawns in cold water, drain and divide into two portions. Finely chop one portion and stir into the cream cheese mixture, together with the chopped dill. Pour 2 tablespoons warm water into a

bowl and stand the bowl in a pan of hot water. Sprinkle with the gelatine and stir until dissolved. Mix the gelatine liquid into the cream cheese and stand briefly in the refrigerator to cool.

Whip the remaining cream until stiff. Fold into the cheese mixture. Rinse out two individual jelly moulds with cold water and pour in the cheese mousse. Smooth the surface, place the moulds in the refrigerator and leave for 3 hours until completely set.

Wash and dry the lettuce leaves and use to line two individual plates. Dip the moulds into hot water for a few seconds and turn the mousses out onto the beds of lettuce. Garnish each plate with a sprig of dill, a few lemon slices and the remaining prawns.

Cream Cheese Tartare

225 g/8 oz full fat cream cheese
150 ml/¼ pint double cream
¼ teaspoon salt
few drops lemon juice
½ red pepper
½ green pepper
1 gherkin
¼ red onion
¼ white onion
small bunch parsley
10 stuffed olives
1 tablespoon pickled green
  peppercorns (optional)
1 teaspoon each paprika pepper,
  caraway seeds, capers and
  freshly ground white pepper

Beat the cream cheese with the cream, salt and lemon juice and arrange in the centre of two individual plates. Wash the red and green peppers, remove the seeds and pith and dice finely. Drain and chop the

gherkin. Peel and finely dice the onions. Wash, drain and finely chop the parsley. Slice the olives. Drain the pickled green peppercorns, if used. Arrange the diced peppers, gherkin, red and white onion, parsley, sliced olive, green peppercorns, paprika, caraway seeds, capers, and white pepper in spoonfuls around the cream cheese on each plate. Mix the cream cheese tartare to taste with the different seasonings and accompaniments at the table, and serve with a choice of breads.

Gourmet Fare

2 large tomatoes
5 tablespoons French dressing
  (see page 88)
100 g/4 oz cottage cheese
2 cooked chicken breasts
¼ lettuce
1 tablespoon capers
4 tablespoons mayonnaise
2 teaspoons anchovy paste
3 tablespoons single cream
1 teaspoon strong mustard
salt and pepper

Wash and dry the tomatoes
and slice vertically down the
centre of each, stopping short
of cutting through the base.
Scoop out the seeds and
sprinkle the insides with a little
French dressing. Fill the half-
open tomatoes with the cottage
cheese. Slice the chicken
breasts and arrange on two
individual plates with the
stuffed tomatoes.
    Wash and drain the lettuce,
cut into strips and toss in the
remaining French dressing.
Arrange the lettuce on the
plates.
    Drain and chop the capers.
Mix the mayonnaise with the
anchovy paste, cream,
mustard, salt, pepper and all
but 1 teaspoon of the chopped
capers. Spoon the dressing
over the sliced chicken and
sprinkle the remaining
chopped capers on top.

Scandinavian Fare

100 g/4 oz fresh or canned
  button mushrooms
2 tablespoons oil
1 tablespoon wine vinegar
1 tablespoon diced onion
salt and pepper
1½ green peppers
½ red pepper
100 g/4 oz ham sausage,
1 pickled cucumber
6 tablespoons mayonnaise
1 teaspoon mustard
2 tablespoons single cream
4 thin wedges honeydew melon
few lettuce leaves
2 smoked trout fillets
2 hard-boiled eggs, halved
1 teaspoon pickled green
  peppercorns, drained and
  chopped (optional)
1 teaspoon brandy

Clean fresh or drain canned
mushrooms. Beat the oil with
the vinegar, diced onion, salt
and pepper, and pour over the
mushrooms. Trim and finely
dice the green and red peppers,
and stir 1 tablespoon of each
into the mushroom salad.
    Remove the skin from the
ham sausage, drain the pickled
cucumber and cut both into
strips. Place in a bowl with the
remaining diced green and red
pepper. Beat 4 tablespoons
mayonnaise with the mustard
and cream, season and stir into
the sausage mixture.
    Peel the melon wedges and
remove the seeds. Divide
the lettuce between two
individual plates and top with
the ham sausage salad.
Arrange the mushroom salad,
trout fillets, melon wedges and
eggs alongside. Beat the
remaining mayonnaise with the
brandy and chopped
peppercorns, if used, and
spoon over the eggs.

Italian Fare

100 g/4 oz thinly sliced Parma
   ham
100 g/4 oz salami
4 tomatoes
½ small onion
12 black olives
1 small head red endive
2 teaspoons French dressing
   (see page 88)
2 tablespoons mayonnaise
1 teaspoon pickled green
   peppercorns (optional)

Divide the ham and salami
slices between two individual
plates. Wash, dry and slice the
tomatoes. Peel the onion and
cut into rings. Arrange the
tomato slices and onion rings
next to the meat, together with
the black olives.
   Wash the red endive,
separate the leaves, drain
thoroughly and cut into strips.
Arrange the endive on the
plates and sprinkle with the

French dressing. Spoon the
mayonnaise over the sliced
tomato and sprinkle with the
green peppercorns, if used.

Shepherd's Fare

100 g/4 oz cottage cheese
1 red pepper
1 head chicory
½ punnet mustard and cress
½ (396-g/14-oz) can artichoke
   hearts
1 hard-boiled egg
1 gherkin
3 tablespoons oil
1 tablespoon wine vinegar
pinch each salt, pepper and
   ground ginger
1 tablespoon chopped fresh
   mixed herbs, (parsley, chives,
   dill)
6 black olives

Spoon the cottage cheese into
the centres of two individual
plates. Wash and dry the red
pepper, slice into rings and
remove the seeds and pith.
Wash the chicory, separate the
leaves, and leave to drain. Snip
the cress, rinse in cold water
and leave to dry. Drain and

halve the artichoke hearts.
Arrange all the salad
ingredients in portions around
the cottage cheese.
   Shell and finely chop the
egg. Drain and chop the
gherkin. Beat the oil with the
vinegar, salt, pepper, ginger,
chopped herbs, egg and
gherkin, and sprinkle the
dressing over the salad.
Garnish both plates with 3
black olives.

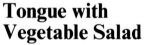

Tongue with Vegetable Salad

225 g/8 oz sliced cooked tongue
1 tomato
2 tablespoons canned sweet corn
½ cucumber
1 strip canned pimiento
salt and pepper
1 carrot
½ head kohlrabi
small bunch parsley
1 tablespoon wine vinegar
3 tablespoons oil
pinch dried oregano

Fold the slices of tongue in half and arrange in a fan shape on two individual plates. Wash, dry and halve the tomato, scoop out the seeds and leave on one side. Drain the sweet corn. Cut two thick slices from the cucumber and finely dice the slices. Drain and chop the pimiento. Mix the tomato seeds with the sweet corn, diced cucumber and pimiento, salt and pepper. Fill the tomato shells with the mixture, and place one tomato half on each plate.

Wash, trim and peel the carrot and kohlrabi and cut into strips, together with the rest of the cucumber. Mix the vegetable strips together and divide between the two plates. Wash, drain and finely chop the parsley. Beat the vinegar with the oil, oregano and chopped parsley, add salt and pepper to taste and pour over the mixed vegetables.

Pork with Persimmon Cream

6 thin slices cold roast pork
few lettuce leaves
1 hard-boiled egg
2 teaspoons lumpfish roe
50 g/2 oz full fat cream cheese
1 ripe persimmon
2 tablespoons double cream
pinch each salt and ground
* ginger*

Arrange the slices of pork on two individual plates. Wash and drain the lettuce and place next to the meat. Shell the egg, cut in half lengthways and top each portion of lettuce with an egg half. Garnish the egg with the lumpfish roe.

Place the cream cheese in a bowl. Wash, dry and quarter the persimmon. Hold each persimmon quarter over the cream cheese so that no juice is lost, and using a pointed knife, cut out the soft flesh. Slice the flesh into strips and place on one side.

Scrape the inside skin of the persimmon thoroughly over the bowl and stir the juice into the cheese, together with the cream, salt and ginger. Whip the cheese mixture until light and fluffy, transfer to a piping bag fitted with a large star-shaped nozzle and pipe one rosette onto each plate. Top the rosette with the strips of persimmon.

Smoked Turkey with Curried Eggs

100 g/4 oz smoked turkey or
*   chicken breast*
½ mango
generous pinch cayenne pepper
1 hard-boiled egg
50 g/2 oz cream cheese
2 tablespoons double cream
generous pinch salt
2 slices wholemeal bread
1 teaspoon curry powder
25 g/1 oz soft butter
generous pinch freshly ground
*   black pepper*
1 large tomato
1 tablespoon chopped chives

Slice the turkey and arrange on two individual plates. Peel and slice the mango, arrange over the turkey and sprinkle with cayenne.

Halve the egg and remove the yolk. Beat the cream cheese with the cream and salt, divide into two portions and spread one portion over the wholemeal bread. Pass the egg yolk through a sieve into the remaining portion, add the curry powder and butter and beat until light and fluffy. Transfer to a piping bag fitted with a star-shaped nozzle and pipe the curry cream into the egg whites. Sprinkle with black pepper.

Wash, dry and slice the tomato. Place one egg half on each piece of bread and arrange on the plates, together with the tomato slices. Sprinkle the tomatoes with the chopped chives.

Sausage 'Rolls' with Carrot Salad

6 long, thin slices streaky bacon
12 cocktail sausages
2 medium carrots
1 small apple
1 teaspoon lemon juice
2 tablespoons single cream
salt and white pepper
½ teaspoon sugar
few lettuce leaves
2 slices wholemeal bread
15 g/½ oz butter

Remove the rind from the bacon and cut the rashers in half widthways. Wrap each sausage in a piece of bacon and secure with a cocktail stick. Grill the sausage 'rolls' under a moderate heat for 8-10 minutes, turning once, until the bacon is crisp. Then place six skewers on each plate and leave to cool.

Trim, peel and grate the carrots. Peel and coarsely grate the apple, mix with the carrot and sprinkle with lemon juice. Beat the cream with the salt, pepper and sugar and stir into the carrot and apple salad.

Wash the lettuce, allow to drain and divide between the plates. Arrange the carrot and apple salad on the lettuce.

Serve with wholemeal bread and butter.

Cold Beef with Fruit Salad

2 oranges
100 g/4 oz green grapes
100 g/4 oz black grapes
1 tablespoon chopped almonds
juice of ½ lemon
2 tablespoons Grand Marnier
    liqueur
¼ teaspoon sugar
225 g/8 oz cold roast beef
1 small grapefruit
3 tablespoons cranberry jelly
1 teaspoon freshly grated
    horseradish, or bottled
    creamed horseradish
2 small lettuce leaves

Slice the oranges in half widthways. Cut out the flesh, remove the thin skin between the segments, and slice the flesh, discarding any pips. Retain two orange shells and discard the other two.

Wash, dry and halve the grapes, and remove the pips. Mix the diced orange, grapes and chopped almonds together in a bowl. Beat the lemon juice with the Grand Marnier and sugar, pour over the fruit salad, cover and leave to stand at room temperature for 30 minutes.

Slice the beef very thinly and arrange on two individual plates. Peel the grapefruit, remove the skin from the segments and dice the flesh, discarding the pips. Mix the grapefruit with the cranberry jelly and horseradish. Wash and drain the lettuce, place one leaf on each plate and top with the grapefruit mixture. Fill the two reserved orange shells with the marinated fruit salad and arrange next to the lettuce. Serve with fresh French bread.

Duck with Artichoke Salad

1 boned duck breast
salt and white pepper
1 tablespoon oil
50 g/2 oz butter
1 teaspoon pickled pink or
    green peppercorns (optional)
½ (396-g/14-oz) can artichoke
    hearts
½ onion
1 small tomato
2 teaspoons chopped parsley
1 tablespoon wine vinegar
3 tablespoons olive oil
few lettuce leaves

Rub the duck breast with a little salt and pepper and brush with the oil. Cover and leave to marinate at room temperature for 2 hours.

Melt the butter in a frying pan and fry the duck breast over a moderate heat for 7 minutes, stirring continuously.

The duck will still be rare; if you prefer it cooked through, continue frying for a further 7 minutes. Leave to cool, cut into slices and arrange on two plates. Drain the pink or green peppercorns, if used, and sprinkle over the duck.

Drain and halve the artichoke hearts. Peel the onion and cut into rings. Peel and quarter the tomato, remove the seeds and dice the flesh. Mix the artichoke, onion, tomato and chopped parsley together in a bowl. Beat the vinegar with the oil, add salt and pepper to taste and pour over the artichoke salad. Wash and drain the lettuce leaves, divide between the plates and arrange the salad on top.

Russian Salad Platter

150 g/5 oz frozen mixed
    vegetables
225 g/8 oz ham sausage,
    unsliced
1 stick celery
2 tablespoons mayonnaise
pinch each salt, celery salt and
    white pepper
½ teaspoon soy sauce
6 tomatoes
1 teaspoon coarsely ground
    black pepper
2 tablespoons double cream
3 hard-boiled eggs
3 teaspoons lumpfish roe

Cook the frozen vegetables
following the instructions on
the packet, drain and leave to
cool. Remove the skin from
the ham sausage and cut the
sausage into thin strips. Wash
and trim the celery and also
slice into strips. Mix the meat
and vegetables together. Beat
the mayonnaise with the salt,
celery salt, white pepper and
soy sauce, and pour over the
salad ingredients.

    Wash, dry and thinly slice
the tomatoes. Arrange the
tomato slices in a ring on two
individual plates. Spoon
the salad into the centre of the
rings and sprinkle the tomato
with coarsely ground black
pepper.

    Whip the cream until stiff.
Shell and halve the eggs, place
three halves on each portion of
salad and top with whipped
cream. Garnish the egg halves
with the lumpfish roe.

Children's Lunch Party

Children have seemingly insatiable appetites, so offer your young guests plenty to eat and a variety of different fruit juices to drink. You can buy a lot of prepared foods, such as cold meats, continental sausages, various kinds of bread and bread rolls, mixed pickles, sauces, crisps and sweets. Brightly coloured paper plates, cups and napkins add a festive note, and have the added bonus of no washing up. Here are some suggestions for home-made party dishes.
Serves 10-12

Meat Loaf Sandwiches
2 onions
100 g/4 oz fresh white
  breadcrumbs
1.5 kg/3 lb minced beef, lamb or
  pork
4 eggs
1 teaspoon paprika pepper
salt and white pepper
2 tablespoons chopped parsley
12 lettuce leaves
24 slices white bread
3 tomatoes
2 hard-boiled eggs

Peel and dice the onions and mix in a bowl with the breadcrumbs, minced meat, eggs, paprika, salt, pepper and parsley. Mix all the ingredients well together, shape into a long loaf and bake in a moderately hot oven (200 C, 400 F, Gas Mark 6) for 40-45 minutes. Leave the meat loaf to cool and cut into twelve thick slices.
  Wash and thoroughly drain the lettuce leaves, place one leaf on each of twelve slices of

bread and top with a piece of meat loaf. Wash, dry and slice the tomatoes. Shell and slice the eggs. Arrange the tomato and egg over the meat loaf and top each sandwich with a second slice of bread.

Potato and Cucumber Salad
1 kg/2¼ lb new potatoes
2 onions
½ cucumber
100 g/4 oz mayonnaise
4 tablespoons natural yogurt
3 tablespoons wine vinegar
salt and pepper
bunch chives

Wash the potatoes, place in a pan containing boiling salted water and simmer over a moderate heat for 20-25 minutes until tender. Then drain, allow to cool, remove the skins and slice. Peel and finely dice the onions. Wash the cucumber and cut into very thin slices. Mix the potato,

onion and cucumber together in a bowl. Beat the mayonnaise with the yogurt, vinegar, salt and pepper and pour over the salad. Wash, drain and chop the chives and sprinkle over the salad before serving.

Spicy Rice Salad
225 g/8 oz rice
1 tablespoon curry powder
450 g/1 lb boned cooked chicken
2 pears
3 slices canned pineapple
½ (425-g/15-oz) can mandarin
  segments
1 tablespoon chopped pistachio
  nuts (optional)
3 tablespoons lemon juice
salt and pepper
5 tablespoons oil

Cook the rice following the instructions on the packet, adding the curry powder to the cooking water. Rinse through with cold water and leave to drain. Remove any skin from

the chicken and dice the meat. Peel, halve, core and dice the pears. Drain and chop the pineapple and mandarins. Mix all these ingredients together in a serving bowl, and add the pistachios, if used.

Beat the lemon juice with the salt, pepper and oil and pour over the rice salad.

Pasta Salad

450 g/1 lb luncheon meat
225 g/8 oz Cheddar or Tilsit
cheese
225 g/8 oz pickled cucumbers
1 red pepper
100 g/4 oz cooked peas
575 g/1¼ lb cooked pasta shells
or noodles
3 tablespoons wine vinegar
salt and white pepper
6 tablespoons oil

Remove the skin from the luncheon meat and dice the meat, together with the cheese. Drain and slice the pickled

cucumbers. Wash and quarter the red pepper, remove the seeds and pith and dice the flesh. Mix the luncheon meat, cheese, cucumber and red pepper together in a bowl and add the cooked peas and pasta shells or noodles.

Beat the vinegar with the salt, pepper and oil and stir the dressing into the salad.

Stuffed French Bread

2 long French loaves
8 tablespoons mayonnaise
100 g/4 oz Mortadella or
Cervelat sausage
100 g/4 oz salami
100 g/4 oz smoked cheese
3 large tomatoes
3 hard-boiled eggs
parsley sprigs
few lettuce leaves
100 g/4 oz blue cheese (Danish
Blue, Dolcelatte)
450 g/1 lb meat salad (bought
ready-made, or use any meat
salad from the salad section)

Cut the loaves in half lengthways and spread the insides with the mayonnaise. Slice the Mortadella or Cervelat, together with the salami and smoked cheese. Fold the slices in half and arrange at intervals along the bottom half of one loaf. Wash and dry the tomatoes. Shell the eggs. Cut 2 tomatoes and 2 eggs into slices, and the remaining tomato and egg into wedges. Arrange the sliced egg and tomato in the intervals between the cold meat and cheese slices. Garnish the loaf with sprigs of parsley and cover with the top half.

Wash the lettuce, drain thoroughly and use to line the bottom half of the second loaf. Slice the blue cheese. Arrange the meat salad in spoonfuls on the lettuce leaves, alternating with slices of blue cheese and the remaining tomato and egg wedges. Top with the other half of the loaf.

Summer Fruit Dessert

225 g/8 oz morello cherries
225 g/8 oz raspberries
225 g/8 oz redcurrants
225 g/8 oz sugar
50 g/2 oz cornflour
250 ml/8 fl oz double cream
¼ teaspoon cinnamon

Pick over the fruit, stone the cherries, place in a pan with 450 ml/¾ pint water, bring to the boil and simmer for 5 minutes. Pass the fruit through a sieve and top up the purée with water to 1 litre/1¾ pints. Add 200 g/7 oz sugar and bring back to the boil. Mix the cornflour with a little cold water, stir into the fruit purée and simmer for 3 minutes, stirring continuously. Pour the fruit mixture into a bowl and leave to set in the refrigerator. Before serving, whip the cream with the remaining sugar until stiff, spoon onto the dessert and sprinkle with cinnamon.

169

Giant Meat Platter

225 g/8 oz ham
225 g/8 oz smoked ham
100 g/4 oz smoked Parma ham
100 g/4 oz salami
225 g/8 oz tongue sausage or
    cooked tongue
225 g/8 oz ham sausage or
    Mortadella sausage
100 g/4 oz meat loaf
100 g/4 oz liver sausage
450 g/1 lb brawn sausage
400 g/14 oz finely minced fillet
    steak
2 onions
salt and white pepper
½ teaspoon paprika pepper
2 egg yolks
few lettuce leaves
2 tablespoons oil
2 teaspoons wine vinegar
1 tablespoon caraway seeds
2 hard-boiled eggs
2-4 tomatoes
bunch radishes
coarsely ground black pepper
GARNISH
parsley sprigs
a selection of pickled vegetables
    such as baby gherkins,
    canned pimiento, canned
    baby sweet corn cobs and
    olives

Arrange all the cold meats
except for the brawn sausage
on a large serving platter or
board, as shown.

Place the minced steak in a
bowl. Peel and dice one onion
and mix half into the minced
steak with the salt, white
pepper, paprika and one egg
yolk. Wash the lettuce, drain
thoroughly and arrange in one
corner of the meat platter. Top
with the minced steak tartare.
Make a well in the centre of
the meat and carefully tip in
the second egg yolk. Place the
rest of the diced onion next to
the egg and sprinkle with a
little paprika.

Arrange the brawn sausage

on a separate flat dish. Peel the
remaining onion, slice into
rings and arrange over the
brawn. Beat the oil with the
vinegar, pour over the brawn
and sprinkle with the caraway
seeds.

Shell and slice the hard-
boiled eggs. Wash and dry the
tomatoes and cut each into
eight wedges. Wash the
radishes and leave to drain.
Arrange the sliced egg and a
few tomato wedges on the
platter, and sprinkle the egg
with coarsely ground black
pepper. Serve the remaining
tomato wedges and the
radishes separately. Garnish
the platter with parsley and a
selection of pickled vegetables,
and serve with various kinds of
bread, rolls and crispbreads.
Serves 8-10

Cook's Tip

You can of course serve
any kind of cold meat at
a buffet and the ones
listed are intended only
as suggestions. The steak
tartare can be replaced
with a meat or sausage
salad, a Waldorf or even
a crab salad. Slices of
pâté, terrine or cold
roast meat can be
substituted for the
brawn sausage, and you
can vary the garnishes
with sliced fresh
cucumber, celery and red
and green peppers,
depending on what is in
season.

Gourmet Platters

SAUSAGE AND MEAT PLATTER
2 heads chicory
4 tablespoons salad dressing
 (see pages 88-89)
1 tomato, sliced
225 g/8 oz garlic sausage
100 g/4 oz smoked ham
6 Veal Tournedos with Broccoli
 Purée (see page 131)
CHEESE PLATTER
225 g/8 oz Stilton cheese
225 g/8 oz Emmental cheese,
 sliced
cheese balls (see page 133)
2 red peppers
3 stuffed olives
225 g/8 oz full fat cream cheese
¼ teaspoon celery salt
1 tablespoon brandy
1 shallot, finely grated

Trim and wash the chicory, cut into fine strips and toss in the salad dressing of your choice. Place the chicory salad in the centre of a large serving platter

and garnish with the tomato slices. Arrange the garlic sausage, smoked ham and Veal Tournedos on the platter.

Cut the Stilton into wedges and arrange on a platter with the Emmental and cheese balls. Slice the peppers into wedges and remove the seeds and pith. Slice the olives. Beat the cream cheese with the celery salt, brandy and grated shallot until well-mixed, transfer to a piping bag fitted with a star-shaped nozzle and pipe onto the pepper wedges. Garnish each with a slice of olive and arrange on the platter. *Serves 6*

Cook's Tip

Serve with a herring salad and a cheese and salami salad.

Country Sausage Platter

100 g/4 oz tongue sausage or
 cooked tongue
100 g/4 oz garlic sausage
225 g/8 oz ham
275 g/10 oz smoked or cold
 roast pork
100 g/4 oz liver sausage
225 g/8 oz Mortadella
 sausage
225 g/8 oz salami, unsliced
few lettuce leaves
275 g/10 oz meat salad
 (bought ready-made, or
 use any meat salad of your
 choice)
GARNISH
gherkins, canned baby sweet
 corn cobs, sliced tomato,
 radishes, parsley

Arrange the sliced cold meats on one or two flat serving dishes, as shown in the photograph. Top one of the

platters with the unsliced salami. Wash and drain the lettuce leaves and arrange on top of the other platter. Place 2 tablespoons meat salad on the lettuce and serve the remaining meat salad in a separate bowl. Garnish the platters with baby gherkins, baby sweet corn cobs, tomato slices, radishes and parsley. Serve with an assortment of breads, rolls and crispbreads. *Serves 6*

Cook's Tip

Cold meat platters can be prepared several hours in advance, if you cover them with cling-film and store in a cool place.

Ham and Salad Platter

175 g/6 oz frozen peas
1 large avocado
1 teaspoon lemon juice
½ red pepper
1 gherkin
100 g/4 oz ham sausage, unsliced
4 tablespoons mayonnaise
salt and white pepper
¼ teaspoon curry powder
few sprigs dill
1 crisp dessert apple
2 tablespoons fresh grated horseradish, or bottled creamed horseradish
250 ml/8 fl oz double cream
generous pinch sugar
400 g/14 oz smoked or boiled ham
450 g/1 lb smoked or cold roast pork
GARNISH
2 hard-boiled eggs
black grapes
2 tomatoes
½ honeydew melon
5 gherkins
5 chillies
canned baby sweet corn cobs
parsley sprigs

Cook the peas following the instructions on the packet, drain and leave to cool. Wash and dry the avocado, cut in half lengthways and remove the stone. Scoop the flesh out of each half, to within ½ cm/¼ inch of the shell, and dice. Sprinkle the diced avocado and the inside of the shells with lemon juice.

Wash and dry the red pepper, remove the seeds and pith and cut the flesh into strips. Drain the gherkin and cut also into strips, together with the ham sausage. Place the peas, diced avocado, red pepper, gherkin and ham sausage together in a bowl and mix well. Beat the mayonnaise with the salt, pepper and curry powder, and stir into the salad. Fill the avocado halves with the salad and garnish each with a sprig of dill.

Peel, quarter, core and finely grate the apple, and place in a bowl with the horseradish. Whip the cream with the sugar until stiff and fold into the horseradish and apple mixture. Taste and adjust seasoning, then transfer the horseradish and apple cream to a piping bag fitted with a large plain nozzle. Cut six slices from the smoked or boiled ham, roll up the slices and pipe horseradish cream into each. Cover a large serving platter with the smoked or roast pork. Arrange the ham rolls on top. Cut a few more slices of ham, fold in half and place at one end of the dish, together with the remaining uncut piece of ham. Arrange the stuffed avocado halves at the other end of the dish.

Shell and slice the eggs. Wash and drain the grapes. Quarter the tomatoes. Cut the melon into wedges and remove the seeds. Drain the gherkins, and slice into a fan-shape, if liked. Garnish the platter with the egg, grapes, tomato quarters, melon wedges, gherkins, chillies, baby sweet corn cobs and parsley. Serve with toasted white bread, brown bread, rye bread and butter. *Serves 6-8*

Cheese Platters with Camembert Cream

6 puff pastry horns (bought
    ready-made)
2 egg yolks, beaten
2 tablespoons grated Cheddar
    cheese
225 g/8 oz full fat cream cheese
pinch cayenne pepper
salt and white pepper
1 teaspoon lemon juice
2 stuffed olives, sliced
few lettuce leaves
100 g/4 oz Brie cheese
225 g/8 oz Camembert cheese
175 g/6 oz soft butter
½ clove garlic
1 small onion
½ teaspoon caraway seeds
1 teaspoon paprika pepper
few sprigs parsley
100 g/4 oz Danish Blue cheese
225 g/8 oz Gruyère cheese,
    sliced
225 g/8 oz Bavarian smoked
    cheese with ham, sliced
225 g/8 oz Cervelat sausage

Paint the pastry horns with
half the beaten egg yolk,
sprinkle with grated Cheddar
and bake in a hot oven (220 C,
425 F, Gas Mark 7) for a few
minutes, until the cheese begins
to melt. Beat the cream cheese
with the cayenne, salt, pepper
and lemon juice, transfer to a
piping bag fitted with a star-
shaped nozzle, and pipe the
mixture into the horns.
Garnish with the olive slices
and arrange on one side of a
serving platter. Arrange the
lettuce and Brie on the dish.
    Crush the Camembert with a
fork and mix with the butter
and the remaining beaten egg
yolk. Peel and crush the garlic.
Peel the onion, cut in half
widthways and slice one half
into rings. Grate the other half
into the Camembert mixture,
and add the garlic, half the
caraway seeds, the paprika and
salt and pepper to taste. Pile
in a bowl and top with onion
rings, parsley, and caraway
seeds.
    Cut the Danish Blue into
wedges and arrange all the
remaining cheeses and the
Cervelat sausage on another
large serving platter. Serve
with radishes, stuffed eggs (see
pages 96-97), fresh bread
and scoops of butter.
Serves 6-8

Cold Platters

Fish Platter

225 g/8 oz frozen prawns
1 medium pineapple
3 tablespoons mayonnaise
5 tablespoons single cream
1 teaspoon lemon juice
1 teaspoon sugar
generous pinch salt
1 teaspoon pickled green
   peppercorns or capers
   (optional)
Trout with Dill (see page 114)
Salmon with Vegetable Salad
   (see page 115)
GARNISH
stuffed eggs (see pages 96-
   97), horseradish and apple
   cream (see page 172), apple
   slices, lettuce, asparagus tips

Place the prawns in a bowl,
cover and leave to thaw at
room temperature, then drain.
Cut a wedge out of the
pineapple lengthways, leaving
a gap measuring one-third of
the whole pineapple. Remove

the rind from the wedge and
dice the flesh, discarding any
hard parts of the core. Beat the
mayonnaise with the cream,
lemon juice, sugar and salt.
Mix the diced pineapple with
the prawns in a bowl, stir in
the mayonnaise dressing and
spoon the prawn salad into the
pineapple cavity. Sprinkle with
the pickled green peppercorns
or capers, if used.
   Arrange the stuffed
pineapple, the trout, the
salmon and the vegetable salad
on serving platters as shown in
the photograph. Garnish with
any of the suggested garnishes,
as liked. *Serves 6-8*

Copenhagen Platter

1 (150-g/5-oz) can prawns
3 strips canned red pimiento
1 tablespoon chopped fresh or
   canned pineapple
3 tablespoons mayonnaise
225 g/8 oz ham
8 tomatoes
few sprigs dill
salt and white pepper
250 ml/8 fl oz double cream
1-2 tablespoons grated fresh
   horseradish, or bottled
   creamed horseradish
pinch sugar
100 g/4 oz thinly sliced streaky
   bacon
few lettuce leaves
400 g/14 oz liver pâté
parsley sprigs
6 hard-boiled eggs
225 g/8 oz meat salad (bought
   ready-made)

Rinse the prawns in cold

water, drain and chop
coarsely. Drain and dice the
pimiento. Place the chopped
prawns and pimiento in a bowl
with the pineapple, and stir in
the mayonnaise. Spread the
slices of ham with this mixture,
roll up and arrange on a
serving platter. Slice two
tomatoes, place a slice on each
ham roll and garnish with dill.
   Cut the end opposite the
stalk off each remaining
tomato, scoop out the seeds
and sprinkle the insides with
salt and pepper. Whip the
cream until stiff and fold in the
horseradish and sugar. Fill the
tomatoes and place next to the
ham rolls. Remove the rind
from the bacon and grill until
crisp. Arrange the lettuce with
the bacon and liver pâté and
top with parsley. Shell and
halve the eggs; mix the yolks
into the meat salad. Spoon into
the egg whites and garnish with
parsley. *Serves 6*

Meat Platters with Pineapple Salad

1.5 kg/3¼ lb assorted sliced cold meats (tongue, meat loaf, roast pork, liver sausage, tongue sausage, garlic sausage, roast beef)
175 g/6 oz frozen peas
1 red pepper
225 g/8 oz Mortadella sausage
225 g/8 oz Edam cheese
2 tablespoons flaked almonds, toasted
4 tablespoons mayonnaise
4 tablespoons natural yogurt
2 tablespoons vinegar
salt and pepper
1 small onion
1 pineapple
1 maraschino cherry
GARNISH
tomato wedges, green pepper rings, stuffed olives, sliced hard-boiled egg, lettuce, canned baby sweet corn cobs, gherkins, pickled cocktail onions, canned pimiento strips, parsley

Arrange the cold meats on several serving platters, as shown in the photograph.

Cook the peas following the instructions on the packet, drain and leave to cool. Trim and quarter the red pepper, remove the seeds and pith, and slice into strips, together with the Mortadella and Edam. Mix the red pepper, Mortadella and Edam in a bowl with the peas and almonds. Beat the mayonnaise with the yogurt, vinegar, salt and pepper. Peel the onion and grate into the dressing, then stir the dressing into the salad. Cut a wedge out of the pineapple lengthways. Remove the rind from the wedge, dice the flesh and mix into the salad. Spoon the salad into the pineapple cavity, top with the maraschino cherry, and place on one of the serving platters. Garnish the platter with any of the suggested garnishes, as liked, and serve with a Seasonal Sausage Salad (see page 52). *Serves 8-10*

Smörgåsbord

Serves 10-12

MEAT PLATTER
1 kg/2¼ lb assorted cold meats
1 hard-boiled egg
HERRING PLATTER
10 pickled herring fillets
5 small cooked carrots
bunch dill
8 maatjes herring fillets
1 onion
2 tomatoes, quartered
RED HERRING SALAD
10 maatjes herring fillets
500 ml/17 fl oz milk
175 g/6 oz pickled beetroot
2 crisp dessert apples
150 ml/¼ pint soured cream
2 tablespoons mayonnaise
1 slice lemon
GREEN HERRING SALAD
10 maatjes herring fillets
3 tablespoons chopped dill or parsley
juice of 2 lemons
6 tablespoons oil

2 green peppers
1 (283-g/10-oz) can green beans
175 g/6 oz pickled cocktail onions
275 g/10 oz canned pimiento
MEATBALLS
50 g/2 oz butter
1 onion
1 tablespoon chopped parsley
450 g/1 lb minced beef
1 egg
6 tablespoons fresh breadcrumbs
salt
½ teaspoon dried marjoram
1 teaspoon paprika pepper
4 tablespoons oil

Arrange the sliced cold meats on a serving platter or board. Shell and quarter the egg and use to garnish the platter.

For the herring platter, drain the pickled herring fillets. Cut the carrots in half widthways and wrap each half in a herring fillet. Garnish with a sprig of dill and arrange in a

circle round the edge of a flat dish. Drain the maatjes herrings and place in the centre of the dish. Wash and quarter the tomatoes. Peel the onion and slice into rings. Garnish the herring platter with the tomato and onion.

To make the red herring salad, soak the salted herring fillets in the milk for 30 minutes, then drain and cut into pieces. Drain and chop the beetroot. Wash, quarter, core and dice the apples. Mix the herring, beetroot and apple together in a bowl. Beat the soured cream with the mayonnaise, and stir into the salad ingredients. Garnish the red herring salad with a sprig of dill and a slice of lemon.

To make the green herring salad, chop the salted herrings and place in a bowl with the dill or parsley, the lemon juice and oil. Trim and quarter the green peppers, remove the seeds and pith, and dice. Drain

and chop the beans, cocktail onions and pimiento. Mix all these ingredients into the herring and leave to stand.

For the meatballs, melt the butter in a pan. Peel and finely dice the onion, and fry in the butter with the parsley. Place in a bowl with the minced beef, the egg, breadcrumbs, salt, marjoram and paprika, mix well together and shape into small balls. Heat the oil in a frying pan and fry the meatballs for 8-10 minutes, turning continuously. Transfer to a serving bowl and leave to cool.

Add variety to a Smörgåsbord by serving stuffed eggs (see pages 96-97), stuffed tomatoes (see page 23) and Gravad Lax, (see page 112) and round it off with a crisp cucumber salad, assorted sliced cheeses and plenty of fresh rolls and butter.

Danish Buffet

Serves 10-12

RED CABBAGE SALAD
20 dried prunes
575 g/1¼ lb pickled red cabbage
1 onion, cut in rings
PRAWN SALAD
few lettuce leaves
450 g/1 lb thawed prawns
juice of 1 small grapefruit
2 tablespoons double cream
1 teaspoon lumpfish roe
HERRING SALAD
6 pickled herring fillets
6 cooked carrots
few lettuce leaves
50 g/2 oz lumpfish roe
4 egg yolks
1 onion, cut in rings
DEEP-FRIED PLAICE
6 plaice fillets
¼ teaspoon salt
4 tablespoons plain flour
2 egg yolks, beaten
6 tablespoons dried breadcrumbs
oil for deep-frying

Remoulade sauce (see page 197)
800 g/1¾ lb cold roast pork
675 g/1½ lb cold roast beef
225 g/8 oz smoked eel
GARNISH
parsley, dill, tomatoes, radishes, lemon slices and grapes

Soak the prunes in enough cold water to cover for 12 hours, then stone them and bring to the boil in a pan with the juice. Drain the red cabbage, add to the pan, and simmer gently over a low heat for 20-30 minutes, until the prunes are tender. Transfer the prunes and cabbage to a bowl and garnish with the onion rings.

For the prawn salad, line a bowl with the lettuce and top with the prawns. Sprinkle with grapefruit juice and garnish with the whipped cream and lumpfish roe.

For the herring salad, drain the pickled herring fillets and

cut into pieces. Slice the carrots. Line one half of a large flat dish with the lettuce, top with the lumpfish roe, and place the egg yolks in their shells on top. Mix the herring, carrot and onion and arrange on the dish.

Rub the plaice with salt and coat first in flour, then in beaten egg yolk and finally in breadcrumbs. Heat the oil in a deep fryer to 190 C/375 F and fry the fillets for 3-4 minutes until golden brown. Serve with the Remoulade sauce.

Arrange the cold meats and the skinned eel on separate platters and finish your Danish buffet with a Gravad Lax (see page 112) and a selection of Danish cheeses. Garnish the dishes with any of the suggested garnishes.

DANISH ALMOND RINGS
1 kg/2¼ lb marzipan
225 g/8 oz granulated sugar
450 g/1 lb icing sugar, sifted

5 egg whites
grated rind of 1 lemon
1 teaspoon lemon juice

Knead the marzipan to a dough with the granulated sugar, half the icing sugar, 3 egg whites, the grated lemon rind and juice. Roll the marzipan into ten finger-thick rolls of varying lengths. Join the ends to make rings; the largest ring should have a diameter of 18 cm/7 inches, and each successive ring measure 1 cm/½ inch less than the previous one. Line two baking trays with greaseproof paper, lay the rings separately on the trays and bake in a cool oven (150 C, 300 F, Gas Mark 2) for 20 minutes, until pale golden. Allow the rings to cool, then stack them as shown. Beat together the remaining icing sugar and egg whites and pipe a fine pattern on the rounds.

177

The Cold Table

Italian Buffet

Serves 6-8

One of the best-known Italian delicacies must be Parma ham with melon, so it would be appropriate to serve it for an Italian buffet with some salami and Mortadella sausage. As the centrepiece of your buffet, why not serve Italian Veal Galantine (see page 39) or Braised Veal 'Mostarda' (see page 126), accompanied by different salads? You can also include a selection of creamy Italian cheeses, such as Gorgonzola, Provolone and goat's cheese (shown above), Bel Paese and Dolcelatte, as well as fresh fruit, olives, white bread, 'grissini' (Italian bread sticks), fruit juices and Italian wines. And finally, no Italian buffet would be complete without pizzas, some recipes for which are given here.

Party Pizzas

PASTRY
1 teaspoon castor sugar
300 ml/½ pint warm water
2 teaspoons dried yeast
900 g/2 lb plain flour
1 teaspoon salt

TOPPINGS
6 large tomatoes
100 g/4 oz canned artichoke
 hearts
350 g/12 oz grated Gruyère,
 Mozzarella or Cheddar
 cheese
175 g/6 oz mixed canned
 shellfish (mussels, prawns,
 shrimps)
10-12 black olives
100 g/4 oz mushrooms
100 g/4 oz salami
6 stuffed olives, halved
2 tablespoons chopped fresh
 mixed herbs
4 tablespoons olive oil

Dissolve the sugar in the warm water and stir in the yeast. Leave to stand in a warm place for about 10 minutes until frothy. Sift the flour and salt into a large warmed bowl, make a well in the centre and pour in the yeast liquid. Mix to a soft, but not sticky dough. Turn out onto a lightly floured surface and knead the dough for 10 minutes or until smooth and elastic. Shape into a ball, place in a bowl, cover with a damp cloth and leave to rise until doubled in size.

To make the toppings, peel the tomatoes, cut two of them into slices and the remaining four into wedges. Drain and halve the artichoke hearts. Divide the grated cheese into three portions. Drain the shellfish. Stone the black olives. Clean, trim and slice the mushrooms. Grease three 18-cm/7-inch sandwich tins. Knead the dough quickly and lightly for 1-2 minutes, divide into three equal portions and pat each portion into one of the tins. Cover the first with the tomato slices, the artichoke halves and the salami. Sprinkle the stuffed olives over the top, followed by one portion of grated cheese. Arrange the shellfish, black olives and half the remaining tomato wedges on the second pizza and top with the second portion of cheese. Cover the third pizza with the sliced mushroom, the remaining tomato wedges and grated cheese and scatter the chopped herbs over the top. Sprinkle each pizza with olive oil and bake in a hot oven (220 C, 425 F, Gas Mark 7) for 30-40 minutes.

Olive Appetisers
2 sticks celery
2 cloves garlic
3 shallots
400 g/14 oz black olives
4 mint leaves
6 tablespoons olive oil

Wash and trim the celery, cut in half lengthways and slice into 5-cm/2-inch pieces. Peel

the garlic and shallots. Finely chop the garlic and cut the shallots into thin rings. Arrange all these ingredients with the olives in layers in a wide preserving jar. Chop the mint leaves and sprinkle over the top. Pour on the olive oil, seal the jar and leave to stand in a cool place for 2 hours.

Tomato and mozzarella Salad
6 large tomatoes
175 g/6 oz mozzarella cheese
salt and freshly ground black pepper
1 teaspoon each fresh oregano and basil, or ½ teaspoon each dried oregano and basil
5 tablespoons olive oil

Wash, dry and slice the tomatoes. Remove the mozzarella from its wrapping, drain and slice thinly. Arrange the tomato and cheese in layers on a plate. Sprinkle with the salt, pepper and herbs, and pour over the oil.

Vegetable Salad with Italian Green Sauce
225 g/8 oz frozen peas
225 g/8 oz frozen diced carrots
300 g/12 oz frozen broccoli
300 g/12 oz frozen French beans
½ (396-g/14-oz) can artichoke hearts
1 small head red endive
few cos lettuce leaves
2 hard-boiled eggs
10 black olives
8 tablespoons chopped fresh mixed herbs (parsley, chives, dill, basil, marjoram)
4 spring onions
1 clove garlic
4 canned anchovy fillets
1 mild chilli (optional)
6 tablespoons olive oil
3 tablespoons wine vinegar
salt and pepper

Cook all the frozen vegetables in separate pans following the instructions on the packets, drain and leave to cool. Drain and halve the artichoke hearts. Separate the red endive leaves,

wash the endive and the lettuce and allow to dry. Shell and slice the eggs. Line one half of a large salad platter with lettuce and the other half with red endive. Arrange the vegetables in portions on the salad leaves, and garnish with the sliced egg and the olives.

To make the sauce, place the mixed herbs in a bowl. Wash, trim and slice the spring onions. Peel and finely chop the garlic. Drain the anchovy fillets. Cut the chilli, if used, in half, remove the seeds and pith, and chop finely, together with the anchovies. Mix the spring onion, garlic, chilli and anchovy with the herbs. Beat the oil with the vinegar, salt and pepper and pour over the top. Transfer the sauce to a sauce boat and serve with the salad.

Italian Fruit Salad
1.25 kg/2-3 lb mixed fresh fruit (pear, melon, persimmon, peach, grapes, figs)
2 tablespoons amaretto liqueur, or peach brandy
100 g/4 oz glacé cherries
1 family-size carton vanilla ice cream
2 tablespoons chopped pistachio nuts

Peel the fruit, remove any pips or stones, cut into thin slices and mix together in a large bowl. Pour over the amaretto or peach brandy. Cover and leave to stand for 30 minutes, then arrange the fruit salad in individual bowls and add the cherries. Top each portion with a scoop of vanilla ice cream. Sprinkle with the pistachios just before serving.

Classic Cold Buffet

Serves 6

For more formal occasions, serve Veal Terrine (see page 39) with preserved kumquats, Roast Stuffed Ham or Pork with Curry Sauce (see page 125), and six of the Trout with Dill (see page 114). Offer two or three salads, a cheese platter, and a light dessert.

Waldorf Salad
2 medium dessert apples
3-4 sticks celery, trimmed
1 (227-g/8-oz) can pineapple
  pieces, drained
100 g/4 oz chopped walnuts
juice of ¼ lemon
100 g/4 oz mayonnaise
salt, white pepper and sugar

Peel, quarter and core the apples and cut into fine strips. Wash the celery and slice also into strips. Mix the apple, celery, pineapple and walnuts and add the lemon juice.

Season the mayonnaise with salt, pepper and sugar and stir into the salad.

Mediterranean Salad
1 Iceberg or Webb's Wonder
  lettuce
3 hard-boiled eggs, quartered
3 tomatoes, quartered
2 onions, cut in rings
½ (283-g/10-oz) can green
  beans, drained
½ cucumber, sliced
8 black or green olives
4 tablespoons olive oil
juice of 1 lemon
1 teaspoon mild French mustard
salt and pepper
1 tablespoon chopped fresh
  mixed herbs

Separate the lettuce leaves.

Mix together the eggs, tomatoes, onions and beans. Add the cucumber and olives. Beat the oil with the lemon juice, mustard, salt and pepper, pour the dressing over the salad and sprinkle with the chopped herbs.

Summer Bavarois
450 g/1 lb Summer Fruit
  Dessert (half quantity of
  recipe on page 169)
450 ml/¾ pint milk
1 vanilla pod
6 egg yolks
175 g/6 oz castor sugar
15 g/½ oz gelatine
300 ml/½ pint double cream

Make the Summer Fruit Dessert and pour into six glasses or bowls to set.

Place the milk in a pan with the vanilla pod and bring to the boil. Cover the pan, remove from the heat, and infuse for 10 minutes. Beat the

egg yolks with the sugar until thick, then gradually pour in the milk, beating continuously. Return to the pan with the vanilla pod and heat very gently. Do not let the custard become too hot or it will curdle. Stir over a low heat for 5-8 minutes until the custard thickens just enough to coat the back of a spoon. Strain into a chilled bowl and leave to cool slightly, stirring from time to time. Pour 2 tablespoons warm water into a bowl and stand in a pan of hot water. Sprinkle with the gelatine and stir until dissolved, then add to the custard. Allow the mixture to cool completely, stirring frequently. Lightly oil six small jelly moulds. Whip the cream until thick and fold gently into the custard. Pour the mixture into the moulds. Leave to set in the refrigerator for 1-2 hours. To serve, dip each mould briefly in hot water and turn out onto the Desserts.

Sunday Buffet

Serves 6

Here is a light summer lunch to serve as a change from the traditional Sunday roast. Have one main cold meat dish such as Vitello Tonnato (see page 131) and a salad platter assorted cheeses and fruit.

Salad Platter
1 small head red endive
100 g/4 oz mushrooms
6 tablespoons oil
2½ tablespoons lemon juice
pinch sugar, salt and pepper
1 tablespoon chopped parsley
50 g/2 oz corn salad or watercress
½ onion
1 tablespoon wine vinegar
1 (142-g/5-oz) can prawns
1 large lettuce leaf
2 tablespoons soured cream
1 tablespoon chopped dill
2 hard-boiled eggs

Wash the endive, separate the leaves, drain and cut into narrow strips. Trim, clean and slice the mushrooms. Beat 4 tablespoons oil with 2 tablespoons lemon juice and divide into two portions. Season one portion with the sugar, salt and pepper, toss the endive in the dressing and arrange in one corner of a large serving dish. Mix the parsley into the remaining portion, season to taste and pour over the sliced mushrooms. Arrange the mushrooms on the platter next to the endive.

Trim the corn salad or watercress, wash thoroughly and allow to drain. Peel and finely chop the onion. Beat the remaining oil with the vinegar, onion, salt and pepper, mix the dressing into the corn salad or watercress and place on the platter.

Drain the prawns, rinse under cold running water and

leave to dry. Wash and drain the lettuce. Mix the soured cream with the remaining lemon juice, the dill, and salt and pepper to taste and pour over the prawns. Arrange the lettuce on the platter and top with the prawns. Shell the eggs, cut into wedges and add to the salad platter.

Cheese Platter with Cheese Salad
225 g/8 oz Stilton cheese
225 g/8 oz Brie cheese or Bavarian Brie with herbs
225 g/8 oz Cheddar cheese
225 g/8 oz fresh Gouda cheese
1 kiwi fruit
100 g/4 oz strawberries
3 tablespoons canned mandarin segments
1 tablespoon lemon juice
2 tablespoons natural yogurt
½ teaspoon sugar
pinch salt
generous pinch cayenne pepper

Cut the Stilton and Brie into wedges and dice the Cheddar. Arrange the cheese on a board.

To make the cheese salad, cut the Gouda into strips. Thinly peel the kiwi fruit, cut into slices and halve each slice. Hull and quarter all but one of the strawberries. Drain the mandarins. Mix the Gouda, kiwi fruit, strawberries and mandarins together in a bowl. Beat the lemon juice with the yogurt, sugar, salt and cayenne, pour over the salad ingredients, cover and leave to stand in the refrigerator. Garnish the salad with the remaining strawberry before serving.

Food for a Feast

The choice of dishes for entertaining larger numbers spans the whole spectrum of food, from canapés to desserts. A truly giant buffet would consist of several smaller ones, including cold meat platters, a cheeseboard, one or two cold roast joints, several light salads, a pâté or terrine or two, a choice of desserts, fresh fruit, and a plentiful supply of bread and rolls. We centred this buffet round Spit-roast Pork with Herb Mayonnaise (see page 126), Glazed Saddle of Venison (see page 127), and Pâté d'Escargots (see page 36), served here with apple and horseradish cream (as for the stuffed ham rolls on page 172). You can find ideas for the cheeseboard on previous pages, for the stuffed eggs on pages 96-97, and for canapés in the section 'For Cocktail Parties' (pages 26-33) – or you may like to try the special Party Canapés shown here. Allow 2 stuffed eggs and 4-5 canapés per person. All the other recipes given below should serve 6-8.

Party Canapés

12 slices white bread
75 g/3 oz butter
12 small slices cold roast pork
6 canned pineapple segments
6 slices banana
3 tablespoons mayonnaise
1 teaspoon curry powder
6 slices truffled liver pâté
3 tablespoons diced Madeira
   aspic (see page 202)
6 orange segments
4 tablespoons Cottage Cheese
   with Herbs (see page 23)
6 thin slices smoked salmon
6 sprigs dill
4 tablespoons Waldorf Salad
   (see page 180)
12 small slices cold roast beef
6 walnut halves

Remove the crusts from the bread, cut each slice in half to make squares or triangles, or into two rounds, as liked, and spread with the butter.

Arrange the pork, pineapple and banana on each of six bread triangles, mix the mayonnaise with the curry powder and pipe a rosette on top.

Place one slice of liver pâté on each of the six squares of bread and top with the Madeira aspic and orange segments.

Spread six more squares with Cottage Cheese with Herbs, roll up the salmon slices and place on top. Garnish with dill.

Spoon the Waldorf salad onto the remaining bread pieces, top with beef and garnish with walnuts.

Prawn and Mushroom Salad

225 g/8 oz button mushrooms
6 sticks celery
450 g/1 lb frozen prawns,
   thawed
1-2 tablespoons chopped chives
300 ml/½ pint mayonnaise
salt and pepper
few lemon wedges

Clean, trim and slice the mushrooms. Wash and chop the celery. Mix the prawns, mushroom, celery and chives together in a bowl and stir in the mayonnaise. Season to taste with salt and pepper, chill and serve with lemon wedges.

Artichoke Salad

1 (396-g/14-oz) can artichoke
   hearts
3 tomatoes
2 shallots
5 tablespoons oil
2 tablespoons wine vinegar
salt and white pepper
2 tablespoons chopped fresh
   mixed herbs

Drain and halve the artichoke hearts. Peel and quarter the tomatoes, scoop away the seeds and dice the flesh. Peel the shallots and cut into rings. Lightly mix all the salad ingredients together in a bowl.

Beat the oil with the vinegar, salt and pepper, mix the dressing into the salad and sprinkle the herbs over the top.

Apple and Rice Salad
225 g/8 oz rice
2 dessert apples
2 small oranges
150 ml/¼ pint double cream
3 tablespoons dry sherry
2 tablespoons lemon juice
generous pinch each sugar and ground ginger

Cook the rice in boiling salted water following the instructions on the packet and drain. Wash, quarter, core and dice the apples. Peel the oranges, remove the skin from the segments and discard the pips. Mix the rice and fruit in a bowl. Whip the cream with the sherry, lemon juice, sugar and ginger, and stir into the salad.

Sweet Corn and Pepper Salad
2 (340-g/12-oz) cans sweet corn
6 peppers, red, green and yellow
3 onions
8 tablespoons oil
3 tablespoons wine vinegar
salt and black pepper
1 tablespoon chopped fresh mixed herbs

Drain the sweet corn. Wash and quarter the peppers, remove the seeds and pith and slice the flesh into fine strips. Peel the onions and cut into rings. Mix all the ingredients together in a bowl. Beat the oil with the vinegar, salt and pepper, pour over the salad and sprinkle with the herbs.

Mixed Salad Bowl
2 lettuces
2 heads red endive
100 g/4 oz corn salad or watercress
2 onions
7 tablespoons oil
3 tablespoons wine vinegar
pinch each salt, white pepper and sugar
bunch chives

Wash the lettuce and red endive, separate the leaves and leave to drain. Thoroughly wash the corn salad or watercress and shake dry. Peel the onions and cut into rings. Mix all these ingredients together in a bowl. Beat the oil with the vinegar, salt, pepper and sugar and stir the dressing into the salad. Wash and chop the chives and sprinkle over the top.

Rich Chocolate Mousse
200 g/7 oz sugar
4 egg yolks
2-3 tablespoons Cointreau
200 g/7 oz plain chocolate
7 g/¼ oz gelatine
750 ml/1¼ pints double cream
¼ teaspoon vanilla essence
1 tablespoon chopped nuts

Beat 150 g/5 oz sugar in a bowl with the egg yolks and Cointreau, stand the bowl in a pan of hot water, and whisk until frothy. Break up the chocolate, stand it over hot water until melted, then stir into the yolk mixture. Dissolve the gelatine in 2 tablespoons warm water and add to the mixture.

Whip the cream with the remaining sugar and the vanilla essence until stiff. Fold all but three tablespoons into the mixture. Transfer to a large bowl to set, and pipe on the remaining whipped cream just before serving. Sprinkle with nuts.

183

Party Drinks

One of the most important and enjoyable aspects of planning any party buffet is deciding on what to drink with the food. From having a few friends to supper to throwing a huge summer party, your meal must be complemented by the drinks you serve, especially if 'drink' itself is not only taken to mean alcohol. Wines and spirits are popular, but there is a whole range of fruit juices to buy or make yourself, as well as still and sparkling mineral waters, ciders and beers to consider.

Aim to suit your drink to the occasion – long, cool drinks and a strawberry cup on summer evenings, hot mulled wine at a Christmas party. Even a simple family meal can be given a special touch if accompanied by a delicious fruit cocktail. Here we give enough suggestions for drinks to match every possible occasion.

Soft Drinks

Soft drinks are all too rarely offered at parties. Yet there are bound to be some guests who prefer something non-alcoholic. Contrary to popular opinion, soft drinks do not have to be boring and you'll find a wide variety of refreshing alternatives to alcohol. Tomato, orange, grapefruit, pineapple and apple juices are the standard alternatives, but you can now find grape, peach, passion fruit and mixed-flavour juices on the market. Only products with no additives – not even sugar or water – are entitled to the name fruit *juice*; if you buy fruit drinks under any other name you are not obtaining pure fruit juice.

You can of course make your own. There is nothing to beat one or two freshly squeezed oranges or lemons, served with ice and a twist of the fruit itself on a hot summer day. If you really enjoy pure fresh fruit juices, then it is definitely worth investing in a juicer. One of these opens a whole new range of possibilities, as juice can be obtained from all kinds of fruits and vegetables – apples, carrots, cucumber and celery, to name a few.

Freshly squeezed juices are full of vitamins. They make healthy and appetising aperitifs, delicious summer cocktails and are fast favourites with waistline-watchers. Here are some unusual ideas, each of which makes one glass:

Cucumber Cocktail

50 ml/2 fl oz cucumber juice
50 ml/2 fl oz apple juice
1 tablespoon celery juice
1 teaspoon lemon juice
pinch each salt and freshly ground black pepper
1 teaspoon chopped parsley

Mix the cucumber, apple and celery juices in a tall glass and season to taste with the lemon juice, salt and pepper. Serve sprinkled with parsley.

Carrot and Apple Juice

50 ml/2 fl oz carrot juice
75 ml/3 fl oz apple juice
1 teaspoon lemon juice
pinch each salt and pepper
1 teaspoon finely chopped dill (optional)

Mix the carrot and apple juices in a glass, season to taste with lemon juice, salt and pepper and serve sprinkled with dill, if liked.

Tomato and Celery Juice

50 ml/2 fl oz tomato juice
40 ml/1½ fl oz celery juice
1 teaspoon lemon juice
2 tablespoons soured cream
pinch each salt, pepper and paprika pepper
1 teaspoon chopped parsley

Beat the tomato juice thoroughly with the celery and lemon juices and the soured cream. Season with salt, pepper and paprika. Transfer to a glass and serve sprinkled with parsley.

Finally, one of the most sophisticated and refreshing drinks is simply clear spring water, still or sparkling. Serve it chilled with ice and a twist of lemon or lime.

Cider and Beer

Cider and beer are obtainable in large party cans or bottles at most supermarkets and off-licences. These are best served chilled, especially lager.

There is a growing trend, however, towards real ale – live beer which is served unpressurised straight from the barrel (as opposed to pressurised beer which has carbon dioxide added). You can often order a barrel of real ale through a brewery or a pub, complete with tap and wooden hammer. See that the beer has time to settle before being served. We would advise having it delivered and set up 24 hours before your party. Draught cider can also be supplied in this way.

Wine

The choosing and serving of wine deserves a book to itself. However, here are some points to remember when handling wines, and tips on the right type of wine to serve with each course.

Handling

Correct handling of wine begins when it is bought. Wine is a 'living' thing and reacts to vibration and changes of temperature. Buy it, if possible, a few days before your party. If you have to buy it on the day itself, carry the bottles home as carefully as you can.

Wine is best stored in a cellar, if you are lucky enough to have one, since a cellar can usually be relied upon to keep a constant temperature. Otherwise, store your wine in a cupboard in a room where you know the temperature is not likely to vary much. Always lay the bottles on their sides so that the wine is in contact with the cork. If stored upright, the cork dries out and shrinks and the bottle is no longer completely airtight.

The temperature at which wine is served has a great effect on the bouquet or aroma of the wine. For the connoisseur, each wine has its optimum serving temperature, but as a rule, white wines are served chilled and red wines at room temperature, with the exception of Beaujolais which should be lightly chilled. Sparkling wines should be served as cold as possible, but real champagne should be only just chilled, otherwise it will lose its bouquet and some flavour. You will know when the temperature is right if your glass mists up when the champagne is poured in. As for sweet white wines, these should be served ice-cold, as they taste warm and syrupy at room temperature.

Red wine which has been stored in a cool place needs to be warmed slowly before drinking. Place the bottles in the room where they are to be served early on the day of your party, or even the night before. Never try to warm them up quickly in the oven or near a heater, as this kind of shock treatment will impair the wine. Many young red wines taste better if you remove the corks about an hour before serving. The oxygen in the air can then bring out their full bouquet.

Old red wines often contain a black sediment which, if shaken up when the wine is poured, makes the wine cloudy. It is therefore a good idea to decant these a couple of hours before serving. Carefully remove the cork, holding the bottle as near as possible to the flat position in which it has been stored, so as not to disturb the sediment, and slowly and evenly pour the wine into a decanter or a glass jug. Before the sediment reaches the neck of the bottle, stop pouring. This will keep the wine clear when serving.

There is an established custom of serving white and red wine and champagne in different glasses, but not everyone has a full range to choose from, and the shape of the glass in no way affects the taste of the wine. What is important is that the glass should be large enough, for white wine should fill the glass no more than two-thirds full, and red wine to only half full. This is to allow the scent and flavour of the wine to develop to its best. To keep the bouquet, the glass should be round or tulip-shaped, tapering at the top, and it should have a stem, so that the heat of your hand holding the glass does not change the temperature of the wine. Finally, part of the enjoyment of wine is its colour, which can be anything from pale gold to deep ruby, with an infinite variety of shades in between. Do not spoil the effect by serving it in tinted glasses.

Once you have your basic glass, you can use it for all kinds of wine, even champagne, the only exceptions being sherry and port.

Serving Wine

Nowadays it does not matter if you break the rules and serve a heavy wine at the beginning of the meal or a white wine with game. You should serve whatever you feel goes best with each course. If you are not sure that other people will share your taste, it might be safer to follow some traditional rules.

As an aperitif, serve a dry sparkling wine or champagne, sherry or vermouth.

With an hors d'oeuvre of artichokes, avocados, tomatoes, cucumber, eggs or smoked fish serve a dry sherry, especially if the hors d'oeuvre contains vinegar, as vinegar is a natural enemy of wine.

With pork, veal, pâtés and continental sausages, serve dry, not too young wines, red or white: Beaujolais and Alsace wines from France, Soave and Frascati from Italy, and almost any wine from southern Germany.

Oysters and shellfish are best eaten with very dry white wines, the classic accompaniments to oysters being Chablis and dry champagne. Moselle and dry Orvieto are also good.

Fish tastes much better served with white rather than red wine, as the sharpness of white wine seems to tone down any excessively fishy taste. Serve white wines such as Rhine and Alsace, white Côtes-du-Rhône and Muscadet.

Hot or cold beef, lamb or game dishes traditionally require full-bodied red wines. These can range from Bordeaux, a comparatively light wine, to the richer Burgundy, according to taste, and include Valpolicella and Chianti from Italy and Rioja from Spain. But you can also serve good, full-flavoured, even slightly sweet white wines such as Rhineland Palatinate, which goes especially well with venison.

Chicken is the perfect dish for the indecisive, as red and white wines go equally well with it and you can serve almost any wine you like according to taste. Turkey follows the same rule, but wild duck, partridge, quail and pheasant, being game birds, really do need red wine.

Cheese is usually eaten with red wine, as you simply continue drinking whatever wine you have had with the main course. If you are serving Stilton however, there can be no better way of rounding off a meal than with a glass of vintage port.

Punches

Making a punch is a good and convenient way of serving drink at a party. Once you have made the basic mixture you can just keep topping it up; moreover, punch lends itself to being adapted to different times of the year. There is a whole wealth of different recipes to choose from, but here is a sample, with one or two general points to bear in mind when making them.

While a lot of punches contain spirits, these do not have to be included. In fact, punches are more economical without. Resist the temptation to use cheap wine in the mixture; your guests may not be able to taste it but they will certainly feel the effects the next day. For the same reason, be careful when sweetening with sugar, as sugar increases the effects of alcohol. Try to use a sweet white wine or sparkling wine instead.

If you are putting fruit in your punch, use only fresh or frozen fruit, not canned or bottled, as the preserving syrup will affect the taste without making it particularly fruity.

Punch is best served chilled, but not over-chilled. Never add ice-cubes to the punch bowl to chill it (unless you are making Sangria); stand the bowl itself in crushed ice instead.

If you have no punch bowl, use a large soup tureen or earthenware pot instead. Use a ladle to transfer the drink to tumblers or wine glasses, half-filling them each time. Replenish the glasses regularly so that cold punch does not become too warm in the glass nor hot punch too cool.

The following recipes will serve 6-8.

Mock Champagne

2 bottles chilled dry white wine
1 lemon
1 bottle chilled soda water, sparkling mineral water or sparkling
*   wine*

Pour the white wine into a large jug or bowl.

Wipe the lemon, peel the rind in a very thin spiral and infuse in the wine for about 15 minutes. Then take out the lemon rind, pour in the soda or mineral water or sparkling wine and stir well. Peel the pith from the lemon and slice the fruit very thinly, discarding the pips. Place a slice in each glass and pour in the wine cup.

Strawberry Cup

350 g/12 oz strawberries
100 ml/4 fl oz water
2 tablespoons sugar
2 bottles light white wine
1 bottle sparkling wine

Hull the strawberries, rinse quickly in cold water if necessary and place in a chilled punch bowl.

Heat the water in a pan with the sugar and stir until the sugar has completely dissolved. Leave to cool and pour over the strawberries. Add 1 bottle white wine, cover the bowl and stand it in a cool place for 1 hour.

Just before serving pour in the second bottle of white wine, followed by the sparkling wine and serve immediately.

Pineapple Cup

1 medium pineapple
100 ml/4 fl oz water
1-2 tablespoons sugar
2 bottles light white wine
1 bottle sparkling wine

Slice the pineapple in half lengthways, scoop out the flesh and cut it into 1-cm/½-inch cubes, discarding any hard core. Place the pineapple in a chilled punch bowl.

Heat the water in a pan with the sugar and stir until the sugar has dissolved. Pour into the punch bowl, followed by 1 bottle white wine and leave to stand in a cool place for 1 hour.

Just before serving, add the second bottle of white wine and the sparkling wine.

Sangria

This refreshing punch from Spain has many variations. It works on a balance between lemon juice and sugar, so take care to adjust the one if you alter the other. Serve as a long drink with plenty of ice cubes.

100 g/4 oz sugar
2 litres/3¼ pints chilled Spanish red wine
1 stick cinnamon
5 cloves
3 oranges
3 lemons
1 litre/1¾ pints chilled water or mineral water

Stir the sugar into the red wine until dissolved and add the cinnamon and cloves.

Wash and dry the oranges and lemons. Peel 1 orange and 1 lemon in a thin spiral and infuse the rind in the wine.

Thinly slice all the oranges and lemons, both peeled and unpeeled, add to the wine, cover the bowl and leave to stand in a cool place for several hours.

Just before serving pour in the water and add a few ice cubes.

Mulled Wine

3 bottles red wine
8 cinnamon sticks
10 blades mace
16 cloves
rind and juice of 4 oranges
1 tablespoon freshly grated nutmeg
225 g/8 oz sugar

Place all the ingredients together in a large pan and heat very gently. Take the pan off the heat and leave the wine to infuse for 1-2 hours. Strain and reheat until just below boiling point. Ladle into suitable glasses.

Never allow mulled wine to boil, as this will ruin its delicate spicy flavour.

Cocktails and Long Drinks

Nobody quite knows who had the inspired idea of mixing two or three different drinks together with a generous supply of ice, pouring the concoction into a glass and serving it with a twist of lemon. Cocktails are said to have been invented in America, but if so, they quickly spread to the rest of the world and are now justifiably popular as one of the most delightful, relaxing and sophisticated ways of party drinking.

There is an enormous range of different cocktails, from the dry and refreshing to the rich and creamy. You can mix them to a certain extent in individual glasses, but if you are planning to make large quantities of different cocktails, here are a few items of useful equipment:

Large bar glass with a lip for pouring
Long-handled metal bar spoon for stirring
Cocktail shaker
Hawthorne strainer with thick twisted wire all around the edge
    to keep ice cubes, lemon pips and other pieces of fruit from
    falling into the glass
Measuring glass with detailed volume scale
Corkscrew and bottle opener
Serrated knife for slicing lemons and other fruit
Ice bucket and tongs
Lemon squeezer
Ice crusher, or hammer
Individual long-handled cocktail spoons and sticks for eating
    pieces of fruit from the drink
Several clean tea towels

Cocktails are nearly always either stirred or shaken. To stir a cocktail, place ice cubes in the bar glass and leave to stand while you prepare the ingredients, then pour off any water from the melting ice. Measure the ingredients in the order stated in the recipe and pour into the glass one after the other. Stir for about 20 seconds with the long spoon, stirring in a spiral from bottom to top. Hold the Hawthorne strainer under the lip of the bar glass to catch any ice or pieces of fruit and strain the drink into the prepared cocktail glass.

To shake a cocktail, place ice cubes in the shaker and stand the shaker on one side while you measure out your ingredients. Pour off any water from the ice and add the ingredients to the shaker. Place the lid on the shaker and wrap in a teatowel. Shake vigorously for about 10 to 20 seconds until the outside of the shaker mists over, then strain the contents into a glass as above.

Most mixed alcoholic drinks are served 'on the rocks'. Some however, particularly long drinks, have to be very thoroughly shaken and served ice-cold. These may require crushed ice. If you do not have an ice crusher, wrap the ice cubes in a clean teatowel, place on a firm surface and smash them with a hammer. You can also buy freezing trays which make small ice balls, and these look very decorative in drinks.

Other decorative ingredients are maraschino cherries, lemon and orange slices, cucumber and mint. It is also quite easy to coat the rim of a glass with sugar frosting. Cut through the centre of a lemon quarter to the rind. Hold the glass upside down, place the rim of the glass in the cut in the lemon and rub the lemon around the rim. Pour some sugar onto a plate or saucer and dip the dampened rim of the glass into it. Serve only sweet drinks in sugar-frosted glasses.

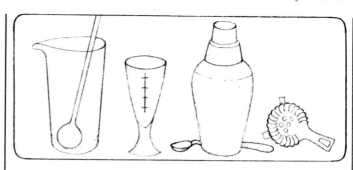

The tools of the barman: large bar glass with a lip for pouring, containing a long-handled metal bar spoon; measuring glass with volume scale; cocktail shaker; Hawthorne strainer to prevent ice cubes and fruit pips from falling into the glass.

The Cocktail Bar

A good stock of spirits, wines, mineral waters and juices naturally enables you to make hundreds of classic cocktails. If you are going into the business seriously, a well-stocked bar should include gin, Scotch whisky, Bourbon whiskey, sweet and dry vermouth, Campari, brandy, vodka, white rum and liqueurs such as Curaçao, crème de menthe, crème de cacao and apricot brandy. Add Angostura bitters, orange bitters and Grenadine (pomegranate syrup), jars of maraschino cherries and green olives, plenty of soda water, tonic water, your favourite mixers, tomato juice, oranges and lemons and a nutmeg and the range should be complete.

In general, there is a distinction between cocktails – short drinks, stirred or shaken and served in small glasses – and long drinks which are more thirst-quenching, contain less alcohol and are served ice-cold in tumblers.

Here is a selection of internationally popular cocktails and long drinks for you to try. Once you have mastered these, you can go on to invent your own. Each cocktail serves one.

(Some recipes call for a 'dash'; this is equivalent to 3-4 drops.)

Cocktails

Classic Martini

Pour 50 ml/2 fl oz gin and 20 ml/1 fl oz dry vermouth into the bar glass and stir vigorously for 20 seconds. Strain the drink into a cocktail glass and add an olive.

Dry Martini

Stir 50 ml/2 fl oz gin with 10 ml/½ fl oz extra dry French vermouth and strain into a glass. Squeeze a small piece of lemon peel over the glass so that the zest goes into the martini. Add an olive.

Rum Martini

Stir 20 ml/1 fl oz dry French vermouth with 50 ml/2 fl oz white rum, add a dash of orange bitters and strain into a glass. Add an olive.

Vodka Martini

Stir 10 ml/½ fl oz dry French vermouth with 10 ml/½ fl oz white Italian vermouth and 40 ml/1½ fl oz vodka. Strain into a glass and squeeze lemon peel over the top.

Old Fashioned Whiskey Cocktail

In a whisky glass, crush ½ sugar cube with 2 teaspoons water. Add a dash of Angostura bitters, followed by 50 ml/2 fl oz Bourbon whiskey and stir well. Add a piece of lemon peel and 2 ice cubes, stir again and serve.

Manhattan Dry

Stir 20 ml/1 fl oz dry French vermouth with 50 ml/2 fl oz Bourbon whiskey and a dash of Angostura bitters, strain into a glass and decorate with a maraschino cherry.

Daiquiri on the Rocks

Pour the juice of ½ lemon or lime into the shaker with 50 ml/2 fl oz white rum. Dissolve 1 teaspoon sugar in 2 teaspoons hot water, allow to cool and add to the shaker. Shake very thoroughly and pour into a glass filled with ice cubes.

Columbus

Shake 10 ml/½ fl oz lemon juice, 10 ml/½ fl oz apricot brandy and 10 ml/½ fl oz white rum thoroughly together and strain into a glass.

Panama

In the bar glass stir 10 ml/½ fl oz white rum with 10 ml/½ fl oz pineapple juice and 10 ml/½ fl oz maraschino liqueur. Strain into a glass and add 2 ice cubes.

Havana

Shake together 20 ml/1 fl oz white rum, the juice of ½ lemon, the juice of ½ orange and 20 ml/1 fl oz dry vermouth in the shaker, strain into a glass and add a slice of orange.

Alexander

Pour 10 ml/½ fl oz single cream into the shaker with 10 ml/½ fl oz crème de cacao, and 10 ml/½ fl oz brandy, shake briefly and strain into a glass.

Caruso

Shake together 10 ml/½ fl oz gin, 10 ml/½ fl oz dry French vermouth and 10 ml/½ fl oz crème de menthe in the shaker. Strain into a glass.

Royal Cocktail

Shake 10 ml/½ fl oz gin with 10 ml/½ fl oz cherry brandy, 10 ml/½ fl oz French vermouth and a dash of maraschino liqueur. Strain into a glass and add a maraschino cherry.

Bronx

Shake 10 ml/½ fl oz orange juice with 20 ml/1 fl oz gin and 10 ml/½ fl oz sweet Italian vermouth, and strain into a glass. Use dry vermouth if you want to make a Dry Bronx.

Paradise

Shake 10 ml/½ fl oz orange juice, 10 ml/½ fl oz gin and 10 ml/½ fl oz apricot brandy together and strain into a glass.

White Lady

Shake together 10 ml/½ fl oz lemon juice, 20 ml/1 fl oz gin and 10 ml/½ fl oz Cointreau and strain into a glass.

Bombay

Shake together 10 ml/½ fl oz lemon juice, 10 ml/½ fl oz Curaçao and 50 ml/2 fl oz arrack and strain into a glass.

Cherry Blossom

Shake 10 ml/½ fl oz orange juice with 10 ml/½ fl oz cherry brandy, 10 ml/½ fl oz brandy, 3 dashes Curaçao and 3 dashes Grenadine. Strain into a glass and decorate with a maraschino cherry.

Raymond Hitch

Shake 50 ml/2 fl oz Italian vermouth with 20 ml/1 fl oz orange juice and a dash of orange bitters.

Champagne Cocktail

Fill a champagne glass with finely crushed ice. Pour 1 teaspoon Grenadine, 1 teaspoon lemon juice, 1 teaspoon brandy and a dash of Angostura bitters into the glass. Add a slice of orange and top up with champagne.

Orange Champagne Cocktail

Stir 10 ml/½ fl oz orange juice with 10 ml/½ fl oz dry vermouth, 10 ml/½ fl oz Curaçao and 10 ml/½ fl oz gin in the bar glass. Pour the cocktail over an ice cube in a wide-rimmed champagne glass and top up with champagne.

Bloody Mary

Pour 20 ml/1 fl oz vodka into the shaker with 50 ml/2 fl oz tomato juice, a pinch of salt, a dash of Tabasco sauce, 2 dashes Worcestershire sauce and the juice of ½ lemon. Shake well for 15 seconds, strain into a glass and sprinkle with pepper.

Flips

A 'flip' is an alcoholic 'base' well shaken with sugar and a fresh egg yolk, and served sprinkled with a little grated nutmeg.

Rum Flip

Shake together 1 egg yolk with 2 teaspoons sugar and 20 ml/ 1 fl oz white rum, strain into a glass, sprinkle with a little grated nutmeg and serve with a straw.

Champagne Flip

Shake 1 egg yolk with 1 teaspoon sugar and 75 ml/3 fl oz white wine. Strain into a large glass and top up with champagne.

Cobblers

A 'cobbler' is made directly in the glass, preferably one with a wide rim like a champagne glass. Fill the glass two-thirds full with crushed ice, top with pieces of fruit and pour in the cocktail mixture. Serve with a spoon and straw.

Brandy Cobbler

Place a few pieces of pineapple and maraschino cherries on the ice. Pour in 1 teaspoon Grenadine, 3 dashes maraschino liqueur, 3 dashes Curaçao and 3 dashes Kirsch. Top up with 20 ml/1 fl oz brandy and serve.

Champagne Cobbler

Place a few grapes and slices of banana on the crushed ice. Pour in 3 dashes maraschino liqueur, 3 dashes Cointreau and 3 dashes Curaçao. Top up with champagne.

Long drinks
Tom Collins

Place 4 ice cubes and 1 teaspoon castor sugar in a tall glass. Pour in the juice of 1 lemon and 50 ml/2 fl oz gin, stir well and top up with soda water.

George Collins

Place 2 cubes of ice in a glass with 20 ml/1 fl oz each of vodka, lemon juice and Cointreau, stir well and top up the glass with bitter lemon. Garnish with a slice of lemon.

Highballs

Highballs are long cool drinks (from the American name for a good-sized tumbler) consisting of a base liquid which does not have to be alcoholic, topped up with soda, ginger ale or any other carbonated drink or mixer except citrus juices. The classic highball is of course whisky and soda, for which you simply place ice cubes in a large tumbler, add 50 ml/2 fl oz Scotch whisky and top up with chilled soda water. Highballs do not have to be shaken or stirred.

Whiskey Highball

Place a few pieces of ice in a large tumbler or balloon glass, pour in 20 ml/1 fl oz Bourbon whiskey and top up with ginger ale. Add a twist of lemon.

Fizzes

'Fizzes' are spirit-based long drinks, thoroughly shaken with fruit juice, crushed ice and some form of sweetener and topped up with any kind of fizzy beverage.

Gin Fizz

Fill the shaker one-third full with small pieces of ice. Add the juice of 1 lemon, 1-2 teaspoons sugar and 20 ml/1 fl oz gin and shake well. Strain into a tumbler, top up with soda water and serve with a straw.

Apricot Fizz

Fill the shaker one-third full with crushed ice and pour in the juice of ½ lemon and ½ orange. Add 20 ml/1 fl oz apricot brandy and shake well, strain the liquid into a glass and top up with soda water.

Brandy Fizz

Place crushed ice in the shaker and add the juice of 1 lemon, 3 teaspoons sugar and 20 ml/1 fl oz brandy. Shake thoroughly, strain into a glass and top up with soda water.

Egg Fizz

Pour the juice of 1 lemon into a shaker containing crushed ice, add 1 egg, 1 tablespoon single cream, 2 teaspoons sugar and 20 ml/1 fl oz brandy. Shake very thoroughly, strain into a glass and top up with soda water.

Golden Fizz

Place crushed ice in the shaker and add 1 egg yolk, the juice of 1 lemon, 2 teaspoons sugar, 3 teaspoons Grenadine syrup and 20 ml/1 fl oz gin. Shake very thoroughly, strain into a glass and top up with soda water.

Whisky Fizz

Pour 50 ml/2 fl oz whisky into a shaker containing crushed ice, add the juice of ½ lemon and 1 teaspoon sugar and shake thoroughly. Strain into a glass and top up with soda water. Add 2 maraschino cherries and 2 ice cubes.

Sours

A 'sour' is very similar to a 'fizz' in that it is a sweetened spirit-based drink thoroughly shaken up with crushed ice and fruit juice, but a sour is not always topped up with soda water. A sour can in fact be either a cocktail or a long drink.
   Place a good deal of crushed ice in the shaker. Add the juice of ½ lemon, 1-2 teaspoons sugar and 50 ml/2 fl oz spirit (gin, brandy, whisky, vodka, rum). Wrap the shaker in a teatowel and shake

vigorously. Strain the drink into a tumbler and add 2 cherries and a slice each of orange and lemon. Top up with soda water, if liked, and serve with a long-handled spoon and a straw. If you prefer, you can use Cointreau or Grenadine as a sweetener instead of sugar.

Whisky Sour

Shake the juice of ½ lemon with ½ teaspoon sugar, 50 ml/2 fl oz whisky and a generous amount of ice, strain into a cocktail glass and decorate with ½ slice lemon.

Crustas

A 'crusta' is a sour served in a balloon glass with a sugar-frosted rim to which you add the rind of a lemon cut into a spiral. Half-fill the shaker with crushed ice and pour in the juice of ½ lemon, 1 teaspoon sugar, 2 dashes Angostura bitters, 3 dashes maraschino liqueur and 20 ml/1 fl oz brandy, whisky, gin, rum or other spirit. Shake the mixture very thoroughly and strain into the glass.

Sorbets

You can serve a sorbet on its own as a dessert, or as the main ingredient in a delightful summer drink. Allow the sorbet to thaw just enough to fold in whipped double cream flavoured with a liqueur or spirit, transfer to a chilled cobbler or champagne glass and garnish with fruit. Top up the glass with chilled still or sparkling wine.

Champagne Sorbet

Pour 20 ml/1 fl oz brandy into a wide-rimmed glass and fill up to two-thirds full with peach, pineapple or strawberry sorbet. Cover the sorbet with slices of the appropriate fresh fruit and top up with champagne.

Pick me ups

Prairie Oyster

This is supposed to be the classic hangover cure. Mix 1 teaspoon tomato juice with 1 teaspoon Worcestershire sauce in a cocktail glass and add 1 egg yolk. Sprinkle with a little salt and paprika pepper. Pour in 1 teaspoon tarragon vinegar and down in one.

Florida Cocktail

Thoroughly shake the juice of ½ lemon and ½ orange with a dash of Angostura bitters and 2 dashes Grenadine. Strain into a cocktail glass and serve decorated with a maraschino cherry.

Tomato Cocktail

Place crushed ice in the bar glass. Pour in 1 teaspoon Worcestershire sauce, 40 ml/1½ fl oz orange juice, and 50 ml/2 fl oz tomato juice, add a pinch of cayenne pepper and stir thoroughly. Strain into a large cocktail glass.

Kitchen Equipment

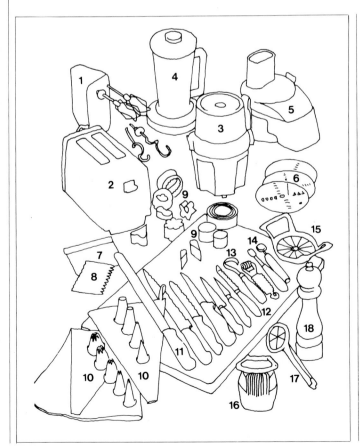

As with all branches of cooking, you will find making salads and cold dishes much easier and more enjoyable if you have the right equipment to start with. Of course you do not need all the equipment shown, nor does this selection cover the entire range of useful utensils. Basically, cooking equipment can be divided into three main categories: essentials (knives, chopping boards, mixing bowls); non-essentials but great time-savers (food mixers and processors); and simple implements, often used for garnishing, a function secondary to the main cooking process but still necessary for party presentations (biscuit cutters, piping bags, melon scoops). This selection should give you an idea of the kind of equipment to choose from:

1. Electric hand-mixer with beaters for beating, whisking and whipping, and dough hooks for kneading firm dough.
2. Toaster.
3. Food mill with attachments, including 4. blender, 5. shredder and 6. individual blades for grating, grinding and slicing.
7-8. Smooth and serrated decorating combs to use with savoury butters, vegetable purées, creamy desserts.
9. Plain and crinkled pastry cutters, decorative biscuit cutters.
10. Piping bags with plain and star-shaped nozzles in varying sizes, used for filling and garnishing.
11. A selection of knives: ham slicer, carving knives, kitchen knife, cook's knives.
12. Decorating knife.
13. Simple butter curler and butter curler with food decorator.
14. Oval vegetable scoop, melon scoop.
15. Apple divider and corer.
16. Egg slicer.
17. Egg wedger.
18. Spice mill.

Kitchen Equipment

Essential knives and cutters

Vegetable and kitchen knives: You will need two or three in different sizes for trimming, scraping, peeling and chopping fruit and vegetables. They are available with plain and serrated blades.

Cook's knives: These have long, wide, pointed blades and strong handles, good for slicing meat and root vegetables. They are also available in different sizes.

Chopping blade: Effectively a knife with two handles, with a sharp, rounded blade in between. The extra control makes it ideal for chopping vegetables and herbs very finely.

Decorating knife: The vertical notches in the blade give a wavy pattern to any food you slice with it.

Tomato knife: This has a serrated blade and a sharp point which breaks the skin cleanly, enabling you to slice tomatoes very thinly without crushing.

Grapefruit knife: Useful for preparing orange and grapefruit halves, the double serrated blade quickly frees the segments from their surrounding skin. The tip of the blade curves slightly, making it easy to cut round the fruit between the pith and the segments.

Paring knife: There are many different varieties of small knives which can be used for peeling very thinly. The important thing is to find one that feels comfortable for you.

Carving set: A true carving set has a long-bladed steel carving knife, a sharpening 'steel' with a strong handle, and a carving fork with a prong on the back that juts out to protect your hand when carving.

Kitchen scissors: It is worth investing in a good, strong pair, preferably ones that can be sharpened, to use for all tasks from snipping mustard and cress to trimming meat.

Slicer and grater: Indispensable for cutting very thin slices or slivers from raw fruit, vegetables, cheese and other foods. It is important that the blades should be very sharp and easy to clean. The rectangular utensil which combines grater and slicer stands firm on its base during use, but the cutting surfaces are rather small, and often do not grate as finely as the separate implements. Hand-operated food choppers and shredders are practical for small quantities but for large quantities it is really worth buying a food processor.

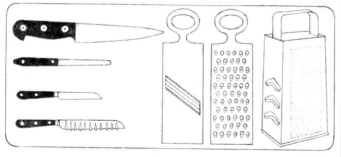

Cook's knife, grapefruit knife, tomato knife and decorating knife, all with stainless steel blades and comfortable handles; individual vegetable slicer and grater and multi-purpose box grater.

Electrical appliances

Food mixer: This mixes and beats food and has separate beaters for whisking egg whites, whipping cream and kneading dough, as well as attachments for blending and shredding.

Food processor: This has the advantage over the mixer in that it slices, grates and shreds fruit and vegetables, chops and minces meat, mixes and liquidises, all inside the machine itself. It cannot whip cream or egg whites very stiffly though, so you would need a separate hand beater for this.

Deep fryer: Useful if you do lots of frying as it controls temperatures thermostatically and cuts down on cooking smells. Otherwise, a deep pan with a frying basket will be adequate.

Small useful implements

Garlic press: This purées a peeled garlic clove very efficiently and saves chopping and crushing with a knife. To give a dish a very delicate garlic flavour, retain the purée and use only the drops of juice produced by the press.

Mortar and pestle: Very useful for pounding herbs and spices to obtain their full flavour, also garlic, capers and pickled green peppercorns.

Spice mill: The difference in flavour between buying ready-ground spices and grinding your own just before use is so great that it is well worth building up a collection of separate mills for caraway seeds, coriander, allspice, mace and other spices, as well as white and black pepper.

Salad dryers: You can buy various kinds of baskets for shaking lettuce dry, as well as salad spinners. Baskets have an advantage in that most types can be stored flat, but they have to be used with more care than salad spinners, if you don't want your kitchen liberally sprinkled with water.

Apple corer: This is a knife with a tubular blade which is pressed into the centre of an apple, swivelled round and extracted, taking the whole core with it. Useful for making neat apple rings.

Melon scoop: Extremely useful for cutting melon and avocado balls. You can improvise with a teaspoon, but the effect will not be the same.

An egg wedger and an apple divider are very useful for cutting hard-boiled eggs and apples into neat, even segments. A melon scoop enables you to scoop decorative shapes out of soft foods such as melon, avocado, mango, cream cheese and butter.

Egg piercer: If you prick an egg at the round end before boiling, the air will be able to escape, making the egg less likely to crack during cooking.

Butter curler: This has a crinkly blade like a decorating knife, but one which curves right round to produce fine, crinkly curls when drawn across a cold, hard block of butter.

Egg slicer: An egg slicer is the most efficient way of cutting hard-boiled eggs into neat slices. You can also use it for other soft foods such as mushrooms.

Egg wedger and apple divider: An egg wedger cuts a hard-boiled egg into six equal wedges, an apple divider slices apples and pears into twelve wedges and simultaneously removes the core.

Pastry and biscuit cutters: You cannot have too many of these. Begin with the basic plain and crinkly round cutters and build up your collection with flowers, stars, animals and other shapes as liked, ranging from tiny 1 cm/$\frac{1}{2}$ inch aspic cutters to 5 cm/2 inch and 7.5 cm/3 inch pastry cutters. They are indispensable for cutting rounds for canapés and biscuits, and shapes for garnishing cold meat and fish platters, stuffed eggs, salads and sandwiches.

Piping bags and nozzles: Use nylon or plastic piping bags for convenience, as linen bags have to be boiled thoroughly after every use. A selection of plain and star-shaped nozzles in different sizes will enable you to give a professional touch to all your cooking, from piping a fine pattern on cakes and biscuits to making rosettes of cream or vegetable purée on main dishes.

Basic Recipes

Although the range of ready-prepared basic foods you can buy is wider now than ever before, there is still plenty of scope for the home cook, from making crusty loaves and creamy mayonnaises to real vanilla ice cream. And there are certain essential cold buffet ingredients which cannot readily be bought, such as good meat stocks and aspics. On the following pages you will find all these necessities, plus a selection of recipes for the basics most frequently used in 'cold table' preparation. For convenience, they can be bought, but they taste much better if they are home-made.

Home-made bread

Baking your own bread is time-consuming, but it is one of the most enjoyable processes in the whole of cooking and once you have tasted a loaf fresh from the oven you will be sold on the idea.

The most important ingredient in any bread recipe is the raising agent, which in most cases is yeast. Yeast is sold either fresh or dried; if fresh, it should be soft and pliable, creamy in colour and crumbly in texture; dried yeast is sold in little packets of granules. Fresh yeast should be stored in an air-tight container or wrapped in cling-film and will keep in the refrigerator for 1-2 weeks, or in the freezer for up to 6 months. Dried yeast will keep indefinitely in an air-tight packet or container. Yeast needs a warm environment if it is to work most effectively. The room temperature of most kitchens should be warm enough to allow yeast to rise, while too hot a temperature will kill the yeast cells and prevent the bread from rising.

All the recipes here specify fresh yeast, but you can use dried yeast instead, as long as you remember that dried yeast is twice as concentrated as fresh, so you should use half quantity. Instead of creaming the fresh yeast with the lukewarm milk or water (depending on the recipe), simply whisk dried yeast into the liquid, leave to dissolve for 5 minutes and pour the mixture into the flour. Then continue as directed in the recipe.

Wholewheat Loaf

150 g / 5 oz wholewheat grains
50 g / 2 oz fresh yeast
750 ml / 1¼ pints lukewarm water
2 teaspoons salt
8 tablespoons clear honey
3 tablespoons oil or melted margarine
900 g / 2 lb wholemeal flour or 450 g / 1 lb wheatmeal and 450 g / 1 lb
  wholemeal flour

Place the wholewheat grains in a bowl with cold water to cover and leave to soak for 24 hours. Drain, rinse through with fresh water and return the damp wheat to the bowl. Cover the bowl and leave the wheat to stand for a further 24 hours, rinse again and drain. The wheat should now have begun to germinate and will be ready to use.

Cream the yeast in a bowl with a little of the water, then add the salt, honey, oil or melted margarine and the rest of the water. Stir in half the flour. Mix well, cover the bowl and leave to rise at room temperature for 30 minutes. Stir in the remaining flour and the germinated wholewheat grains and knead well to a smooth, elastic dough. Cover and leave to rise in a warm place for 30 minutes or until doubled in bulk.

Lightly grease two baking trays. Knead the dough thoroughly, shape into two loaves, and place one on each tray. Allow to rise for a further 15-20 minutes, then using a sharp knife, cut a cross into the top of each loaf and brush with water. Sprinkle with a little flour and bake in a moderately hot oven (200 C, 400 F, Gas Mark 6) for 40-50 minutes.

Basic Recipes

French Bread

1 kg/2¼ lb strong plain white flour
40 g/1½ oz fresh yeast
750 ml/1¼ pints lukewarm water
4 teaspoons salt

Sift the flour into a large mixing bowl and make a well in the centre. Cream the yeast with a little of the water, add the remaining water and pour the mixture into the flour. Sprinkle a little of the flour over the liquid, cover the bowl and leave to stand in a warm place for 20-30 minutes. Add the salt and mix all the ingredients together to a dough. Knead the dough for about 5-10 minutes until it becomes smooth and elastic. Sprinkle the surface with flour to prevent a crust forming, cover the bowl and leave the dough to rise at room temperature for 5 to 6 hours.

Sprinkle a large baking tray with flour. Quickly knead the dough on a floured surface and divide it into four or five pieces. Shape each piece into a long roll and place the rolls on the baking tray. Cover and leave to rise in a warm place for a further 15 minutes.

Using a thin, sharp knife cut diagonal lines at intervals along the tops of the loaves and brush with lukewarm water.

Bake in a hot oven (220 C, 425 F, Gas Mark 7) for 15 minutes, then turn the oven down to moderate (180 C, 350 F, Gas Mark 4) and bake for a further 15-20 minutes.

Savoury Peasant Bread

BASIC SOUR DOUGH
2 tablespoons milk
6 tablespoons lukewarm water
1 teaspoon oil
15 g/½ oz fresh yeast
1 teaspoon castor sugar
2 teaspoons salt
100 g/4 oz strong plain flour
RYEBREAD DOUGH (PEASANT BREAD DOUGH)
20 g/¾ oz fresh yeast
300 ml/½ pint warm water
100 g/4 oz streaky bacon
1 teaspoon salt
100 g/4 oz Emmental or Edam cheese, grated
50 g/2 oz chopped almonds
1 tablespoon chopped parsley
225 g/8 oz rye flour
100 g/4 oz strong plain flour

Make the sour dough first by bringing the milk to the boil in a pan with 4 tablespoons of the water and the oil. Take the pan off the heat and allow to cool until lukewarm. Dissolve the yeast with the sugar in the remaining warm water and leave to stand for 5 minutes. Sift the flour into a bowl. Add the yeast liquid and the salt to the milk mixture, stir into the flour until well blended, cover the bowl and leave to stand for 12-18 hours.

Cream the yeast for the ryebread dough in a bowl with a little of the water, pour in the remaining water and add the sour dough. Stir well together.

Remove the rind from the bacon, lightly grill the rashers and chop finely. Drain on absorbent kitchen paper and leave to cool. Mix the bacon, salt, Emmental or Edam, almonds, and parsley into the yeast mixture. Sift in the rye flour and plain flour, knead well, shape into two round loaves and place on a floured baking tray. Brush the surface of the loaves with water, sprinkle with a little flour and cut a criss-cross pattern on the top. Leave to rise for 1½ hours. Bake in a hot oven (220 C, 425 F, Gas Mark 7) for 20-30 minutes.

Strong Rye Bread

half quantity sour dough (as for Savoury Peasant Bread)
7 g/¼ oz fresh yeast
150 ml/¼ pint warm water
100 g/4 oz rye flour
100 g/4 oz strong plain flour
1 teaspoon salt

Make the sour dough following the recipe for Savoury Peasant Bread and leave to stand overnight.

Cream the yeast with a little of the water, pour in the remaining water and stir in the sour dough. Sift the rye flour, plain flour and salt into the mixture, knead well and shape the dough into a ball.

Line a large baking tray with cooking foil. With floured hands form the dough into a small round loaf, place on the tray and leave to rise at room temperature for 1½-2 hours. During this time, brush the top of the loaf several times with lukewarm water to help prevent cracks appearing. With a sharp knife, cut a criss-cross pattern on the top of the risen loaf and bake on the bottom shelf of a moderately hot oven (200 C, 400 F, Gas Mark 6) for 30 minutes.

Poppyseed Rolls

450 g/1 lb strong plain white flour
1 teaspoon salt
25 g/1 oz fresh yeast
250 ml/8 fl oz lukewarm milk
50 g/2 oz butter or margarine
1 egg
generous pinch each pepper and grated nutmeg
GLAZE
1 egg yolk
1 tablespoon milk
2 tablespoons poppy seeds

Sift the flour and salt into a mixing bowl and make a well in the centre. Cream the yeast with a little of the milk, add the remaining milk and pour into the flour. Sprinkle some of the flour over the liquid, cover and leave to stand in a warm place for 30 minutes until frothy.

Melt the butter or margarine and beat in the egg, pepper and nutmeg. Add the mixture to the bowl. Knead all the ingredients together to a smooth dough, cover and leave to rise for a further 20 minutes or until doubled in bulk.

Grease two baking trays. Lightly knead the dough and with floured hands break off pieces, each weighing about 40 g/1½ oz. Shape the pieces into balls and place at intervals on the baking trays. Flatten the rolls slightly with the palm of your hand, cover the trays and leave to rise for a further 20 minutes.

Beat the egg yolk with the milk. Brush the rolls with the mixture, sprinkle with poppy seeds and cut a cross into the top of each. Bake in a hot oven (230 C, 450 F, Gas Mark 8) for 15-20 minutes.

Basic Recipes

Crusty Rye Rolls

half quantity sour dough (as for Savoury Peasant Bread)
15 g/½ oz fresh yeast
450 ml/¾ pint lukewarm water
450 g/1 lb rye flour
1 teaspoon salt

Make the sour dough following the recipe for Savoury Peasant Bread and leave to stand overnight.

Cream the yeast with a little of the water, add the remaining water and stir in the sour dough. Sift the flour and salt into the mixture and knead well until smooth and elastic. With floured hands, divide the dough into 50 g/2 oz pieces and shape into balls. Sprinkle two baking trays with flour, place the rolls on the trays and brush them with water. Dust with sifted flour and make a cut in the top of each with a knife. Leave to rise for about 1 hour, then bake in a hot oven (230 C, 450 F, Gas Mark 8) for 20-25 minutes.

Poppy Seed Plaits

450 g/1 lb strong plain white flour
40 g/1½ oz fresh yeast
250 ml/8 fl oz lukewarm water
1 teaspoon salt
2 tablespoons poppy seeds

Sift the flour into a mixing bowl and form a well in the centre. Cream the yeast with a little of the water, add the remaining water and pour into the flour. Sprinkle some of the flour over the top, cover and leave to stand in a warm place for 30 minutes until frothy.

Sprinkle the salt over the flour and work all these ingredients together to a dry, light dough. If the dough is too stiff, add a little more lukewarm water. Cover the dough and leave to rise in a warm place for a further 30 minutes, or until doubled in bulk.

With floured hands, divide the dough into 50 g/2 oz pieces. Form three long thin strands from each piece, each measuring about 15 cm/6 inches in length, and weave together into small plaits, tucking under the ends. Brush the surface of the plaits with a little water and sprinkle with the poppy seeds. Place on a greased baking tray and leave to rise in a warm place for a further 30 minutes. Bake in a hot oven (230 C, 450 F, Gas Mark 8) for 10-20 minutes and serve while still hot.

Garlic Bread

You can make garlic bread with bought or home-made French loaves – either way, the taste of the hot, savoury, crispy garlic bread straight from the oven is irresistible. It goes specially well with a fresh green or mixed salad.

100 g/4 oz butter
3 cloves garlic (more if preferred)
generous pinch salt
1 tablespoon each chopped parsley and chives (or other fresh herbs)
1 (450-g/1-lb) French loaf

Beat the butter until light and fluffy. Peel and crush the garlic and beat into the butter with the salt and chopped herbs. Taste and adjust seasoning. Make diagonal cuts at 2.5 cm/1 inch intervals all along the French loaf, stopping short of cutting through the base. Spread the cut surfaces with the garlic butter, wrap the loaf in cooking foil and place on a baking tray. Bake in a moderately hot oven (200 C, 400 F, Gas Mark 6) for 15 minutes.

Mayonnaise Variations

Although you can buy many kinds of good quality ready-made mayonnaises and salad creams, there is still nothing to beat the home-made variety. Here is a basic recipe for mayonnaise, together with some ideas for different flavourings.

Classic Mayonnaise

2 egg yolks
generous pinch each salt and sugar
pinch pepper
1 teaspoon mild French mustard
1 teaspoon lemon juice
250 ml/8 fl oz oil
1 tablespoon wine vinegar
1 tablespoon warm water

Make sure all the ingredients are at room temperature.

Beat the egg yolks with the salt, sugar, pepper and mustard until frothy. Add the lemon juice and leave the mixture to stand for a few minutes, then whisking continuously, add the oil a few drops at a time, until the mixture is thick. Stir in a little vinegar, then continue adding the oil in a slow, steady stream, whisking all the time. Keep adding a few drops of vinegar whenever the mayonnaise becomes thick, so that it can absorb more oil. Continue in this way until all the oil is incorporated, then gradually whisk in the warm water.

The mayonnaise mixture will easily curdle if the oil is poured in too quickly, or if too much oil is added in relation to the vinegar. You can remedy this by beating another egg yolk in a separate bowl and gradually whisking in the curdled mixture.

Remoulade Sauce

3 hard-boiled eggs
1 onion
1 teaspoon capers
2 canned anchovy fillets
1 pickled cucumber
bunch fresh mixed herbs
1 recipe Classic mayonnaise

Shell and finely chop the eggs. Peel and dice the onion. Drain the capers, anchovies and pickled cucumber and chop as finely as possible. Wash and chop the herbs. Mix all the ingredients into the mayonnaise, transfer to a sauceboat and serve.

Quick Mayonnaise

1 tablespoon cornflour
150 ml/¼ pint water
1 egg
1 teaspoon mild French mustard
generous pinch each salt and sugar
pinch pepper
150 ml/¼ pint oil
1-2 tablespoons wine vinegar

Stir the flour into the water, bring to the boil in a pan and simmer for a few minutes, stirring continuously. Leave to cool.

Whisk the egg with the mustard, salt, sugar and pepper until frothy. Gradually pour in the oil, whisking continuously. Stir in the cooled flour mixture, a spoonful at a time, season the mayonnaise with vinegar and add more salt, sugar and pepper as necessary.

Basic Recipes

Mushroom Mayonnaise

100 g/4 oz mushrooms
7 g/¼ oz butter
salt
2 hard-boiled eggs
bunch parsley
100 g/4 oz Classic mayonnaise
1 (150-g/5.3-oz) carton natural yogurt
1-2 teaspoons lemon juice
pinch each pepper and grated nutmeg

Trim, clean and chop the mushrooms. Melt the butter in a pan, add the mushrooms and season with a little salt. Cover the pan and sauté gently for a few minutes until soft. Shell and finely dice the eggs. Wash, drain and finely chop the parsley. Beat the mayonnaise with the yogurt, lemon juice, pepper and nutmeg and stir in the mushroom, chopped egg and parsley.

Herb Mayonnaise

100 g/4 oz Classic mayonnaise
1 (150-g/5.3-oz) carton natural yogurt
pinch pepper
generous pinch garlic salt
½ punnet mustard and cress
bunch fresh mixed herbs (parsley, dill, chives)

Beat the mayonnaise with the yogurt and season to taste with pepper and garlic salt. Snip the cress and wash in cold water, together with the mixed herbs. Shake them dry, chop finely and stir into the mayonnaise.

Olive Mayonnaise

100 g/4 oz Classic mayonnaise
1 (150-g/5.3-oz) carton natural yogurt
1 teaspoon lemon juice
1 teaspoon paprika pepper
pinch pepper
10 stuffed olives
1 clove garlic

Beat the mayonnaise with the yogurt, lemon juice, paprika and pepper. Halve the olives, peel and crush the garlic and stir both into the mayonnaise.

Tomato Mayonnaise

2 tomatoes
100 g/4 oz Classic mayonnaise
1 (150-g/5.3-oz) carton natural yogurt
3 tablespoons tomato purée
salt and pepper
1 teaspoon paprika pepper

Put the tomatoes into boiling water, leave for a few seconds, then plunge them into cold water and peel. Quarter the tomatoes, scoop away the seeds and dice the flesh. Beat the mayonnaise with the yogurt and tomato purée. Season to taste with salt, pepper and paprika and stir in the diced tomato.

Pickle Mayonnaise

100 g/4 oz Classic mayonnaise
½ (397-g/14-oz) can condensed milk
2 tablespoons mild French mustard
1 (269-g/9½-oz) jar mixed pickled vegetables

Beat the mayonnaise with the condensed milk and the mustard. Drain the pickled vegetables, retaining 1 tablespoon of the liquid on one side, chop finely and stir into the mayonnaise, followed by the reserved pickling liquid.

Curry Mayonnaise

1 crisp dessert apple
1 banana
100 g/4 oz Classic mayonnaise
1 (150-g/5.3-oz) carton natural yogurt
2 teaspoons curry powder

Peel, halve, core and finely grate the apple. Peel the banana, cut in half lengthways and slice the halves. Beat the mayonnaise with the yogurt and curry powder and mix in the grated apple and sliced banana.

Apple Mayonnaise

3 tablespoons double cream
100 g/4 oz Classic mayonnaise
1 tablespoon white wine
3 tablespoons apple purée
1 teaspoon grated fresh horseradish or bottled creamed horseradish
generous pinch each salt and sugar

Whip the cream until thick but not stiff. Stir into the mayonnaise, followed by the white wine, apple purée and horseradish. Season to taste with salt and sugar.

Anchovy Mayonnaise

100 g/4 oz Classic mayonnaise
1 (150-g/5.3-oz) carton natural yogurt
6 canned anchovy fillets

Beat the mayonnaise with the yogurt. Drain the anchovy fillets, chop very finely and stir into the mayonnaise.

French dressing and vinaigrette dressing are, like mayonnaise, classic accompaniments to salads and other cold dishes. Recipes for these can be found on pages 108 and 165 respectively.

Basic Recipes

Pâtés, Terrines and Galantines

Some confusion exists over these terms and it is true to say that their traditional meanings have changed over the years. Strictly speaking, the main difference between a pâté and a terrine is that a true pâté (literally translated as 'pastried') should always have a pastry crust, although nowadays they are often made without. A terrine is baked sealed in an ovenproof earthenware dish from which it takes its name and the dish itself stands in a large container such as a roasting tin filled with hot water (this is known as a bain-marie). The point of the bain-marie is to allow the dish to cook gently at an even temperature without 'baking' or drying out. In all other respects, pâtés and terrines are made in the same way, except that the filling for a pâté tends to be smooth whereas a terrine can contain chunks of meat. Nowadays the term pâté seems invariably to be applied to both dishes, but we have kept the traditional distinction for the purpose of this book.

Galantines are made from poultry, game or meat, boned out and stuffed and served cold. The stuffing itself is prepared in a similar way to that for pâtés and terrines.

The pie crust for a pâté can be made from brioche dough or puff pastry, but the classic and most popular dough is savoury shortcrust pastry.

Savoury Shortcrust Pastry

The quantity given below is enough to line a 25-cm/10-inch round cake tin or a 450-g/1-lb loaf tin, including a pastry lid and trimmings. It will also make 8 pastry tartlet cases or 12 pastry 'boats'.

350 g/12 oz plain flour
½ teaspoon salt
175 g/6 oz soft butter or margarine
100 ml/4 fl oz lukewarm water
2 egg yolks

Make sure all the ingredients (except the water) are at room temperature.

Sift the flour and salt into a bowl. Flake the butter or margarine and rub into the flour until the mixture resembles fine breadcrumbs. Make a well in the centre of the mixture and pour in the water and one egg yolk. With cool hands, quickly knead all the ingredients into a dough, working from the centre of the mixture outwards. (The quicker the mixing, the smoother the pastry.) Wrap the dough in greaseproof paper or cling-film and leave to stand in the refrigerator for 30 minutes to 1 hour.

Grease the base and sides of a cake or loaf tin, if used. Divide the dough into the number of pieces you need for the base, sides, and top of the pâté, depending on the kind of tin being used, and roll out these pieces in turn on a lightly floured surface. Meanwhile, leave the portions you are not using to chill in the refrigerator.

Line the tin (see page 232), if used, with the pastry pieces, and spoon in the filling. Alternatively, if you are not using a tin, wrap the filling in the pastry and pinch the edges together to join. Roll out any left-over pastry until quite thin and cut out decorative shapes such as leaves, rings and crescents.

Beat the remaining egg yolk and use half to brush the top of the pastry. Arrange the decorations on the pâté and coat the whole surface once more with the remaining egg yolk. Bake in the oven as directed in the individual recipes.

Brioche Pastry

The quantity given will make between 18 and 20 individual brioches, each weighing 50 g/2 oz, or 12 filled brioche pasties.

450 g/1 lb strong plain white flour
25 g/1 oz fresh yeast
100 ml/4 fl oz lukewarm milk
150 g/5 oz butter
2 eggs
½ teaspoon salt
½ teaspoon sugar
1 egg yolk, beaten

Sift the flour into a mixing bowl and make a well in the centre. Cream the yeast with a little of the milk, add the remaining milk and pour the mixture into the well. Sprinkle a little flour over the yeast mixture and leave the bowl to stand in a warm place for 20-30 minutes until the yeast is frothy. Melt the butter, cool slightly and mix with the eggs, salt and sugar. Pour it into the yeast mixture and knead all the ingredients together to a smooth, dry dough. Cover the bowl and leave the dough to rise at room temperature for 30 minutes, until doubled in bulk. The dough will now be ready to use, but if you want an even lighter consistency, knead it again for a few minutes and leave to rise for a further 15-20 minutes.

To make individual brioches, take three-quarters of the dough and shape into about 20 small balls. Fit each ball into a brioche tin and indent the top of the dough slightly. Divide the remaining dough into 20 smaller pear-shaped pieces and place on top of the first pieces, with the narrower end in the indentation. Brush the brioches with beaten egg yolk and leave to rise in a warm place for 15 minutes. Bake in a hot oven (220 c, 425 f, Gas Mark 7) for 15 minutes, until golden brown.

If you are making individual pasties, shape the dough into a long roll and cut into twelve equal pieces. Cut one-third of each piece and place on one side. Roll out the larger pieces of dough and use to line 12 brioche moulds or deep patty tins. Place the required filling in the moulds and roll out the remaining pieces of dough to the same thickness to form lids. Brush the edges of the pastry with beaten egg yolk, place the lids over the filling and press the pastry edges firmly together. Trim away any excess pastry, roll out flat and cut into decorations. Arrange these on the brioches and brush the whole surface with the remaining egg yolk. Finally pierce the top of each pasty with a skewer, or cut a small opening in the pastry, to allow the steam to escape.

Hints for using Puff Pastry

Making your own puff pastry is time-consuming, and you can produce almost as good a result with ready-made frozen puff pastry unless you are an expert cook. Here are some general points to help you when using frozen puff pastry.

Always allow the pastry to thaw out at room temperature before use. This should take 1-2 hours.

Roll out puff pastry on a very lightly floured surface. Remember never to roll in one direction only, but from top to bottom as well as from left to right. If rolled only in one direction, the pastry will not rise evenly during baking.

Cut puff pastry with a very sharp pastry wheel or a thin sharp knife to avoid pressing down on the layers and causing the edges to stick together during baking. If you are using a pastry cutter, dip it in cold water before cutting out the pastry.

When brushing the surface of the pastry with egg, keep this away from the cut edges as beaten egg will also make the layers stick together and prevent it rising.

Any left-over pieces of puff pastry can be gathered together and rolled out again. This pastry will not rise so well but is ideal for cutting out decorations.

Basic Recipes

Always place puff pastry on a baking tray or in a tin which has been lightly sprinkled with cold water. Leave to stand in a cool place for 15 minutes before baking.

Lining a Pâté Tin

Flour the work surface well before rolling out the pastry to a 3-mm/⅛-inch thickness. Place the tin in the centre and mark out the base in the pastry, either by lightly drawing round it with the point of a knife or pricking out the shape with a pin or the end of a fine skewer. Turn the tin over on its side and mark the measurements in the pastry in the same way, allowing an extra 2.5 cm/1 inch along the top edge. Do this with each side in turn, then, using a sharp knife or a pastry wheel, cut along the outside edge of the pattern. Place the tin upside down on the remaining pastry and cut all round the shape of the tin to make a lid. Leave this on one side.

Grease the tin. Lightly sprinkle the main piece of pastry with flour, fold the sides gently together and place in the tin. Open the piece out again and, using a small ball of dough, press each pastry side into the corresponding side in the tin. Press the edges and corners firmly together to seal, and trim all round the upper edge of the pastry with scissors, to leave an even border of about 2 cm/¾ inch.

Spoon the pâté filling into the pastry case, pressing it well into the corners and smoothing over the top. Fold the edges of the pastry over the stuffing and press down lightly. (You can if you like fill the small gap between the pastry edges with an extra strip of pastry, as shown, but this is not essential as the lid should be enough to seal the pâté.) Top with the pastry lid, press the joins firmly together and seal the pâté well by pressing all along the edges of the lid with the tip of a teaspoon.

Prick the surface all over with a skewer to allow the steam to escape or, better still, cut one or two holes through the pastry down to the filling, using a knife or small pastry cutter. Fold a double thickness of cooking foil round your finger to make a chimney and insert into the opening. The chimney prevents meat

Mark the shape of the tin in the pastry and cut it out, allowing 2.5 cm/1 inch extra on the top edge.

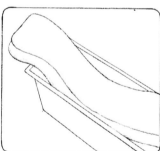

Lightly fold the sides of the pastry together and place it in the greased tin.

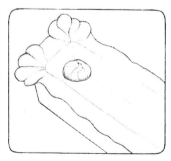

Open the pastry out and press the sides into the sides of the tin, using a ball of dough.

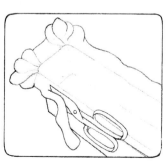

Trim round the upper edge to leave a 2-cm/¾-inch border.

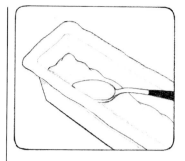

Use a spoon to press the pâté filling smoothly into all the corners.

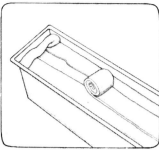

Fold the pastry edges over the filling. If you want to, you can seal the centre with a pastry strip.

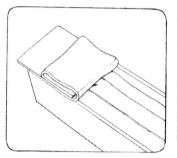

Top the whole pâté with the pastry lid.

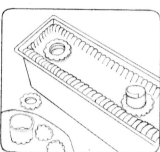

Decorate holes for the steam with pastry trimmings. Insert foil 'chimneys' to protect the surface.

juices spilling out onto the top of the pie and spoiling its appearance. It is also useful for testing whether the pâté is cooked or not: insert a thin skewer through the chimney into the centre of the pâté and leave it for 30 seconds. If when you remove the skewer it feels hot to the touch, the pâté is ready; if cold, the pâté is not yet done and if burning hot, it is overcooked. For round pâtés one chimney in the centre will be enough; rectangular pies will need two.

Finish the pâté by brushing the top with beaten egg yolk and decorating it with pastry shapes. Coat the top once more with egg before baking.

Once the pâté is baked, remove the cooking foil and pour a little hot aspic (see page 234), if liked, through the chimney. This will fill the gap which sometimes appears between the filling and the pastry case during baking.

Lining and Cooking a Terrine

A classic rectangular terrine mould should be lined with thin slices of fresh white pork fat (use rindless streaky bacon instead). Cut the slices large enough – or use enough of them – to leave a generous margin above the edges of the terrine and line the base and sides of the dish as shown (page 233). The slices or rashers should overlap to create an unbroken layer. Spoon in the filling and fold over the top edges of the fat or bacon to cover the filling completely. Garnish the surface with herbs and spices, and place the lid on the terrine.

You *can* make a terrine without either fat or bacon, provided that you grease the inside of the mould very thoroughly and cover the filling with a double sheet of greaseproof paper brushed with oil. But you will inevitably lose some of the flavour.

The lid of the terrine should be tightly fitting with a hole both to allow steam to escape and for the terrine to be tested with a thin skewer in the same way as a pâté (see above). To ensure that the terrine is thoroughly sealed it is a good idea to fill all round the crack between the lid and the terrine mould with luting paste (see page 233), a simple mixture of flour and water.

Line the base and sides of the terrine with slices of pork fat or rindless bacon.

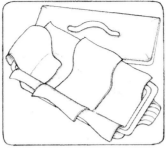

Make sure the slices overlap to give an unbroken lining of fat.

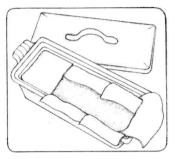

Place the filling in the terrine and fold over the edges of the fat to cover completely.

Garnish the surface with spices and sprigs of herbs.

To cook the terrine, place it in a large bain-marie (a roasting tin will do) and fill the bain-marie with boiling water to 2.5 cm/ 1 inch below the top of the terrine. Cook on the lowest shelf of a moderate oven (180 C, 350 F, Gas Mark 4) for the time indicated in the given recipes.

Luting Paste

200 g / 7 oz plain flour
250-300 ml / 8-10 fl oz water

Sift the flour into a bowl, make a well in the centre and pour in 250 ml/8 fl oz of the water. Mix with your fingers to a smooth paste firm enough to shape, adding a little more water if necessary. Transfer the paste to a floured surface and roll out into a rope long enough to fit round the top of the mould. Place the rope all along the crack between the mould and the lid, pressing down firmly. The paste will harden and provide an effective sealing agent.

Cooking a Galantine

Galantines are cooked on top of the oven in a rich meat, poultry or game stock, at a constant temperature of 80 C (175 F). Heat the stock first, add the galantine and cook in an open pan for the time given in the individual recipe. Do not allow to boil. Leave the galantine to cool in the stock.

Stocks and Aspics

While a rich stock is the classic basis for all good cooking, in buffet cookery it plays a special rôle in making aspic, a vital ingredient of dishes for the cold table. Not only does aspic allow you to prepare dishes in advance without the danger of their drying out, it also gives the food a succulent and appetising appearance.

Aspic takes time to prepare, but it's time well spent if you want to make a particularly attractive party dish, or serve the more familiar smoked fish, cold meats and vegetables in an unusual way. You can make aspic from any kind of meat or fish stock, but the result will be especially good if you use beef or veal bones, or even a calf's foot or pig's trotters for a meat stock. Bones, particularly those from young animals, contain a rich store of flavour and gelatine. Ask the butcher to chop the bones for you.

Light Meat Stock for Aspics

900 g / 2 lb chopped beef or veal bones
450 g / 1 lb shin of beef
pinch salt
about 3.5 litres / 6 pints water
2 leeks
1 carrot
1 stick celery
1 onion
4 peppercorns
1 bay leaf

Place the bones in a large pan with enough cold water to cover and bring to the boil. Then drain, rinse both the bones and the pan thoroughly and fill the pan with fresh water. Add the bones, beef and salt, bring once more to the boil and simmer gently over a low heat for 1½ hours. Skim the froth from the top of the liquid from time to time until no more appears, then partially cover the pan and continue cooking.

Wash, trim and chop the leeks, carrot and celery. Peel the onion and add all the vegetables to the stock, together with the peppercorns and bay leaf. Remove the lid from the pan and simmer gently for a further 1½ hours. You should end up with about 1 litre/1¾ pints rich stock.

Stock for making aspics has to be entirely fat-free. Skim the surface with a spoon and use absorbent kitchen paper to soak up the fat that rises to the top. If there is time, allow the stock to cool thoroughly and the fat to set; it will be much easier to remove from the surface. Strain the stock through a fine sieve to catch any remaining pieces of fat.

This rich stock can be used for soups and sauces as well as aspic. Vary the ingredients according to the type of stock needed in each recipe, using chicken meat and bones for a chicken stock, fish and fish bones for a fish stock (see below), and so on.

If you reduce the stock by further simmering, it will eventually jellify as it cools, especially if veal bones are used.

Basic Fish Stock for Aspics

Melt 15 g/½ oz butter in a large saucepan, add 675-700 g/1½ lb rinsed white fish bones, such as sole or plaice, a sliced onion, a few white peppercorns, the juice of ½ lemon and a little salt. Leave the pan, covered, over a low heat for about 10 minutes, then add 1.2 litres/2 pints water. Bring to the boil, skim thoroughly, then lower the heat and simmer the stock gently for about 20 minutes. Take the pan from the heat, strain the stock and allow to cool, if not for immediate use. Refrigerate until required.

To clarify fish stock, bring it again to the boil, add 1 whisked egg white and simmer for 2 minutes. Take the pan off the heat

Basic Recipes

and leave to stand until the egg white gathers on top of the stock, then strain it through a piece of clean muslin or a sieve lined with a treble thickness of absorbent kitchen paper. Use as directed in each recipe.

White Wine Aspic

The egg whites in the following recipe clarify the stock, making it crystal clear and suitable for aspic, so use this method whenever clarified stock is specified. You may not always have time to simmer it as long as is necessary, in which case 5-10 minutes' simmering should be enough to absorb most of the impurities. A really clear stock though does require the full cooking time.

2 egg whites
1 small onion
1 leek
50 g/2 oz celeriac or 1 stick celery
sprig parsley
pinch salt
8 white peppercorns
½ bay leaf

1 litre/1¾ pints fat-free clear meat stock
100 ml/4 fl oz white wine
40 g/1½ oz aspic crystals or gelatine

Beat the egg whites until thick and frothy but not too stiff. Peel and dice the onion. Wash, trim and finely chop the other vegetables and the parsley, and beat all the chopped ingredients thoroughly into the egg whites with the salt, peppercorns and bay leaf, using a wooden spoon.

Heat the meat stock and wine together in a large pan, stir in the egg white mixture and bring to the boil over a high heat, whisking vigorously to prevent the egg white sticking to the bottom or sides of the pan as it coagulates. As it does so, it will rise to the surface, collecting all the impurities in the stock on the way. Once the egg white has risen to the top of the pan, stop whisking. Continue simmering the stock over a very low heat for 40-50 minutes but do not allow to boil.

Strain carefully through a sieve lined with a double thickness of filter paper or absorbent kitchen paper. Pour 2 tablespoons of the stock into a bowl and stand in a pan of hot water. Sprinkle with gelatine or aspic crystals, stir until dissolved and return the liquid to the rest of the stock. If the stock has cooled too much during filtering, heat it again before adding the gelatine or aspic crystals, without letting it boil.

Stir well and leave to cool, stirring from time to time. Wait until the aspic is just beginning to set, then use as directed in each recipe, or leave to set completely in the refrigerator when it can be chopped and used as a garnish.

The occasional recipe requires you to line a mould with a thin layer of aspic. To do this, chill the mould first, pour in the aspic just on the point of setting and turn the mould slowly round between your fingers to coat each side. Chill to set before arranging a filling on top.

This basic method can be adapted to make port, sherry, muscatel or Madeira aspic, using meat, chicken, game or fish stock depending on the recipe.

For Madeira aspic, substitute 100 ml/4 fl oz Madeira wine for the white wine in the basic recipe.
For muscatel aspic, substitute 100 ml/4 fl oz muscatel wine for the white wine in the basic recipe.
For port aspic, substitute 100 ml/4 fl oz port wine for the white wine in the basic recipe.
For sherry aspic, substitute 100 ml/4 fl oz dry sherry for the white wine in the basic recipe.

Making a Chaudfroid

This is a savoury jelly similar to aspic, except that being based on a sauce it is opaque rather than clear. Like aspic, it protects meat and poultry dishes from drying out, makes them look attractive and adds a very special flavour. Use a light chaudfroid to cover cold roast or boiled veal and poultry, and a dark one for beef and game. The following recipe makes 1 litre/1¾ pints sauce.

Light Chaudfroid

1.5 litres/2¾ pints fat-free light veal, chicken or fish stock
25 g/1 oz cornflour
1 tablespoon dry white wine
20 g/¾ oz gelatine
300 ml/½ pint double cream
salt and white pepper

Bring the stock to the boil in a pan and simmer over a moderate heat until reduced by half. Whisk the cornflour into the white wine, pour into the stock, bring to the boil again and simmer over a moderate heat, stirring continuously, for 1 minute.

Pour 2 tablespoons warm water into a bowl and stand in a pan of hot water. Sprinkle with gelatine, stir until dissolved and mix well into the stock. Pour in the cream. Strain through a fine sieve, season to taste and leave the sauce to cool. Use just as it is beginning to set, as you would an aspic.

Dark Chaudfroid

40 g/1½ oz butter
1 small onion
3 tablespoons plain flour
1 tablespoon tomato purée
150 ml/¼ pint water
150 ml/¼ pint red wine
2 tablespoons beef extract
salt and pepper
1.5 litres/2¾ pints fat-free game or meat stock
1 tablespoon Madeira wine
15 g/½ oz gelatine

Melt the butter in a pan. Peel and finely dice the onion and fry in the butter until golden brown. Sprinkle in the flour and brown over the heat, stirring continuously. Add the tomato purée, gradually stir in the water and wine and bring to the boil. Simmer the brown sauce over a low heat for 10 minutes, stirring all the time. Mix in the beef extract and season with salt and pepper.

Bring the game or meat stock to the boil in a separate pan and simmer over a moderate heat until reduced by half. Take the pan off the heat and pour in the Madeira. Gradually stir the hot stock into the brown sauce, then bring the mixture to the boil and remove the pan from the heat.

Pour 2 tablespoons warm water into a bowl and stand it in a pan of hot water. Sprinkle with gelatine, stir until dissolved and mix the liquid into the hot sauce. Strain the sauce through a fine sieve, adjust the seasoning, leave to cool and use just as it is beginning to set.

For desserts

Finally, two classic extras for the dessert course.

Sweet Wine Sauce

This rich, foamy sauce is delicious poured over both hot and cold desserts. Serve it as a special accompaniment to fruit salads.

4 eggs
100 g/4 oz castor sugar
1 teaspoon cornflour
250 ml/8 fl oz sweet white wine
juice of 1 lemon

Separate the eggs. Whisk the whites until very thick, but not stiff. Stir in 1 tablespoon sugar, then continue whisking until completely stiff.

Beat the egg yolks in a separate bowl with the remaining sugar. Dissolve the cornflour in a little cold water and stir into the egg yolks, together with the white wine and lemon juice. Place the bowl in a pan of hot water and stir the sauce over a gentle heat until it thickens and turns creamy. Remove from the hot water, fold in the egg white and serve hot or cold.

Vanilla Ice Cream

Home-made ice cream tastes so much better than the bought variety, so it is well worth making it yourself. The secret of ice cream is to beat it as often as possible while setting; the more you beat it, the finer it will be.

3 egg yolks
75 g/3 oz castor sugar
250 ml/8 fl oz milk
1 vanilla pod
250 ml/8 fl oz double cream

Beat the egg yolks with the sugar until pale and frothy. Heat the milk very gently in a pan with the vanilla pod but do not allow to boil. Strain the milk, setting the vanilla pod on one side, and pour the flavoured milk gradually into the egg yolks, whisking continuously. Transfer the mixture to the top of a double boiler, or to a bowl standing in a pan of hot water, add the vanilla pod and stir over a low heat until the mixture thickens enough to coat the back of a spoon. Allow to cool and remove the vanilla pod.

Whip the cream until stiff and fold into the mixture. Transfer to an ice cream maker or freezer tray and place in the freezer or the freezing compartment of the refrigerator. If you do not have an ice cream maker, take the ice cream out of the tray after 10 minutes or just as it is beginning to freeze at the edges, allow to thaw slightly and beat well to remove any ice crystals, or blend in the liquidiser. Return the ice cream to the freezer and repeat this process every 10-15 minutes, until the ice cream sets completely. You will probably have to beat or blend it three or four times.

Index